the TIME-CRUNCHED
TRIATHLETE

the TIME-CRUNCHED
TRIATHLETE

Race-Winning Fitness in 8 Hours a Week

CHRIS CARMICHAEL
and JIM RUTBERG

BOULDER, COLORADO

The Time-Crunched Triathlete is part of the TIME-CRUNCHED
ATHLETE™ series.

Copyright © 2010 by Chris Carmichael and Jim Rutberg

1830 55th Street
Boulder, Colorado 80301-2700 USA
(303) 440-0601 · Fax (303) 444-6788 · E-mail velopress@competitorgroup.com

Distributed in the United States and Canada by Ingram Publisher Services

Library of Congress Cataloging-in-Publication Data
Carmichael, Chris, 1960–
The time-crunched triathlete: race-winning fitness in 8 hours a week /
Chris Carmichael and Jim Rutberg.
    p. cm.
    Includes bibliographical references and index.
ISBN 978-1-934030-61-5 (pbk.: alk. paper)
1. Triathlon—Training. 2. Physical fitness. I. Rutberg, Jim. II. Title.
GV1060.73.C37 2010
796.42'57—dc22

For information on purchasing VeloPress books, please call (800) 811-4210
ext. 2169 or visit www.velopress.com.

This book is printed on 100 percent recovered/
recycled fiber, 30 percent postconsumer waste,
elemental chlorine free, using soy-based inks.

Cover design by Jason Farrell
Cover photograph by Nils Nilsen; back cover photograph by Joel Strayer
Interior design and composition by Anita Koury
Interior photographs by Brad Kaminski

Text set in Whitman 11.5/16

10   11   12 / 10   9   8   7   6   5   4   3   2   1

To all the age-group athletes out there
striving to balance career, family, and fitness:
You inspire me,
and I stand united with your efforts.

Contents

Preface

The very first e-mail I received upon release of *The Time-Crunched Cyclist* was short and to the point: "Great book, when are you going to write *The Time-Crunched Triathlete*?" With a chuckle, I forwarded the e-mail to Ted Costantino at VeloPress, who had championed the *TCC* and worked tirelessly to get it published. The irony was that we had just finished talking about writing a book that would provide triathletes with the highly effective time-crunched training program my coaches and I use with busy triathletes, and we had decided to wait until we had more feedback from readers.

Ted's response pretty much summed it up: "So much for waiting. When can you start?"

Time waits for no one—not athletes in training, not coaches creating training programs, and certainly not coaches writing training books. And so we pushed some other projects aside and put *The Time-Crunched Triathlete* at the top of our to-do list.

In fairness, the idea of writing this book was originally broached by my coaching staff at Carmichael Training Systems (CTS), who accurately noted during the writing of *The Time-Crunched Cyclist* that there are significant differences (beyond the obvious inclusion of running and swimming) between programs that work for cyclists and programs that work for triathletes with limited training time. There are certainly some aspects of sports science and nutrition that are common to all endurance athletes, and as athletes we do approach our sports with the same basic physiology. But when it comes to training and competition, the only things cyclists and triathletes really have in common are their commitment to training and the time on their bicycles. In all other respects, triathlon is a sport unto itself, complete with its own culture, unique physical demands, and time challenges. It also requires a complex training program, one that can account for the demands of the three disciplines and yet also allow for enough recovery time between sessions to maximize training gains.

Triathlon appeals to highly motivated individuals, some of whom are drawn to the sport because they were originally single-sport athletes and were looking for a greater challenge. The great thing about being an endurance athlete is that you can be active your entire lifetime. And that means there's a lot of time to explore all that endurance sports have to offer, including triathlon. For some, triathlon is their entry point into endurance sports; for others it's an opportunity to combine their passions or discover new ones.

The triathlon community encompasses all age groups, ability levels, and professions, but one common challenge unites the majority of triathletes—time. Training at a high level for even one sport takes a major commitment; training for triathlon's three disciplines really burns up the clock. Unless you're a professional athlete, you have priorities that come before training, making your schedule that much tighter. Your family is more important than your workouts, and your career is what keeps a roof over your head, food on your table, and gear in your garage. As much as you want to be a stronger, faster, and more competitive triathlete, you have to face the reality that you can't put aside your family and career to make room for more training time. So now what?

Now, you embrace the fact that you are a time-crunched athlete. That means that *now* is the time to change the way you approach training so that you can get bigger benefits out of fewer training sessions. *Now* is the time to sharpen your focus and your goals to events that are best suited to the type of fitness you can develop within your limited training time. And *now* is the time to take steps to protect and preserve your identity as a high-performance athlete, because triathlon is not just something you do on the weekends; being a triathlete is a crucial component of who you are.

The Time-Crunched Triathlete Program is the solution that's working right now for busy age-group triathletes who are balancing their sporting goals with full-time jobs and family commitments. It's backed by science, it's been proven effective by real athletes, and it's the program that will deliver the fitness necessary to achieve your goals in your next triathlon.

If you're ready to move away from antiquated ideas and try something new, then it's the program for you. So let's get started.

Abbreviations

Workout Abbreviations

BIS	BaseIntervalSet
CR	ClimbingRepeat
EM	EnduranceMiles
FR	EnduranceRun
FI	Fartlek Interval
KSS	KickSwimSet
LTS	LactateThresholdSwim
NSR	NegativeSplitRun
OU	OverUnder Interval
PI	PowerInterval
PSS	PaceSwimSet
RS	RunningStrides
SPS	SwimPullSct
SS	SteadyState
SSR	SteadyStateRun
T	Tempo
TR	TempoRun
VOS	VO_2Set

Other Abbreviations

ATP	adenosine triphosphate
CP	creatine phosphate
CTS	Carmichael Training Systems
GPS	global positioning system
HR	heart rate
HR_{max}	maximal heart rate
ITU	International Triathlon Union
kcal	kilocalorie
Kj	kilojoule
kph	kilometers per hour
LT	lactate threshold
PR	personal record
PWR	power-to-weight ratio
RBI	rest between intervals
RBS	rest between sets
RMR	resting metabolic rate
RPE	rating of perceived exertion
rpm	revolutions per minute
USAT	USA Triathlon
VO_2max	maximum aerobic capacity

1

A FRESH OUTLOOK FOR TRIATHLON

Do you remember what you used to think "busy" was? Maybe you thought you were busy in college when you were balancing classes with a part-time job. You might have thought you were busy in the first few years of your career. But that was probably 10 years ago, maybe more, and if you compare the commitments you had back then to the demands on your time right now, it's probably no contest. Just about everyone I know has more going on today than a decade ago, and there's no sign that trend is going to change anytime soon. It's an especially dangerous trend for endurance athletes, because in a battle for time and energy, your family and your job will always win over sport. As you become busier and busier, your identity as a competitive triathlete is in danger of being smothered by the ever-growing number of demands on your time.

Well, you are not alone. There are tens of thousands of triathletes facing similar challenges, who have been forced—many times by positive changes in their families or careers—to redefine the role that triathlon plays in their lives. That's perfectly understandable, but I am here to tell you that a busy lifestyle doesn't doom you to middling finishes in races, nor does it mean you should "participate" in triathlons instead of "race" them. Advances in training methods and technology provide opportunities to get more done in less time, enabling time-crunched athletes to remain competitive or regain their competitive edge. The Time-Crunched Triathlete Program uses those advances and technology to create a training program that builds competitive fitness in as little as eight hours per week.

That doesn't mean this program is a shortcut to fitness; there is no such thing. You still have to work hard and dedicate yourself to your training, and you need to understand and accept that you have certain limitations. But if you're seeking greater performance from a dwindling number of training hours, it's time to take a new look at the way you train for triathlon.

Training to Win in the Time You Have

You're a triathlete. You don't think of yourself as a working professional who happens to do triathlons on the weekends. Being a triathlete is a significant component of your identity, and triathlon impacts every aspect of your personal and professional life. That's not to say that you've prioritized triathlon before your career or your family, but rather that you've made choices to ensure that you're able to meet your obligations at work and at home while still training and competing as a triathlete.

But life is not static, and changes in our personal and professional responsibilities mean we have to frequently reevaluate our goals and reallocate our time and resources. Maybe last year, or in the years before that, you were able to commit 15 or more hours to training each week. Perhaps you committed to an Ironman® or half-Ironman race and the double-workout days and long runs and rides that ensued. But then your personal life changed, or your job became more demanding, or both.

For Aimee Harvey, a runner turned triathlete who was one of the first athletes we worked with under what would become the Time-Crunched Triathlete Program, that's exactly what happened. Aimee began working with CTS Coach Kirk Nordgren in 2005 because she was interested in triathlon as a way to continue competing without the persistent injuries she had been suffering as a single-sport runner. Due to her history with running injuries, Kirk started using a low-volume training program with her from the very beginning. As her experience with triathlon increased and her ambitions for longer events grew, Kirk had to design training programs that increased Aimee's speed and stamina without dramatically increasing the time she had to commit to training. And it wasn't just the potential for injuries that kept Aimee from adding more training time to her schedule. Aimee's job—in the human resources department of a major corporation—was demanding and required her to travel a few times a month.

But the turning point that really kicked Aimee into the time-crunched athlete category was her promotion to director of human resources. Now her workload and responsibilities were even greater, and her travel schedule put her on the road nearly every week! There simply wasn't time to commit to the traditional triathlon training schedule of up to 10 individual workouts each week. Aimee had reached a crucial tipping point in her life as a triathlete; she needed to reframe her approach to training or turn her back on the sport she'd grown to love.

The Time-Crunched Triathlete Program worked for Aimee, and it will work for you. The Time-Crunched Triathlete Program is an effective and efficient alternative to traditional triathlon training. It leverages the power of high-intensity interval training and utilizes workouts designed specifically to make you a faster triathlete—not just a more fit endurance athlete. The program's combination of specificity and intensity will enable you to accomplish more with fewer workouts each week. Make no mistake: The workouts themselves are strenuous, and some athletes may not see any decrease in their total number of weekly training hours. The Time-Crunched Triathlete Program is in no way a shortcut to competitive fitness, but it's the most successful way I know to wring greater performance gains out of the time you have available to train. In most traditional training models, the path to greater performance includes an increase in weekly or monthly training volume. You know the old model: If you want to go faster, you need to train more. But when more training *volume* is not an option, you have to be resourceful and find another way. The Time-Crunched Triathlete Program is that way forward.

Finding a New Path

Aimee wasn't alone in facing a serious dilemma as an athlete. When I started CTS in 2000, the original group of athletes who signed up for coaching had large amounts of free time to commit to training. My coaches and I used the training methods I'd developed during my tenure at USA Cycling and my work with Lance Armstrong to make them better, faster, and stronger. Peter Reid was one of the athletes I worked with right at the beginning of CTS, and after I helped him prepare for a winning performance at the 2000 Ironman World Championship, the number of triathletes signing up for coaching really started to rise.

A few years later, however, in about 2004, I began noticing an increase in the number of athletes—across all sports—who were not achieving the goals they had set for themselves. Even more disconcerting to me was the feedback I was getting directly from my coaching staff; they were reporting that even among the athletes who were achieving their goals and were quite happy with their performances, there was a rising number who were not responding to the training programs as well as we expected. Since the training methodology and the principles that govern effective training hadn't changed, I started wondering if something had changed with the athletes.

Upon further investigation, it turned out that the facts supported my suspicions. Over the first four years that CTS was working with athletes, the appeal and awareness of endurance coaching had increased dramatically, and the composition of our athlete base had shifted to include more athletes who were leading busier work and family lives. The methods I'd adapted from coaching elite athletes were based on the classic endurance training model, which relies on a high volume of training to achieve the desired workload and adaptations. Even though the amateurs we were working with weren't training as many hours a week as the pros, the most successful amateurs were still committing 12 to 16 hours a week to their workouts. But by 2004, many of the athletes working with CTS coaches were too busy for such time-consuming training schedules. For these athletes, we had stripped as much volume as possible from their training programs, but once we got below about 8 hours a week, we found that the programs were no longer effective.

Time and intensity add up to workload, and athletes make progress only when the workload of training is high enough to stimulate positive adaptations in muscles and the cardiovascular system. As training time declines, while intensity remains relatively unchanged, you eventually reach a point where the resulting workload falls below the threshold necessary to provide a positive training stimulus. As an athlete, you keep doing your workouts, but your progress stagnates and you stop seeing improvement. After a few weeks or months of working and making no progress, you get frustrated and start skipping workouts or giving less than a complete effort during intervals, and then your fitness falls away even more. It becomes a downward spiral that eventually leads an athlete to conclude that there are more enjoyable ways to spend Sunday afternoons than to burn a ton of energy—and still keep getting slower! Let's face it. Being slow isn't much fun, and triathlon is far too difficult to bother with when it ceases to be fun.

We'd reached the breaking point for the traditional approach to endurance training. With the types of workouts featured in classically structured triathlon training programs, there wasn't enough time to generate workloads sufficient to lead to positive training adaptations. Now I have no problem asking professional and aspiring professional athletes to make sacrifices so they can focus more time and effort on their athletic goals, but for the majority of athletes my coaches and I work with—people like you who have full-time jobs and families—it would be irresponsible to recommend those sacrifices. It's one thing for your athletic goals to affect the amount of time you spend watching television or going out on the town at night. But you're not a professional athlete and you're not making a living based on your performance as a triathlete. After you've squeezed training into every nook and cranny of your available free time, and when the only way to obtain more is by cutting back on the time you spend with your kids, diminishing the attention you pay to your job or spouse, or sleeping fewer hours—which will ultimately hinder your athletic performance—the cost of what you're giving up is completely out of proportion to the value of what you're gaining as an athlete.

But in order to find a new path to competitive fitness, it's important to understand more about the pros and cons of the traditional model of endurance training.

The Classic Endurance Training Model

The classic endurance training model has always taken a top-down approach, meaning we've taken principles proven at the elite level and adapted them to the needs of novice and amateur athletes. Consider the concept of periodization, which has been around in various rudimentary forms for thousands of years. The modern and almost universally accepted version of periodization—systematically changing the focus and workload of training to maximize the positive impact of overload and recovery on training adaptations—was constructed largely by Tudor Bompa and other Eastern bloc coaches in order to win Olympic medals in the 1950s. Back then, the Olympics were as much about the battle of East versus West as they were about athletic achievement.

Before Bompa, German scientist Woldemar Gerschler took the relatively informal but highly effective training practices of Swedish running coaches and, in the 1930s, refined them into what you and I recognize today as "interval training." At the time, the Swedes were using changes in terrain to interject periods of intensity and recovery into their longer runs. They referred to the practice as "fartlek" running, and it's still widely used because it's remarkably effective. But Gerschler eliminated the unpredictability of fartlek training by adding structure, in the form of precise times, distances, and paces, so he could quantify both the work done and the recovery taken between efforts. But neither Bompa nor Gerschler had *you* in mind when they were pushing the boundaries of sports science. Bompa had to earn Olympic medals in order to show the world the power of the Soviet system, and Gerschler was working to find a way to help his athletes—including eventual record holder Roger Bannister—break the coveted 4-minute barrier in the 1 mile run. But the science they discovered changed the face of endurance training for athletes at all levels. Can you think of any training program—any effective training program, that is—that you've seen in the past 20 years that hasn't included periodization, or some form of interval work, or both?

Though I wouldn't compare myself to Bompa or Gerschler in terms of my contributions to endurance training, like them I didn't care much about you at the beginning of my coaching career. I was working with elite athletes, future Olympians and pros, and one future seven-time Tour de France champion. Before being a coach, I had been an Olympian and a professional athlete myself. As a result, I was a disciple of the classic endurance training model, and as a coach, I stuck to the only version of endurance training I knew and understood.

For working with elite athletes, training volume can be as high as the athletes can physically handle. Before sports scientists really understood the relationship between stress and recovery, champion athletes were those who could endure the highest workloads without falling apart. Just look through the stories of champion athletes from the early twentieth century; some barely trained and relied instead on natural talent, while others trained like maniacs and excelled because no one else could cope with the workload.

The classic endurance training model relies heavily on being able to commit to a high training volume. The progression from the low point of seasonal fitness to peak racing condition is gradual, and very slow. It typically starts with long, unstructured training sessions at low to moderate intensities and, after a few months, shifts to workouts that feature long intervals at sustainable aerobic and sub–lactate threshold intensities. Only

after another six to eight weeks do athletes progress to shorter, harder intervals and more competition-specific training activities. Up to this point,
training volume remains high, even as more intensity is added. This is
feasible because the classic endurance periodization plan is very long, and
the months of lower-intensity training build such a foundation of aerobic
fitness that you can layer intensity on top of volume without crushing the
athlete. Only as the goal event approaches, after several months, does the
training volume finally abate as the athlete begins tapering for competition. The exact length of a taper depends on the athlete and the event he
or she is preparing for, but the general idea is to reduce overall workload
and hang on to all the positive adaptations you've gained while enabling
the cumulative fatigue of training to melt away.

Traditional triathlon training has followed the top-down protocol of
the classic endurance training model, but triathlon is also a relative new-
comer to the landscape of endurance sports. Originating in Mission Bay,
California, in 1977, and establishing its marquee event—the Ironman Triathlon in Kona, Hawaii—in 1978, the sport of triathlon recently passed
its thirtieth birthday. In comparison, athletes have been competing in its
component sports for more than a century (cycling) and in some cases
more than a millennium (running and swimming). Perhaps because of
its youth or because it's a product of a San Diego beach community in
the 1970s, triathlon has always been more open-minded than older sports
that carry with them the weight of their history and traditions. The sport
wasn't built by bureaucrats or overburdened with arcane rules. For instance—and this was pointed out to me by CTS Coach Abby Ruby, who
researched gender issues in endurance sports while writing her doctoral
dissertation on exercise addiction in Ironman triathletes—triathlon never
excluded women from participation, never had different distances based
on gender, and has long offered equal prize money for men and women
in the sport's biggest races.

The laid-back and open attitude of triathlon belies the seriousness with
which triathletes approach training and performance, but age groupers
have not always been best served by following the training methods of

the sport's elite. As often happens, amateurs look to the best in the sport and figure that by doing what the pros are doing, they too will maximize their performances. The trouble was, at the beginning, the best in the sport didn't have many tools or resources available to them; there was plenty of science on training techniques for running, cycling, and swimming as individual sports, but none on how to combine them effectively. In this environment, the athletes who could cope with the highest workloads were the ones who excelled, and that in turn created the archetype for what would become traditional triathlon training. With the marquee event being a 140 mile race that takes from 9 to 17 hours to complete, the typical manner of achieving this high workload was to train long hours at relatively moderate intensities.

Over the past 30 years, and especially in the last 10 years, a great deal of science has been applied to the sport of triathlon. From aerodynamics to nutrition and hydration research, heat acclimatization, and event-specific training, the science of triathlon has pushed the speeds and performances of athletes to new heights. But when I've looked across the spectrum of training protocols for triathlon, and especially when I focus on the training programs designed for age-group competitors, what's striking to me is that at their core, they're still largely based on single-sport workouts featuring long-duration, moderate-intensity efforts. Thanks to advances in sports science, you have the opportunity to gather more data than ever before, and more ways than ever to analyze the data, but the actual training that you're monitoring and evaluating hasn't appreciably changed in decades.

When an athlete has the time and focus to commit to working through a training program based on the classic endurance training model, the program works beautifully and can produce incredible athletic performances. But there's a fundamental flaw in the classic endurance training model: It works only if you have enough time to commit to a high number of weekly training hours and/or a high frequency of weekly workouts over several long months. You don't have that kind of time anymore, so we need to change the training model in order for you to stay competitive.

COMMUNITY IS KING

I'VE OFTEN THOUGHT ABOUT WHY TRIATHLON IS SO APPEALING, ESPECIALLY TO people who are busy building careers and families and are relatively new to being endurance athletes. When I was at USA Cycling, the topic used to come up in relation to membership: What was it about triathlon that was drawing so many more newcomers to the sport? Both cycling and triathlon feature a wide variety of challenging events and opportunities for participation and competition across many age groups and ability levels. If anything, the barriers to entry—at least in terms of expense and the time necessary for success—were higher for triathlon than for cycling. But USA Triathlon membership numbers were steadily outpacing USA Cycling's (and still are). As a lifelong cyclist, I believe the critical difference, then and now, is not in the specifics of the two sports, but in the nature of their communities.

The triathlon community is one of the most supportive, positive, and encouraging environments in all of sport. Part of it has to do with the very structure of triathlon competitions. Everyone starts together and competes on the same course at the same time. Yes, there are wave starts, but age groupers and novices are still racing with—even if not against—the pros and higher-level amateurs they admire. There is something very special about being in the middle of your competition and seeing an athlete you admire—whether that person is a pro, a coach, a training partner, a friend, or even a celebrity or inspirational figure—covering the same ground in pursuit of his or her own best performance. That almost never happens in cycling, especially because the most common cycling competition in the U.S. is the criterium, a race held on a closed circuit of 0.6–1.5 miles. The nature of a criterium course requires that races be run one category at a time, which only reinforces the segregation between groups. Most other cycling races, from mountain bike to cyclocross, track racing to long road races, are run in a similar fashion. Charity rides and gran fondos—mass-start cycling road races popular in Europe and gaining popularity in the U.S.—are about the only events in which large groups of cyclists experience something close to the competitive atmosphere of a triathlon.

The fact that triathletes participate together while competing in separate age groups is a crucial component of the sport's supportive community. On the start line of a triathlon, everyone has an individual goal, and except for the handful of people truly aiming to win their age group or the overall competition, everyone can achieve his or her personal goal without diminishing the chances that others will achieve theirs. There's no reason *not* to be supportive of the person next to you, even if you want to get to T1 or the finish line before that person. In amateur bike racing, you're most often competing as a pack for a specific number of laps or minutes. There's one winner per category and you're racing to earn upgrade points so you can move up to the next category. The Category Vs (beginners) want to move up to Category IV, and the riders who are already in Cat. IV rarely want anything to do with the Cat. Vs. That mentality continues right up the ranks, which is part of the reason why athletes who are new to cycling often note that it seems cliquish or elitist. Triathlon doesn't suffer as much from that negative perception because there's not as much separation between competitors of different ability levels.

Because the competitions keep triathletes of varying abilities and experience levels together, they tend to stick together in training as well. Sure, training groups split up based on skill level and workout needs, but at least they gather at the same starting point and at the same time! Generally speaking (and I apologize to all the cycling groups who are genuinely trying to change this perception), I have found there to be greater cooperation and dialogue in the triathlon community—between veterans and beginners, experts and novices, men and women—than in the cycling community.

Adapting Pro-Level Training for Amateurs

For pros, the trouble with having all the time in the world to devote to training is that you will adapt the training to fill the time. Because elite athletes have 20-plus hours a week to train, their training can be designed to take advantage of long, moderate-intensity sessions. If anything, these moderate-intensity sessions are the only way you *could* train for that amount of time each week. Twenty-plus hours of high-intensity training wouldn't be effective because the workload would be so high that the athletes could never recover and adapt. Yet historically, even though age groupers frequently have less than half the time to train, the predominant training methods used with time-crunched athletes have been remarkably similar to what the pros do. The individual workouts have been shorter and the interval sessions have featured fewer or shorter efforts, but the overall training philosophy has been the same.

Effective training comes down to applying a workload to an athlete that is both specific to his or her goal activity and appropriate for that person's current levels of fitness and fatigue. The load has to be high enough to stimulate a training response from the body, but not so great that it creates more fatigue than the body can cope with. And you have to give the body enough recovery time to replenish energy stores and adapt to the applied stress. Physically, the principal differences between training an elite athlete and an amateur are the workloads necessary to achieve positive adaptations, the workloads the athletes can handle, and the time athletes have available to train.

Amateur athletes can't—or shouldn't—train like pros because they don't have the time necessary to commit to training effectively or, if they do have the time, because they can't physically handle the workload in a way that's beneficial for performance (surviving a training program is not the same thing as thriving on one). Fortunately, you don't need to achieve the same workload that a pro does in order to make significant improvements in your performance. And therein lies the opportunity that time-crunched athletes can exploit. Because you have less training time to fill, you have the opportunity to use your time differently than a high-volume athlete would.

Overview of the Time-Crunched Triathlete Program

Triathlon is a unique sport that places demands on your body that are different from those experienced by single-sport cyclists, runners, and swimmers. Traditionally, triathlon training programs have largely segregated these individual disciplines and trained them individually. The Time-Crunched Triathlete Program leverages the specificity principle of training—which I will explain in more detail in Chapter 2—to improve triathlon performance with fewer training sessions per week. The overall number of hours in the programs found in this book may not be much lower than what you'll find in standard triathlon training programs; the innovation is in the structure of the program. The fact is, for athletes preparing for sprint and Olympic-distance events, eight hours of training per week is sufficient to achieve the fitness necessary for high performance, especially for experienced athletes who may already have longer events (such as the half-Ironman, also known as the 70.3, and the Ironman) under their belts.

As my coaches and I worked with more and more time-crunched triathletes, we found that the critical problem wasn't the overall time commitment, but the frequency of training sessions. As your personal, professional, and family schedules become busier, it becomes increasingly difficult to schedule more than one training session per day, and yet traditional training programs often call for up to 10 individual workouts each week. For many athletes, there is not even enough time available for six daily workout sessions per week (assuming one rest day each week). And as a time-crunched triathlete attempts to shoehorn more workouts into his or her schedule, training becomes a source of lifestyle stress—on top of being a physical stress. You become a slave to your training program.

The goal of the Time-Crunched Triathlete Program is to achieve greater adaptations from fewer training sessions, enabling you to be a successful, fit, and competitive triathlete in as few as four training sessions and 8 hours per week. In order to achieve the training adaptations necessary for high performance from so few training sessions, most of the workouts featured in the programs are "bricks," or sessions that feature two disciplines within the same training session. As you'll see in Chapter 2, there's plenty of research to support a heavy reliance on brick training. More than just a timesaving device, brick training allows for a greater degree of training specificity, which in turn leads to bigger improvements in each leg of your triathlon.

There are some limitations to what the programs described in this book can deliver. I will go into each of them in more detail in the coming pages, but it's important that you have a basic understanding of what you can expect to accomplish with this program. The Time-Crunched Triathlete Program is designed for athletes competing primarily in sprint and Olympic-distance triathlons. And I use the word *compete* on purpose. These programs are designed to improve competitive performances in these races, not merely to enable you to reach the finish line. You can already do that, and many of you have done much more than just finish sprint, Olympic, 70.3, and even Ironman races. Your time constraints have placed some of these longer events out of reach, at least for the time being, but have not diminished your competitive drive or your desire to achieve race-winning or personal-best performances.

You will undoubtedly note that I have included a training program for 70.3 events as well. I felt it was important to include a half-Ironman program in this book because research conducted by USA Triathlon indicates that as triathletes gain experience in the sport, they continue to set their sights on longer and longer events. Within five years of entering the sport, many progress to the point where they want to step up to the 70.3 and full Ironman distances. The Time-Crunched Triathlete Program will not prepare you for a full Iron-distance event, and a 70.3 event will be a stretch as well. I have included a training program for 70.3 events because my coaches and I have successfully used these time-crunched principles with athletes we're coaching for this distance, but there is a catch. Where the Time-Crunched Triathlete Program develops the speed necessary to make you competitive in sprint and Olympic-distance events, it's not likely to develop the endurance necessary to make you *competitive* at the 70.3 distance. You'll have the fitness to finish and have a good race, but you probably won't be setting a personal best or contending for a position on the podium.

Since there is more to preparing for a triathlon than merely following a training plan, this book also includes information about optimizing sports nutrition for your training sessions and competitions (Chapter 4), recommendations about optimizing your racing strategy to take advantage of the fitness this program will provide (Chapter 6), and a strength training program (Chapter 8) to keep you fit and injury-free between periods when you're specifically preparing for a triathlon competition.

I should also point out what this book is not: It is not a beginner book. If you're new to triathlon, the programs in this book will work for you, but the book itself won't teach you how to be a triathlete. You won't find information about how to select a wetsuit or adjust your position on the bike. There's not much information about the specifics of swimming or running technique, either. These are all important topics, but they've been covered extensively elsewhere, and there are great resources available for beginners. I recommend *Your First Triathlon* by Joe Friel.

Why *The Time-Crunched Cyclist* Doesn't Work for Triathletes

As this book was taking shape, I fielded a ton of e-mails from triathletes who were attempting to integrate the cycling program from *The Time-Crunched Cyclist* (*TCC*) into their triathlon programs. Almost universally, I advise against it. Here's why: *TCC* is a high-intensity, low-volume training program designed for single-sport athletes. The reason the interval workouts prescribed in that book can be so strenuous is they are the *only* workouts prescribed. There's just enough time between them to allow for adequate recovery and adaptation, which means that putting an additional training load on top of that program will most likely result in inadequate recovery, diminished performance, and in some cases, injury.

Unfortunately, some triathletes failed to heed my advice and learned the hard way. They substituted their normal cycling workouts with *TCC*

Pick Your Distance

THERE'S A TRIATHLON TO FIT EVERY ATHLETE'S FITNESS LEVEL AND PERSONAL goal. Sprint events are a great entry point into the sport, but they can also be incredibly intense competitions for more experienced racers because the distances are so short. As the race distance increases, the intensity and average pace decline. That doesn't diminish the challenge; it just changes its nature. At all distances, triathlon challenges athletes to walk the fine line between speed and endurance. Going too fast may mean faltering before you cross the finish line; focusing only on endurance will get you to the finish but rarely, if ever, first.

Although there are some standard event distances for triathlons, as listed below, it's important to realize that many triathlons are of a more approximate distance. In other words, it's not unusual for a local to regional event to be called a sprint-distance event and have a 500 m or an 800 m swim, or a 25 km bike instead of a 20 km bike. The same variations can be found in local and regional Olympic-distance events.

Sprint: 750 m swim, 20 km bike, 5 km run

Olympic: 1.5 km swim, 40 km bike, 10 km run

Long course/70.3 (half-Iron): 1.9 km swim, 90 km bike, 21.1 km run

Ultradistance (Ironman): 3.8 km (2.4 mi.) swim, 180 km (112 mi.) bike, 42.2 km (26.2 mi.) run

workouts, while keeping their running and swimming programs un-changed, and for a few weeks at least, they saw measurable improve-ments in their cycling performances. Soon, however, the fatigue from those high-intensity sessions caught up with them and not only hindered their cycling progress, but dragged their running and swimming perfor-mances down as well.

Other triathletes wanted to go a step further and apply the scientific premise behind the TCC to their entire triathlon program, meaning they wanted to transition to shorter, higher-intensity workouts for cycling, running, and swimming. I more forcefully advised against that, and as far as I know, they listened. Increasing the intensity of cycling workouts doesn't dramatically increase the stress applied to joints and connective tissues (assuming your riding position is good, and therefore not increas-ing your chances of developing an overuse injury). On the other hand, running or swimming faster or longer than you're physically prepared for can lead to injuries within a few weeks, at which point you go from be-ing a time-crunched athlete to being a time-crunched physical therapy patient—which is a lot less fun.

The training plans in the TCC were designed for not only single-sport athlete but cyclists specifically. Being a nonimpact, weight-supported sport, the risks associated with increasing the intensity of a cyclist's train-ing program are minimal. Sure, you can overdo it with training load, but the athlete gets tired and generally realizes it's time to back off. In fact, the harder the program, the more evident it becomes to an athlete when he or she has reached an overfatigued, or underrecovered, state. Performance doesn't just diminish slightly. It falls off a cliff. But with weight-bearing sports like running and triathlon, you can't be as cavalier when increasing the workload because increased workload brings increased risk of injury. And what's crucial about that increased risk is that the injury process may be well under way before you realize the workload is too high.

The e-mails from triathletes trying to adapt components of the TCC into their training programs only added to my motivation to get this book written. There's no doubt you can be an effective and competitive time-crunched triathlete; you just need a time-crunched program that's unique to triathlon.

The Promise of a New Paradigm

The Time-Crunched Athlete Programs, from cycling to triathlon, running, and other endurance sports, are all about turning a disadvantage into an advantage. In cycling that means increasing the intensity dramatically in order to benefit from the largely untapped potential of short, extremely difficult interval workouts. In triathlon it means combining efforts to maximize the specificity of your training to multisport events. We're going to reduce the number of training sessions you need to integrate into your busy schedule each week, maximize the impact that each one will have on your sport-specific fitness, and get you onto the start line of your next triathlon ready to compete, have fun, and feel proud.

I'm a dreamer when it comes to what's possible, but a pragmatist when it comes to getting the job done. You're leading a busy lifestyle, and there's nothing you can really take off your plate. You're not going to leave your job or take a pay cut so you can train more. Your kids are growing up quickly, and spending time with them has a huge impact on their future success in life. On top of all that, your spouse or significant other deserves a partner, not a roommate. Being a triathlete—and being a fit, fast, and powerful triathlete at that—can help you be better at your job, be a fully engaged parent and great role model for your kids, and be a more supportive and loving partner. It's for all of these reasons that I don't like to see athletes walk away from training due to a lack of available time, because walking away means they are turning their backs on one of the most important and beneficial aspects of their identities. Similarly, it kills me to hear stories about amateur athletes who end up divorced or unemployed—or both—because their passion for training turned into an unhealthy obsession. For motivated athletes who have run out of available time, the Time-Crunched Triathlete Program is the key to staying in the game and keeping your athletic ambitions in a healthy perspective relative to areas of your life that are, quite frankly, more important than winning any triathlon.

Even as we all get busier, it's imperative that we retain and strengthen our identities as athletes. Being an athlete shapes our perspective of the world; makes us part of a positive, supportive, and uplifting community; and gives us another opportunity to guide our children toward healthy and active lifestyles. Being an athlete is an asset, so it's unacceptable for your job or your mortgage to steal this crucial component of who you are. I know from experience. I've been there, and I once made the choice to stop being an athlete in order to focus on building a career. It was one of the worst decisions of my life, and as I lost my identity as an athlete, my focus and performance in all areas of my life eroded. My weight ballooned, my health deteriorated, I was lethargic and disinterested, and those changes had a negative impact on my personality and my relationships with my wife, my children, my friends, and my coworkers. I am a time-crunched athlete and I'm committed to using all the sports science and coaching resources I can get my hands on to ensure that each of us has the means to stay engaged, stay competitive, and stay at the front of the pack.

I refuse to accept that a reduction in training time automatically dooms you to the misery of being a slow, ineffective, and noncompetitive triathlete. There is another way, and if you're ready to leave antiquated training methods behind, if you're ready to work hard, and if you're open to new ideas and methods for triathlon training, then the Time-Crunched Triathlete Program is your ticket to being fit, fast, and competitive in your next triathlon.

THE SCIENCE OF THE TIME-CRUNCHED TRIATHLETE PROGRAM

Whether you have unlimited time to train or only a few hours a week, your performance depends on developing the same physical systems, and since we're going to be discussing the ways in which you can best improve your performance, a brief review of physiology is a good starting point. Because this is a book for time-crunched athletes, however, this will by no means be an exhaustive treatise on exercise physiology. As an athlete, you probably have a small library of training books already, and those have most likely provided you with a reasonable education in this area, so I'm going to review this material quickly and move on to how it applies to the real question at hand: how to improve your triathlon performance with fewer weekly training sessions.

The Energy Systems

Let's begin with a quick overview of where you get the energy you need for endurance sports. The human body has three primary energy systems that power all activities: the immediate energy system (adenosine triphosphate (ATP) and creatine phosphate (CP), the aerobic system, and the glycolytic (anaerobic) system. The end product of all three is ATP, which releases energy when one of its three phosphate bonds is broken. The resulting adenosine diphosphate is then resynthesized to ATP so it can be broken again, and again, and again. The best way to think of these three energy pathways is from the viewpoint of demand.

IMMEDIATE ENERGY: DO OR DIE

The ATP/CP system supports high-power efforts that last less than about 10 seconds. You use it when you have to jump out of the way of a speeding bus, and from an athletic standpoint it's most important in power sports like football. As an endurance athlete, you mostly use this system for a powerful standing start on a bicycle. During those few seconds, you demand energy faster than either the glycolytic or aerobic energy system can deliver it. The ATP/CP system is immediate because the ATP part is the energy-yielding molecule produced by the other systems. The very limited supply that is stored in your muscles can provide energy without the more than 20 steps required to produce ATP through the aerobic system. However, because endurance sports don't rely heavily on this energy system, triathletes have little reason to focus on it during training.

THE AEROBIC ENGINE

The aerobic system is the body's primary source of energy, and it's an utterly amazing machine. It can burn carbohydrate, fat, and protein simultaneously and can regulate the mixture it burns based on fuel availability and energy demand. It's a flex-fuel engine that's remarkably clean and efficient; when the aerobic system is done with a molecule of sugar, the only waste products are water and carbon dioxide. In comparison, the glycolytic system (discussed in more detail below) produces energy faster, but it can only utilize carbohydrate, produces less ATP from every molecule of sugar it processes, and produces lactate as a by-product (more on that later, too).

The rock stars of the aerobic system are little things called *mitochondria*. These organelles are a muscle cell's power plants: Fuel and oxygen go in and energy comes out. For an endurance athlete, the primary goal of training is to increase the amount of oxygen your body can absorb, deliver, and process. One of the biggest keys to building this oxygen-processing capacity is increasing mitochondrial density, or the size and number of mitochondria in muscle cells. As you swim, bike, and run, having more and bigger power plants running at full capacity gives you the ability to produce more energy aerobically every minute.

When training increases the power you can produce aerobically, you can maintain a higher pace before reaching the point where you're demanding energy faster than the aerobic engine can deliver it—the intensity level otherwise known as *lactate threshold*. But increasing your power or pace at lactate threshold (LT) is only part of the equation. With specific training at intensities near your LT, you can also increase the amount of time you will be able to perform at and slightly above threshold.

THE GLYCOLYTIC ENERGY SYSTEM

There's been a lot of confusion about the glycolytic system, mainly because of semantics. This is the system people often refer to as "anaerobic," which literally means "without oxygen." This terminology causes confusion because it implies that the body has stopped using oxygen to produce energy, which is not the case. As exercise intensity increases, you reach a point at which your demand for energy matches your aerobic engine's ability to produce it in working muscles. Then you decide to push the pace to get on someone's heels in the water, or you turn into a headwind on the bike, or you need to dig deeper to maintain your running pace on a hill. Your energy demand increases, and in order for your mitochondria to continue producing enough energy, your body uses a metabolic shortcut called *anaerobic glycolysis*. Although the actual process involves many chemical reactions, to put it most simply, glycolysis rapidly delivers the ATP necessary to meet your increased energy demand by converting glucose (sugar) into lactate in order to keep other energy-producing reactions moving.

Lactate is a partially utilized carbohydrate that leads to trouble when it builds up in your muscles. The molecule is created as a normal step in aerobic metabolism, and lactate is constantly being broken down to usable energy. The problem isn't really that more lactate is being produced; rather, the problem is that as exercise intensity increases, you reach a point where lactate removal or processing can no longer keep up with production. A disproportionate amount of lactate builds up in the muscle and blood, and this accumulation is what we look for when we're determining an athlete's lactate threshold.

The conversion of glucose to lactate in order to keep energy production going is a lot like using a credit card. You're getting the currency you need as you need it, but you don't have unlimited credit, and sooner rather than later you're going to have to pay back every cent you borrowed. What's more, you have to cut back on spending while you're paying it back, which means you have to slow down. As an endurance athlete, one of the key adaptations you're seeking is an improvement in your ability to get that lactate integrated back into the normal process of aerobic energy production so it can be oxidized completely. The faster you can process lactate, the more work you can perform before lactate levels in your muscles and blood start to rise. Put into the financial analogy, a stronger aerobic system puts more cash (aerobic metabolism) in your pocket so you're not so quick to use credit.

VO$_2$MAX

Lactate threshold (LT) is the point at which your demand for energy outstrips the aerobic system's ability to deliver it, but lactate threshold doesn't define the maximum amount of oxygen your body can use. When your exercise intensity reaches its absolute peak, and your body is pulling in, absorbing, and burning as much oxygen as it possibly can, you're at VO$_2$max. This is your maximum aerobic capacity, and it's one of the most important indicators of your potential as an endurance athlete.

An exceedingly high VO_2max doesn't automatically guarantee you'll become a champion; it just means you have a big engine. To make a comparison to car engines, some people are born with eight cylinders, whereas others have four (and extremely gifted athletes are born with twelve). A finely tuned four-cylinder Acura can go faster than a poorly maintained V8 Corvette, and while twelve-cylinder supercars can beat everything, they can be finicky and difficult to control. And while it's true that you have to have a big engine to be a pro, no matter what size engine you start with, you can optimize your performance with effective training.

THE TRIATHLETE'S NEED FOR SPEED

IT TAKES A GREAT EFFORT TO REACH INTENSITIES NEAR YOUR VO_2MAX, AND during VO_2max-specific workouts you generate an enormous amount of lactate and burn calories tremendously fast. But the reward is worth the effort because increasing your power and pace at VO_2max gives you speed. Triathletes sometimes suffer from a one-pace mentality, which is bred partly by a focus on achieving specific split times. When your goal is to run 7:30 miles for the run leg of an Olympic-distance triathlon, it seems to make the most sense to use primarily endurance and some lactate threshold workouts to get to the fitness level necessary to sustain that pace. It's the *sustainable* aspect of triathlon that keeps too many triathletes from venturing into more threshold and ultimately VO_2max training. The perception is that the sport is all about making steady forward progress, that one only needs endurance, and that somehow speed comes naturally from greater endurance. When you were a novice, finishing was a noble goal. Now it's time to get faster, and it's going to take more than additional time in the saddle and more miles in the legs at endurance pace to get the job done.

We need to get away from this "tortoise" approach to training. One of the lessons we've learned from champions like Craig Alexander is that

CONTINUES

CONTINUED

harelike speed can be advantageous in triathlon. It's absolutely necessary for performing well in sprint and Olympic-distance triathlons (which are the primary distances in this book), and speed was of primary importance in Alexander's victories at the 70.3 Ironman World Championships. CTS Premier Coach Nick White worked with him as he made his transition to Ironman, and has been fond of saying, "Craig had an advantage when he moved up to the Ironman distance; he already had the speed of an Olympic and 70.3 competitor. Building the endurance for Ironman is a cinch when you already have the speed."

Someone is certainly going to point out that, in the tortoise-and-hare fable, the tortoise won the race. But the hare didn't lose because he was fast; he lost because he was an idiot.

Speed is important for competitive performances in sprint and Olympic-distance events, and speed results from training efforts at and above lactate threshold. Triathletes may not have as much need as single-sport cyclists and runners to surge ahead of a group of competitors, but there are times when a powerful effort for one to three minutes is necessary and effective. The first few minutes of an open-water swim, for instance, can be a mad dash to get into position to draft off a fast group of swimmers. Passing competitors on a steep hill during the bike leg can push you way over lactate threshold for a few minutes, and then of course there's the chance you're going to be digging deep in the final half-mile of the race to hold off the competition and win. These efforts, though they represent a very small percentage of the time you'll spend competing, can completely alter the face of your race and your result.

But the true value of high-intensity training for triathletes is that VO_2max training further improves your ability to process lactate. That means VO_2max training complements your interval work at, and just below, lactate threshold; it boosts the LT work you're already doing, which leads to larger, more rapid gains in your maximum sustainable power on the bike and maximum sustainable running and swimming paces.

The Endurance String Theory

Delineating the various ways your body can produce energy is both a blessing and a curse. On the positive side, knowing how each system works gives us the information necessary to design training that makes each system produce energy more quickly and sustainably. On the downside, the same information has inadvertently led people to believe that these systems operate independently of each other. Sports scientists and coaches, me included, have told you that training at 86 to 90 percent of your maximum sustainable power output on the bike will target your glycolytic energy system and increase your power at lactate threshold. And although that is true, the glycolytic system isn't the only one doing the work at that intensity, nor is it the only one that will reap a training benefit.

You are always producing energy through all possible pathways, but your demand for energy determines the relative contribution from each. At low to moderate intensities, the vast majority of your energy comes from the aerobic engine (mitochondria breaking down primarily fat and carbohydrate). As your intensity level rises above about 60 percent of VO_2max, the contribution from the glycolytic system starts to increase, and then it really ramps up quickly once you reach lactate threshold. Because glycolysis only burns carbohydrate, the overall percentage of energy coming from carbohydrate increases dramatically as your intensity increases from lactate threshold to VO_2max. You're still burning a lot of fat, however, because your mitochondria are also still chugging along as fast as they can.

Rather than seeing your various energy pathways as separate and distinct, it's better to think of them as segments of one continuous string, arranged according to the amount of work you perform with each. At one end is the immediate energy system, which can only power your muscles for a handful of seconds. Next comes a large segment representing the aerobic system, because it could theoretically power your muscles at a moderate intensity level forever if there were sufficient oxygen and fuel available. After that is the glycolytic system, which can do a lot of work but can only run at full tilt for a limited period of time before lactate accumulation causes you to reduce your exercise intensity. And finally, we have the segment for VO_2max, which is the maximum amount of work you can do, but represents an intensity that is sustainable for only a few minutes. Training to improve your performance at VO_2max is like pulling up on the VO_2 end of the string—all the other segments rise with it. Focusing your training entirely on improving aerobic performance is like picking up the string in the middle: Power and speed at lactate threshold will dip a bit relative to performance, and power and speed at VO_2max will move very little. All the systems are interconnected, and how you focus your training affects the amount of work you can do, not only with the system you're focusing on, but with all the others as well.

You Are What You Train

All endurance athletes train the same physical systems, but the way you structure your training has a tremendous impact on which events you're going to be optimally prepared for. As events get longer, the overall intensity of the effort gets lower. That's not to say that Ironman is easier than a sprint triathlon, just that the challenges are different. In a sprint triathlon, you might ride at 90–95 percent of your maximum sustainable power output for 25–45 minutes, but during an Ironman you might ride at 75–80 percent of max sustainable power for 5.5 to 6.5 hours. And during a sprint triathlon you may be able to maintain a running pace just slightly slower than your 5K pace from running-only competitions, whereas your marathon pace during the running portion of an Ironman will be significantly slower than if you were competing only in a marathon. When you're training for shorter events, it's essential that you spend more time focused on efforts at a higher intensity level. Because this book is focused primarily on sprint and Olympic-distance events, the time spent at higher intensities (closer to lactate threshold and above threshold) is greater than in programs for long-course triathlons. Because this book also focuses on reducing the number of training sessions you need to schedule each week, you'll find more time at higher intensities compared to most other programs designed for similar events.

Lest you believe *The Time-Crunched Triathlete* (*TCT*) is just a rehashed version of *The Time-Crunched Cyclist* (*TCC*), this is where the two programs diverge. In the *TCC*, the central premise is that incorporating more training at or near VO_2max delivers performance improvements for cyclists that are similar to the gains they can make with programs featuring twice as many hours. The training programs in that book are very, very strenuous and the results are dramatic: Cyclists experience significant improvements in their power at VO_2max and the amount of time they can sustain that power, they improve their power at lactate threshold, and they gain the speed necessary to accelerate off the front of a race or a fast-paced group ride. But while the science supports the use of high-intensity interval training in cycling, and to a lesser extent in running, true high-intensity interval training—that is, training with heavy doses of VO_2max work—is of more limited use in triathlon training. That's not to say it's entirely without merit; as I will explain shortly, the science supporting high-intensity interval training is absolutely applicable to triathlon training. But it must be applied in a different manner—and with different considerations—than in single-discipline sports.

Individually, each of the component sports of triathlon responds well to high-intensity interval training, but when training is combined to specifically prepare an athlete for triathlon, those same high-intensity workouts accumulate too much fatigue. Hard workouts break an athlete down and recovery provides time to build back up. But when the workload is too high, there's not enough time for the body to recover adequately and adapt to the stress. It is this inadequate recovery that causes a wide range of problems for an endurance athlete, from diminished training performance and disturbed sleep to nagging injuries or illnesses.

As a result, the training programs in *The Time-Crunched Triathlete* feature only as much intensity as we can safely and effectively incorporate for triathletes. For athletes who are familiar with a wide range of published training plans and methods, you may notice that the intensities featured in individual workouts are somewhat higher than in programs of similar length and designed for similar athletes. But a moderate increase in intensity, while effective, doesn't provide enough additional training stimulus to allow for a significant decrease in the number of training sessions scheduled each week. To achieve this additional training stimulus, we have to revisit the core principles of training: overload and recovery, progression, individuality, specificity, and a systematic approach.

Principles of Training

Just as all endurance athletes work to improve the same basic physical systems, our training progress is governed by a common set of principles. I've described these principles in a variety of publications over the past 10 years, so some of you may recognize the material in the coming pages, but it's important to revisit these concepts in the process of describing how the Time Crunched Triathlete Program works to improve your performance.

When you distill the world's most successful training programs across all sports, you arrive at five distinct principles of training:

1. Overload and recovery
2. Progression
3. Individuality
4. Specificity
5. Systematic approach

OVERLOAD AND RECOVERY PRINCIPLE

The human body is designed to respond to overload, and as long as you overload a system in the body properly and also allow it time to adapt, that system will grow stronger and be ready for the same stress in the future. All forms of physical training are based on the body's ability to adapt to stress (or overload). To achieve positive training effects, this principle must be applied to individual training sessions as well as entire periods of your training. For instance, a lactate threshold interval workout must be difficult enough and long enough to stress your glycolytic energy system, but lactate threshold workouts must also be scheduled into a block of training so that the training loads from individual workouts accumulate and lead to more significant adaptations.

Organizing training into blocks of similar workouts is one of the hallmarks of a modern periodization plan. Rather than train all systems at once using a schedule that includes base aerobic, lactate threshold, and VO_2max workouts each week, we've found that it's more effective to focus your training on developing each system one at a time. I'll discuss this more when I get to the systematic approach principle, but I mention it here because organizing training into blocks of similar workouts plays an important role in achieving the overload necessary for making big improvements.

Many novice athletes start out training all systems every week, and they make steady gains despite the flaws in that method because they are beginners. The simple act of training will lead to significant improvement when you're just starting out. But that progress stalls relatively quickly because you reach the point where the stimulus applied to each individual system is not great enough, or consistent enough, to lead to further adaptation.

On the other hand, focusing your training on one area for a number of weeks, as you can do with a block of lactate threshold training, targets your workload and training time on overloading that one system. Because you're not trying to build everything at once by cramming in a bunch of additional workouts at higher and lower intensity levels, you have the time to schedule adequate amounts of recovery each week.

At the other end of the spectrum, there's recovery. Recovery is not merely the absence of workouts, but rather a crucial component of training. Days off should not be viewed as missed opportunities to get in another ride, run, or swim session. In reality, the periods between your workouts are when the really important stuff happens in your body. When you're in the middle of a training run, you're not improving your fitness. You're just applying stress and accumulating fatigue. But when you back off, sleep, hydrate, and provide your body with adequate and proper nutrition, *that's* when your fitness improves. So the next time one of your Type A buddies, who's trained every day of the past four years, chastises you for sitting on the couch or going for a walk with the dog instead of taking a 60-minute run, just smile and tell him or her you're busy adapting.

Gains are made when you allow enough time for your body to recover and adapt to the stresses you have applied. This is why I don't separate recovery from training. Recovery is part of your training, and thinking of it in that way helps you remain as committed to recovering as you are to working out.

Table 2.1 shows general guidelines for recovery following specific amounts of time at given intensities. Remember that these are only guidelines. Recovery from training varies among individuals.

ADAPTING THE OVERLOAD AND RECOVERY PRINCIPLE FOR TIME-CRUNCHED TRIATHLETES

Triathletes have earned a reputation as the hardest-working men and women in endurance sports, but that's not entirely a compliment. With three disciplines to train for and three modes of exercise to use (four, if you include strength training), triathlon makes overachievers salivate. But it's exactly that fervor for training that gets the age-group triathlete in trouble. For athletes training 10, 12, or more hours a week, there's no problem accumulating enough stimulus to reach overload. If anything, endurance athletes leading busy lives and training on higher-volume training plans have more trouble setting aside enough time for recovery. But as a time-crunched triathlete making the transition to a program featuring fewer weekly training sessions, you have an advantage over your higher-frequency compatriots: You have built-in recovery days!

Reducing the number of training sessions each week allows us to increase the intensity of each workout because the structure of the program incorporates more recovery between sessions. We've increased the amount of stress each workout places on your body, but lengthened the rest periods between strenuous workouts to allow you to adapt and prepare for the next training session. When I look at a traditional triathlon

TABLE 2.1: Guidelines for Recovery

VOLUME OF INTENSITY	SUGGESTED TIME NEEDED FOR RECOVERY
0–6 hours at aerobic endurance intensity	8 hours
30–60 minutes at tempo intensity	8–10 hours
75–120 minutes at tempo intensity	24–36 hours
15–45 minutes at lactate threshold	24 hours
60–90 minutes at lactate threshold	24–36 hours
10–30 minutes above lactate threshold	24–36 hours
45 minutes or more above lactate threshold	36–48 hours

training program next to the Time-Crunched Triathlon Programs I feel as if there's more "breathing room" in this method. We can talk about science all day long, but what the sports scientists sometimes forget is that athletes are not machines. You have emotions; you feel stressed, overjoyed, frustrated, bored, harried, or overwhelmed. As a coach, I understand and use sports science, but I also know that overscheduled athletes don't respond to training as well as athletes who have some downtime.

When your personal, professional, and training tasks are dictating your schedule and keeping you moving at all times, the tail is wagging the dog. For nearly every athlete I know—and *all* the highly successful athletes I know—that's an intolerable scenario. You want to be in control so *you* can make decisions instead of having your decisions made for you. Personally, I can't stand it when my calendar fills to the point where I have back-to-back obligations from sunup to sundown. I feel rushed and confined all day, like a caged animal or a lion in the circus, even if some of the items on my calendar are training related.

The tension that results from being overscheduled carries into your training sessions. Even though workouts can serve as crucial pressure valves to relieve everyday stress, your primary reason for training is to prepare for competition; stress relief is a bonus. To optimize the impact your training sessions have on your race performance, it's helpful to be rt the training session in the first place. Being a physiologically compromised position be- ormone called cortisol in stressful situations, , a test in school, or a confrontation with your stinguish between stressors; it just knows it's hibits recovery and leads to muscle breakdown in athletes, and the more you're stressed, the more cortisol is released. As an athlete reliant on quality recovery for recuperation and physiological adaptation, you want to minimize conditions where your cortisol levels rise higher than absolutely necessary. Everyday stress will increase your cortisol levels, just as doing a hard track session will, so it is best to keep cortisol levels as low as possible whenever you can do so. Take the cortisol hit on the track, not in the boardroom, and you will be better able to tolerate the training program and make positive adaptations from your workouts. As an added bonus, both your increased fitness and reduced everyday stress will help you be a healthier, happier, and more engaging person.

With fewer training sessions each week, there's plenty of recovery time built into the Time-Crunched Triathlete Program to ensure proper adaptation. The challenge then is to accumulate the workload necessary to cause an overload, and the question is whether you can accomplish this task with so few workouts. Fortunately, the relationship between volume and intensity is not linear. Training workload is the product of volume *and* intensity, and increasing intensity results in an exponential increase in workload as compared to the effect of increasing volume. As a result, even modest increases in intensity can lead to significant increases in training workload and the resulting adaptation. In fact, it is unwise to increase intensity without decreasing volume because the resulting effect is too great of an overload for many athletes to tolerate. So by increasing intensity, you've already started saving time, while still accomplishing the work necessary to make progress. Keep in mind that the workload necessary to achieve overload—and hence the amount of time necessary to recover from workouts—changes as your fitness level rises and falls.

The overload and recovery principle must be applied across all workouts, individual weeks of training, seasons, and even years. And to keep moving forward, you need to do more than overload your body and let it rest.

PROGRESSION PRINCIPLE

Training must move forward progressively in order to deliver continued gains in performance. As you utilize the overload and recovery principle, you adapt to the stress of training and grow stronger. But if your training workload stays stagnant, there is no more incentive for your body to continue adapting. If you want to get faster, you have to increase your training workload as your body adapts to the training you've already completed. Those athletes you know who are pretty good but never seem to get any better could use a refresher course in progression.

Time and intensity are the two most significant variables you can use to adjust your workload. For instance, you can increase the number of hours you devote to training (otherwise known as increasing volume), or you can increase the overall intensity of your workouts by including more intervals. You can make the intervals more intense, make them longer, or shorten the recovery periods between the intervals. You can use these variables to manipulate training a hundred different ways, but the end result must be that you're generating a training stimulus great enough to make your muscles and aerobic engine adapt. Just as important, once you adapt and grow stronger, you have to manipulate the time and intensity variables once again so you further increase the workload to generate another training stimulus. In other words, as you adapt to the training load, you must then undertake a bigger workload to overload the stronger system you've built.

Interestingly, some of the most compelling evidence supporting the effectiveness of high-intensity interval training relates to the principle of progression. Neither training time nor intensity is limitless, even for professional athletes. There are only 24 hours in the day, and the human body can only be pushed so hard. Professional athletes across the entire range of endurance sports are pretty much maxed out in terms of the annual hours they can accumulate while still performing at a high level. Indeed, studies have shown that even if highly trained athletes could add more training volume, additional volume wouldn't lead to improvements in VO_2max, power at lactate threshold, or mitochondrial density (Laursen and Jenkins 2002). With volume effectively maxed out and therefore not a limiting factor for improvement, you can really see the impact of increasing an athlete's workload with high-intensity intervals.

In Ironman races, the duration of the event results in a lower average intensity level. Ironman triathletes, even the pros, spend the vast majority of the race below lactate threshold and virtually no time at intensities approaching VO_2max. Yet the top professionals vying for the Ironman World Championship in Hawaii do incorporate high-intensity intervals in their training. They incorporate a lot of interval work above lactate threshold because no amount of moderate-intensity training volume would be enough to generate the power necessary to stay in contention during the bike leg, or the speed needed to rip a sub-2:50 marathon and run down Ali'i Drive as Ironman champion. To make the additional progress necessary for success at the highest levels of the sport, pros have to incorporate high-intensity intervals—on top of the intensity they get in races—into their training programs.

As a time-crunched athlete, you aren't maxed out in terms of training volume, but you are maxed out in terms of the time you can devote to training. Even though there are advantages to training more than eight hours a week, and perhaps advantages to training with more frequency than what's featured in the Time-Crunched Triathlete Program, the other commitments in your life mean you have to do what you can in the time you have. To achieve progression without adding hours or workouts, this program manipulates the type and number of intervals, as well as interval duration and the recovery between efforts. Progression is fast in this program, and by the end of either six or eight weeks (depending on which program you choose) the workouts you thought were challenging at the beginning will look like child's play. But around the same time, you'll also notice that your power and speed in the water, on the bike, and on your feet have increased dramatically and you'll be ready to have a great experience and result on race day.

INDIVIDUALITY PRINCIPLE

The individuality principle simply states that the training program that works for you, right down to the individual workouts and interval intensities, has to be based on your physiological and personal needs. Training is not a one-size-fits-all product. All parts of your program—the total mileage, the number and type of intervals, and even the terrain—must be personalized. That doesn't mean that you can't train with your friends or training partners; it just means that while you're with them you have to stay true to your own training program. Individuality is rarely a problem for time-crunched athletes, because your busy schedule already means training at different times and with different workouts than your friends who have more free time on their hands. Once you start on the Time-Crunched Triathlete Program, your training is going to be extremely different from what they're doing, so much so that you may spend even more time training by yourself and your friends may question the wisdom of your choices. But don't give in to the peer pressure to revert back to a training model that's no longer relevant for you. Let them tell you this is crazy; the best way to convince them that the Time-Crunched Triathlete Program works is to do the program and then surprise them with a stellar performance at your next event!

Now, before you send me an e-mail about the seeming contradiction between the individuality principle and the static training programs in this book, let me say that I see the paradox. Believe me, no one understands the value of individual coaching better than I do. Ideally, every athlete would work with a coach and get a training program built from scratch, but I understand that personal coaching is not an option for everyone. Therefore, the workouts and training programs in this book are rooted in the principles my coaches and I use to create custom schedules for our athletes, and you will be able to apply the individuality principle to them when you establish your personal intensity ranges and fit the workouts into your busy work and family schedule.

SPECIFICITY PRINCIPLE

Your training must resemble the activity you want to perform. In a broad sense, this means that if you want to be a runner, you should spend the vast majority of your training time running. In a narrower sense, it means you have to determine the exact demands of the activity you wish to perform and tailor your training to address those demands. Conversely, it also means that your training is going to prepare you optimally for specific events and activities.

The success of the Time-Crunched Triathlete Program depends a great deal on leveraging the power of the specificity principle. Remember, we can't dramatically increase the workload of your training program by ramping the intensity up into the stratosphere, and I said in the beginning of this section that we had to look more closely at the principles of training in order to find a source for additional training stimulus. That source is specificity, and the additive effect of a moderate increase in workout intensities and of training sessions that are most specific to triathlon performance provides the total training stimulus we were looking for—and that you need.

Traditionally we talk about narrowing the focus of a broad endurance training program in order to enhance the specific skills and paces or power outputs that will lead to success in goal events. But you don't have the time to build broad endurance fitness in the first place, so you need to look at specificity from the opposite direction. With very limited time available for training, the fitness you're going to develop with the Time-Crunched Triathlete Program will be best applied to a specific set of events and goals. You will have the fitness to be successful (probably more successful than you'd be right now if you've been struggling to conform your time-crunched lifestyle to a higher-volume program). However, there are some inescapable consequences to having fewer hours or training sessions available to train for an endurance sport, and I explain these consequences in more detail in the section "Terms and Conditions" later in this chapter.

SYSTEMATIC APPROACH

When it comes to achieving high-performance fitness to be competitive in your next event, you need a training program that integrates and addresses all the principles of training. This is especially true for athletes who have limited training time. A systematic approach to training integrates all of the crucial components of training: overload and recovery, progression, individuality, and specificity. Focusing on any one of the principles while neglecting others will take your training off course. As a time-crunched triathlete, you don't have the time to bumble your way through a training plan that is not systematic; you won't see the results you deserve for all of your hard effort.

Athletes using high-volume training programs have the luxury of being able to waste some percentage of their training time without experiencing much of a penalty. With 10 or more workouts in a single week, there are plenty of opportunities to make up for a poor performance in an individual session, and while high-volume training programs can carry more risk for underrecovery, one benefit of all those training hours is a very deep base of aerobic fitness. That huge foundation means that high volume programs are more forgiving, in that small transgressions (poor or skipped workouts) aren't enough to knock an athlete off course. The less time you have available for training, however, and the fewer workouts you have scheduled for the week to begin with, the greater the penalties for wasted or missed efforts.

In order to leverage the benefits of each of the previous four principles of training, they need to be combined into a systematic approach to improvement. Appropriate levels of overload and recovery must be established based on your individual needs, and manipulated so that you achieve progression. And a training program doesn't do you much good unless it prepares you for the specific and unique demands of your goal event.

You can apply any of the previous four principles individually, but if you do so, you're not likely to be satisfied with the results. A common failure of training results from achieving mastery of overload and recovery and of progression while completely neglecting individuality and specificity. I most often see this with the data junkies, the athletes so focused on numbers, graphs, and training logs that all they care about is the trend of the data, even if it's leading them away from the fitness they need to perform at their best in their goal event.

Another problematic scenario is created by neglecting individuality and progression. This is typically an issue for the social triathletes, the athletes who value the social environment of the triathlon community so highly that they substitute socializing for progression and individuality, which causes their training progress to stall or even collapse. These athletes are essentially going through the motions or treading water, and for short periods of time that can be OK. In fact, of the two, I prefer social triathletes to the data junkies. Data junkies will follow their numbers down a rabbit hole, and even when they're sitting in the dark, some of them lack the common sense to dig themselves out. Social triathletes at least maintain a base level of sport-specific fitness and stay fully engaged in the triathlon community. For many serious and devoted athletes it's a safe and enjoyable place to rest between periods of heightened focus. For instance, we often see athletes go from spending a full year focused on Ironman competitions, sometimes including Ironman Kona, to becoming more of a social triathlete for a few months. The athlete feels less pressure to keep pushing his or her fitness upward, but still achieves the satisfaction of training and being an active triathlete.

Some people seem to be able to remain superfit regardless of what they do or how much they do. Some stay thin regardless of what they eat. These people are the fortunate anomalies. Most athletes, even those who like to think of themselves as rebels, thrive on structure and benefit significantly from approaching training systematically. As you embark on the Time-Crunched Triathlete Program, remember that with limited training time, every hour and every interval counts, and all workouts are connected through the principles of training.

The Science of Specificity in Triathlon

The proof that triathlon needs to be considered a sport unto itself, and not an aggregate of three individual sports, can be found by looking at the most successful triathletes in the world. From the sport's beginnings, and with only a few exceptions (John Howard, for example), the best triathletes have been well-rounded endurance athletes rather than highly specialized, top-tier competitors in single-discipline races. Recent "invaders" have come into triathlon from other endurance sports— professional cyclists, elite middle-distance runners and marathoners, even elite swimmers—but they have generally not succeeded in rising to the top of the triathlon ranks. And if they eventually do reach the upper echelons of triathlon, it is only after several years of adapting to its rigors. If all that was needed to be an elite triathlete was a giant aerobic engine, then the transition into triathlon would be far easier than it has proven to be for many elite single-sport athletes.

Every triathlete knows that running off the bike feels very different from lacing up running shoes and laying down a fast 10K on fresh legs. And yet, most triathlon programs continue to train each discipline in isolation, combining them only occasionally as major events approach. As such, those programs are not fully leveraging the power of training specificity.

As early as 1998, Kreider and colleagues documented the physiological differences of biking after swimming and of running after both swimming and biking. They found that "triathlon performance elicited cardiovascular and thermal adjustments not experienced when performing the events independently. Findings appear to be the result of thermoregulatory and cardiovascular adaptations combined with a decrease in mechanical efficiency observed during prolonged triathlon performance." In other words, cycling after swimming causes different physiological responses in the body than does cycling without a prior swim session. Run stride and run efficiency are also affected by prior cycling efforts, as opposed to running on fresh legs. Millet and Vleck (2000) were able to quantify the cost of this decreased run efficiency. They found a 10 percent increase in the total energy cost of running off the bike opposed to running on fresh legs. They reasoned, "This may be due to exercise intensity, ventilatory muscle fatigue, dehydration, muscle fiber damage, a shift in metabolism toward fat oxidation, and depleted glycogen stores after a 40 km cycle." Quadriceps muscle fatigue may also account for some of the increased energy cost by affecting running gait patterns and run economy.

Investigating the specific differences in run biomechanics and run economy that account for the increased energy cost, Hausswirth et al. (1997) monitored the gait patterns and body positioning of high-level marathoners and Olympic-distance triathletes. Looking at the final 45 minutes of a 2:15 marathon and the final run portion of a 2:15 Olympic-distance triathlon, these investigators found greater stride length in the run portion of the triathlon than in the final 45 minutes of a marathon. They also found that "after cycling, the triathletes adopted a more for-ward leaning posture and the trunk gradient was less marked during the marathon." These alterations in gait pattern not only further substantiate the claim that running off the bike is a different sport from isolated run-ning but may also account for the increased energy cost and decreased economy of running following cycling.

The run portion of the triathlon is not the only segment affected by the cumulative effects of performing different disciplines. Delextrat et al. (2005) found that cycling after swimming, compared to cycling after a cycling-specific warm-up, elicited a lower efficiency and a higher blood lactate concentration while riding. Thus, the energy demands of cycling after swimming are greater than the energy demands of cycling after completing a warm-up routine on the bike.

Further research documents the peripheral effects of triathlon in terms of muscular recruitment patterns by testing electromyography (EMG) activity—the electrical activity in muscles—in lower-leg muscles during running after a cycling session. Heiden and Burnett (2003) recorded "changes in muscle function when changing from cycling to running [indicating] a need to train specifically for the cycle to run transition." So not only is blood lactate higher in triathletes running off the bike, but muscle recruitment patterns are actually different from when they are running without an initial bike segment. The way you use your muscles to power yourself through the running leg of a triathlon is different from the way you power yourself through an isolated running workout.

When you put the research together, it becomes clear that although triathlon appears to be a succession of distinct and isolated efforts (swim, bike, run), the fact is that each activity has a significant impact on the next—so much so that there is an undeniable opportunity to apply the principle of training specificity to triathlon and reap gains over and above those experienced by athletes training each component in isolation.

What triathletes have known all along, and what sports science must now accept, is that triathlon is its own unique sport with highly specialized activities that place unique cardiovascular and muscle recruitment demands on your body, compared to its single-sport components. The exercise physiology research shows it, and it's finally time that the training plans reflect it. To say that the old methods are adequate because they have been used successfully for more than 20 years is to deny that innovation and new research can lead to improved performance. For too long, the standard training protocols for triathlon have clung to the antiquated idea that it is wise to train all three disciplines in isolation and expect the body to put it all together because you do a handful of multidiscipline workouts before race day. Emerging science shows that when triathlon training is designed to more closely resemble the actual sequence of multisport competitions, athletes can make greater performance gains. In practice, applying this science to real athletes has shown my coaches and me that these gains can also be accomplished with fewer training sessions. As a result, the Time-Crunched Triathlete Program actually trains triathletes to ride faster after exiting the water, and to run faster after having already completed the swimming and cycling legs of a triathlon.

By leveraging the science and power of specificity, the Time-Crunched Triathlete Program has proven itself to be both time-efficient and better at preparing athletes to perform at their best during all three disciplines on race day. The specificity principle has been lacking in much of triathlon training to date, and this program corrects that flaw while simultaneously maximizing your precious little training time. By combining a greater focus on specificity with the proven science of high-intensity training, time-crunched athletes have the opportunity to realize performance gains that have previously been out of reach.

The Science of High-Intensity Interval Training

Over the past several years, I've become more of a proponent of high-intensity interval training, especially for athletes who have limited time available to train. I cited much of the research below in making the case for the cycling training programs in *The Time-Crunched Cyclist*, and even though I've stated several times already in this book that it's unwise to apply the level of intensity found in those single-sport programs to multisport athletes, the same research can be used to show that applying an appropriate amount of high-intensity interval training can improve race-day performances for time-crunched triathletes as well.

If you take the time to compare the training plans in *The Time-Crunched Cyclist* with the plans in this book, you will notice that there is less intensity in the triathlon plans. I use the word "less" cautiously, however, because while there are fewer VO_2max workouts—and hence fewer overall minutes spent at intensities approaching VO_2max—the amount of time spent at these high intensities is greater as a percentage of total weekly workout time than is typical in sprint and Olympic-distance triathlon training plans. In other words, while you won't be doing 20 minutes of PowerIntervals (maximum-effort cycling intervals designed to improve power at VO_2max) over the course of a one-hour cycling session, you will instead be doing 15 minutes of work at or near your lactate threshold power output during a 45-minute cycling session, followed by eight 1-minute VO_2max efforts during a 20-minute run. So, in a workout that totals 75 minutes, you will amass 23 minutes of work at intensities at and above lactate threshold, which turns out to be 3 minutes more than you would have accomplished during those 20 minutes of PowerIntervals, and you'll accumulate that work in a triathlon-specific sequence. The Time-Crunched Triathlete Program incorporates more intensity per workout than many other plans that focus primarily on endurance and subthreshold work. In a typical plan, about 20–30 percent of your weekly training volume would consist of threshold work, whereas the program presented here has well over 50 percent of total time spent training at threshold and above.

While we do utilize high-intensity interval training—particularly during run sessions off the bike—we do not incorporate high-intensity work into each and every segment of each and every workout. Doing so would greatly increase the risk of injury and compromise the quality of the workout. For example, imagine a superhard swim session with 25 and 50 meter/yard all-out efforts, followed by PowerIntervals on the bike, followed by a run with fartlek intervals (the running version of max-effort intervals designed to improve pace at VO_2max). By the time you got to the run portion of your workout, your pace during the fartleks would likely be no faster than your normal endurance or tempo run pace. The time already spent way above lactate threshold during your swimming and cycling sessions would render you incapable of adequately completing high-intensity running intervals. Remember, in order to be effective, intervals must be completed at the pace or intensity level that stimulates your body to adapt and grow stronger. When your pace is too low—even if your perceived exertion is extremely high—you're operating at a level your body can already handle. It will see no need to adapt, and therefore the efforts—as strenuous as they may seem—are fruitless.

If we overload you with intensity in the first 20 minutes of a 90-minute workout that features both swimming and cycling, or cycling and running, the subsequent 70 minutes are not likely to yield positive results. And in this scenario, overdoing it during the first portion of the workout will mean missing out on achieving the full benefit of training specificity. By applying the right amount of intensity to both portions of a two-discipline workout, you will make the sport-specific gains you're after in rides after swims, and runs after rides. Running off the bike is a different sport from running on fresh legs in that there are differing muscle recruitment patterns, different fuel utilization, and different physiological functions. To make you a faster triathlete and to give you the ability to race the run instead of survive it, your workouts need to be designed to maximize your performance in this specific circumstance.

During the Time-Crunched Triathlete Program, you will often complete threshold work in one discipline and VO_2 work in another. You will most often train on the bike after swimming, and you'll most often run after cycling. In order to maximize the value of high-intensity training, we need to spread out the hard efforts throughout the entire workout in order to ensure that you can accomplish the whole workout safely and effectively. In single-sport programs, the hardest work is almost always done first, when the athlete is freshest, but this will not always be the case in the Time-Crunched Triathlete Program. There will be times when the hardest interval work is done last, after less-intense work has been completed in a different discipline. It is the careful application of threshold and high-intensity interval training over three disciplines and in a triathlon-specific manner that allows these programs to generate significant improvements in performance over a six- to eight-week period.

The Research on High-Intensity Training

High-intensity training has been studied extensively, and the basic premise of a training program that utilizes intervals above lactate threshold intensity and approaching VO_2max is that efforts at this intensity level lead to many of the same physiological adaptations that result from more traditional endurance training models. In fact, Burgomaster et al. (2005) found that high-intensity interval training doubled an athlete's time to exhaustion on a ride performed at 80 percent of peak VO_2. Esfarjani and Laursen (2007) also found that high-intensity interval training protocols improved runners' performances at the 3,000 meter distance by 8 percent and improved the amount of time runners were able to sustain VO$_2$max by as much as 32 percent. These results are appealing to the time-crunched athlete because the efforts required are up to five times shorter than the traditional intervals used to target power at lactate threshold. I know that many athletes are genuinely interested in the science of performance, so let's take a closer look at the science that supports a high-intensity, low-volume training program.

What Constitutes Improvement?

At the end of the day, improvement can be measured by whether you can go faster at the same relative effort level than before and/or whether you can sustain that pace longer than you could before. On the bike, this can also be measured by an increase in the power output you can sustain, and for how long. In any endurance sport, if you can go faster from point A to point B (in similar conditions) after training, then you have made progress. But many factors are involved in getting from A to B more quickly, including a learning curve that helps athletes become faster over familiar territory and through similar conditions, even when they have made no improvement in fitness. So how do you know whether an athlete's improved performance is due to physiological changes or the fact that he or she has learned how to perform better when tested? You look inside the muscles.

Having more mitochondria in muscle cells allows you to oxidize more fat and carbohydrate through aerobic metabolism. For a long time we thought the most effective way to increase mitochondrial density was to perform long workouts at moderate intensities. And although there's still debate about the exact mechanism at work, evidence suggests that the depletion of ATP in muscle cells, which happens when intense exercise leads you to consume ATP faster than it can be produced, may kick-start a cascade of biochemical processes that ends with increased production of mitochondria (Willett 2006). Studies examining the effectiveness of short, high-intensity cycling intervals for improving aerobic performance have shown an increase in muscles' oxidative capacity (the maximum amount of oxygen a muscle can utilize) and in levels of key enzymes used in the process of aerobic metabolism. In 1982, Dudley and colleagues reported that intensities of 95 percent and above throughout a 20-minute maximum power output on the bike are required to create the largest concentration of mitochondrial enzymes. Conversely, they also reported that there is no increase in muscle enzyme density after 60 minutes of continuous work. Although the original research was completed using rat muscle fiber, the study was corroborated in later research performed on athletes. It has been suggested that the lack of increased muscle enzyme activity after 60 minutes of continuous work (such as during a long, moderate-intensity endurance ride or run) is because the increased exercise duration lowers the athlete's power output and pace below what is needed to stimulate up-regulation of enzymes.

When considering Dudley and colleagues' findings in relation to classic triathlon training protocols, especially those that focus primarily on long, subthreshold training sessions to achieve overload via volume, it becomes more obvious why classic triathlon programs are good at improving an athlete's endurance, but less successful at making athletes fast enough to be competitive. Long efforts at steady intensities will provide the endurance necessary to keep moving all day long, and there is certainly room for that in the overall scope of being an endurance athlete. But if you want to be fast and competitive, intervals are the best way to get there.

You can also measure an athlete's VO_2max to determine whether a training program has improved his or her capacity to utilize oxygen. In 1986, Dempsey found a 19 percent increase in VO_2max (from 50 to 61) using a 12-week cycling program of four workouts a week, featuring 3-minute intervals at VO_2max and 2-minute recovery periods between efforts. Rodas et al. (2000) were able to take the research a step further because of advances in power meter technology, and they reported a 30-watt increase in maximal load and an increase in VO_2max from 57.3 to 63.8 in their high-intensity interval training. Barnett et al. (2004) found a 7.1 percent increase in mean power output and an 8 percent increase in peak VO_2. Their research also showed a 17 percent increase in resting intramuscular glycogen content, and this increase in the amount of carbohydrate fuel a muscle can store is another indicator of improved aerobic conditioning.

Laursen et al. (2002) found that it took only four high-intensity training sessions to bring about a 4.4 to 5.8 percent improvement in 40K time trial performance. Hawley et al. (1997) found that after only four to six interval sessions performed over two to three weeks, peak power output was increased by 15 to 20 watts, which can translate to riding 1.5 to 2 km/hr. faster in a 40K time trial, or a 90- to 120-second improvement. These findings support the notion that after training with high-intensity intervals, athletes are able to sustain work at a higher percentage of their peak VO_2 (90 percent versus 86 percent in the Hawley et al. study). Hawley and colleagues stated that this improvement is likely due to an increased efficiency in fatty acid metabolism and a "decreased reliance on carbohydrate as a fuel source" due to an increased density of mitochondria in muscle cells.

Similarly, Brooks and Mercier (1994) reported a reduction in carbohydrate oxidation and lactate accumulation following high-intensity interval training when subjects were asked to perform at the same absolute work rate as they had at the beginning of the study. This is crucial for understanding how high-intensity training ends up increasing endurance performance. After the high-intensity training, when athletes ride at higher power outputs, they will be less reliant on the glycolytic system and derive a higher percentage of energy from the aerobic system. As a result, they will use more fat for energy and produce less lactate. Harmer et al. (2000) also found a reduction in glycogen utilization and lactate accumulation following a high-intensity training protocol. Additional physiological adaptations to high-intensity interval training have been found in runners as well.

Helgerud et al. (2007) found both stroke volume and VO_2max improvements using high-intensity interval training protocols. Researchers compared four groups of runners: (1) a long slow distance group (70 percent maximal heart rate, or HR_{max}); (2) a lactate threshold group (85 percent

HR_{max}); (3) a short interval group (15 seconds of running at 90–95 percent HR_{max}, followed by 15 seconds of active resting at 70 percent HR_{max}); and (4) a long interval group (4 minutes of running at 90–95 percent HR_{max}, followed by 3 minutes of active resting at 70 percent HR_{max}). Each group's workouts were standardized so all performed similar work as measured in terms of total oxygen consumption. And each group exercised three days per week for a total of eight weeks. The short interval group and the long interval group increased their VO_2max by 5.5 percent and 7.2 percent, respectively, as compared to the long slow distance group and the lactate threshold group. Additionally, in both interval groups there was a 10 percent increase in stroke volume after interval training. Thus Helgerud et al. conclude that "high-aerobic intensity endurance interval training is significantly more effective than performing the same total work at either lactate threshold or at 70 percent HR_{max} in improving VO_2max." Another study, conducted by Bickham et al. (2004), found a 15.3 percent increase in time to exhaustion in endurance-trained runners who underwent a six-week high-intensity training protocol. High-intensity interval training is thus very effective and leads to marked physiological benefits and improved performance in both cycling and run training.

Terms and Conditions

There was a time when I wanted to be all things to all people, but that method doesn't really work, at least not for athletes who want to achieve a high level of performance. The truth is that programs and guidance designed to apply to everyone are effective for only a portion of the population—usually the beginners. But this book and these programs aren't for beginners, and they may not even be right for all experienced triathletes. The Time-Crunched Triathlete Program is not meant to be all things to all athletes, but it's the right program for a large number of triathletes who already have sport-specific experience, at least a few races under their belts, and a desire to be competitive despite having limited time available for training.

If you're one of those triathletes, you've come to the right place. But before you dive in, there are some terms and conditions you need to accept, because while these programs offer time-crunched athletes great opportunities, it's important for you to understand that there are limits to the types and lengths of events for which you can expect to be optimally prepared. After all, there are some inescapable consequences to training for an endurance sport on limited training time.

The 3-Hour Limit

The reason training volume is so beneficial is that it builds an incredibly deep foundation of aerobic fitness. More than that, high-volume training that incorporates high-intensity intervals prepares triathletes to uncork amazing run performances at the end of triathlon. Pro triathletes aiming to win Ironman events need that combination of high-volume and high-intensity interval work because they need the endurance to get to

DOES IT MATTER HOW STRONG YOU ARE NOW?

RESEARCH HAS SHOWN THAT IF AN ATHLETE HAS A VO$_2$MAX OVER 60 ML/KG/MIN., endurance performance will not improve without high-intensity interval training (Londeree 1997). Londeree also found that even with a VO$_2$max lower than 60 ml/kg/min., after three weeks of training there will be very few positive training adaptations unless there is an increase in training stimulus. As a matter of perspective, a moderately trained triathlete will have a VO$_2$max of about 50 to 55, a well-trained triathlete (age-group winner) will likely be between 55 and 65, and a high-level amateur or pro is likely to have a VO$_2$max above 70 ml/kg/min. Laursen and Jenkins (2002), who defined "moderately trained" athletes as having a VO$_2$max less than 60 ml/kg/min., provided a very useful summary of relevant research. They defined high-intensity training as an interval of 30 seconds to 5 minutes

CONTINUES

CONTINUED

at intensities above lactate threshold, and they looked at a wide range of markers to identify improvement in aerobic metabolism, including changes in muscle fibers and the small blood vessels (capillaries) that deliver oxygenated blood to muscle tissue:

High-intensity training in sedentary and recreationally active indi-
viduals improves endurance performance to a greater extent than
does continuous submaximal training alone. This improvement ap-
pears due, in part, to an up-regulated contribution of both aerobic and
anaerobic metabolism to the energy demand, which enhances the
availability of ATP and improves the energy status in working muscle.
An improved capacity for aerobic metabolism, as evidenced by an

TABLE 2.2: Summary of Findings in High-Intensity Interval Training (HIT) Studies in Highly Trained Endurance Athletes[a]

REFERENCE	N	HIT SESSIONS	REPS	INTENSITY (% P_{peak})
Lindsay et al.	8	6	6–8	80
Weston et al.	6	6	6–8	80
Westgarth-Taylor et al.	8	12	6–9	80
Stepto et al.	4	6	4	80
Stepto et al.	4	6	8	85
Stepto et al.	4	6	12	90
Laursen et al.	7	4	20	100
Stepto et al.	3	6	12	100
Stepto et al.	44	6	12	175

[a] Changes indicated based on statistical significance at the $p < 0.05$ level.

3-HCoA = 3-hydroxyacyl coenzyme A dehydrogenase activity; **CHO**ox = carbohydrate oxidation rates; **CS** = citrate synthase activity; **HK** = hexokinase activity; **N** = number of participants; **PFK** = phosphofructokinase activity; **P**peak = peak aerobic power output;

increased expression of type I fibers [otherwise known as slow-twitch muscle fibers and in contrast to type II, or fast-twitch muscle fibers], capillarization and oxidative enzyme activity, is the most common response to high-intensity training in untrained or moderately active individuals. (Laursen and Jenkins 2002)

Although far less research has been conducted on professional-level athletes (it tends to be difficult to get professionals to participate in a study that requires them to try something different), Laursen and Jenkins put together a table that summarizes the results of research on the effectiveness of high-intensity training for highly trained endurance athletes (see Table 2.2).

WORK DURATION	REST DURATION	HIT DURATION (WEEKS)	RESULTS
5 min.	60 sec.	4	$\uparrow P_{peak}$, $\uparrow TF_{150}$, $\uparrow TT_{40}$
5 min.	60 sec.	4	$\uparrow P_{peak}$, $\uparrow TF_{150}$, $\uparrow TT_{40}$, $\uparrow ß$, $\leftrightarrow HK$, $\leftrightarrow PFK$, $\leftrightarrow CS$, $\leftrightarrow 3$-HCoA
5 min.	60 sec.	6	$\uparrow P_{peak}$, $\uparrow TT_{40}$, $\downarrow CHO_{ox}$
8 min.	1 min.	3	$\leftrightarrow$
4 min.	1.5 min.	3	$\uparrow P_{peak}$, $\uparrow TT_{40}$
2 min.	3 min.	3	$\leftrightarrow$
1 min.	2 min.	2	$\uparrow P_{peak}$, $\uparrow T_{vent}$, $\uparrow TF_{100}$
1 min.	4 min.	3	$\leftrightarrow$
30 sec.	4.5 min.	3	$\uparrow P_{peak}$, $\uparrow TT_{40}$

Reps = repetitions; **TF100** = time to fatigue at 100%; **TF$_{150}$**= time to fatigue at 150% of P_{peak}; **TT40** = 40K time trial performance; **T$_{vent}$** = ventilatory threshold; **ß** = buffering capacity; $\downarrow$ = decrease; $\uparrow$ = increase; $\leftrightarrow$ = no change.

Source: Laursen and Jenkins 2002.

the run feeling fresh, and the aerobic capacity to race the run instead of just survive it.

With far less time available to train, you can still build the fitness necessary to finish a triathlon with a great run, but your best performances will come in events that are 3 hours or shorter. Sprint triathlons certainly fit within this range, with beginner finishing times typically under 2 hours, moderately fit athletes finishing in 60 to 90 minutes, and fast finishers crossing the line in less than 1 hour. Olympic-distance events are also well suited to the 3-hour limit. Typically, a moderately fit, moderately experienced triathlete can finish an Olympic-distance event in 2:30 to 3:00, with faster competitors coming in at about 2 hours and beginners at around 3:30. Keep in mind, these numbers are broad generalizations and racecourses and conditions vary widely from event to event. What's become clear over the years my coaches and I have been working with time-crunched triathletes, however, is that the Olympic-distance triathlon marks the upper limit when it comes to events at which time-crunched triathletes can expect to perform at their best.

Before you label me a heretic or cast me off as someone who just doesn't understand how dedicated and talented you are as an endurance athlete, let's take a look at how the 3-hour limit is actually going to impact your training and racing. When you pore over triathlon calendars looking for competitions, the vast majority feature swims of 1,500 meters or less, bike legs of 40 kilometers or less, and runs of 10 kilometers or less. There is a smattering of events that might incorporate a longer run or a longer ride, maybe a longer swim, but rarely all three. And while half-Iron distance events are certainly growing in popularity, I have yet to see a regional triathlon calendar packed with 1.2 mile swim/56 mile bike/13.1 mile run events. The truth of the matter is that events under 3 hours are the bread and butter of age-group triathlon competitions. These are the races that are easiest to get to and easiest to fit into your busy work and family schedules, and fortunately, they're also the events for which you can be really well prepared!

I'm not saying that as an athlete you're incapable of preparing for a half- or full-Iron-distance event. What I *am* saying is that with the current constraints on your time, there are advantages to focusing your efforts on events you can finish in 3 hours or less. It's a matter of being pragmatic. You want to feel strong and fast on race day, be competitive in your age group, and be within striking distance of your personal-best performances. We can do that by focusing your training efforts on the demands of these shorter events. Instead of generalized aerobic training to build endurance across swimming, cycling, and running, the Time-Crunched Triathlete Program focuses on developing the physiology needed to run faster for 10, 12, and maybe 15 kilometers—especially after you've already completed a strong swim and ride. The cycling portion of the program isn't going to give you all-around cycling fitness, either; it's designed to make you faster for rides lasting about 60 to 75 minutes—and after swimming. And as for the swim itself, this program focuses on getting you out of the water after 750 to 2,000 meters as fresh as possible so you have the energy for great rides and runs. A good swim that sets up the energy scenario that leads to a superfast run is more beneficial than a great swim that costs you the opportunity to have a great run.

Here's the bottom line, and the value proposition I offer to time-crunched athletes in any sport: Do you want to be mediocre at every distance, or is it OK to be strong enough to be really good at a smaller selection of the distances and events within your sport? A 3-hour limit covers a large percentage of the events most amateur athletes participate in, and I'm betting that you don't like being mediocre at anything. That's why I regard the 3-hour limit in a positive light: By accepting that you may not be optimally prepared for every event on the calendar, the Time-Crunched Triathlete Program gives you the opportunity to excel in the events you most frequently participate in anyway.

Of course, presenting a training program for an Ironman 70.3 event in this book flies directly in the face of the 3-hour limit, right? Even fast age-group competitors take more than 4 hours to complete half-Iron-distance races, and most take more than 5 hours to reach the finish line. The 3-hour limit defines the dividing line between events at which you can be competitive and events you can expect to finish. My coaches and I have successfully used the 70.3 program in this book with our athletes, but those athletes went into their events with clear expectations and often with at least 3 years of racing under their belts. The Time-Crunched Triathlete 70.3 Training Program will prepare you to have a good day and a positive experience at a half-Iron-distance race. It is a good choice for triathletes who have significant experience in shorter events and a desire to step up to long-course racing and see if they enjoy it. However, if you fall in love with 70.3 events and decide you want to achieve competitive fitness for long-course triathlons, you're also going to need to step up to a higher-volume training program that builds both the endurance and speed necessary for success.

The 3-hour limit was derived purely from anecdotal evidence and initially through our work with cyclists. My coaches and I noticed that cyclists on the Time-Crunched Cyclist Program experienced a significant change in their performance about 3 hours into long rides. They got noticeably tired, stopped talking, started skipping pulls, and struggled on climbs. It took longer to realize that the 3-hour limit also applies to triathletes, because individual training sessions tended to be shorter than 3 hours and the early adopters of the program rarely attempted rides, runs, or bricks longer than 3 hours, in training or competition. A high-intensity, low-volume training program delivers many of the same physiological adaptations we see in higher-volume training programs, but it stands to reason that there are some adaptations that actually require more time in the saddle, in the water, and on your feet.

Before moving on from the 3-hour limit, I want to make sure you put this "limitation" in the proper perspective. Big days filled with outdoor activities are crucially important for endurance athletes, even if they have nothing to do with competition or even the specific sport for which you're training. I run a business, travel a great deal for work, and have a loving wife and three children. And I live in Colorado, at the foot of Pikes

Peak, with the Rockies stretching hundreds of miles to the west, north, and south. When the weather is good and the timing is right, I head into the mountains on my road bike, my mountain bike, or in hiking boots for all-day excursions. I'm a time-crunched athlete too, and these epic rides and hikes aren't necessarily part of the program, but they are absolutely part of my identity as an endurance athlete.

The 3-hour limit is not meant to stop you from taking advantage of outdoor activities that require more than 3 hours to complete. It doesn't mean you aren't allowed to go out for epic rides, runs, or hikes; it just means your best performances will be in events shorter than 3 hours. You can still take advantage of that weekend when your family leaves you behind for a few days, or there is an impromptu snow day and you are just dying to get out on your new snowshoes; in fact, I encourage you to do that. Those adventures are our reward for being endurance athletes. They are rides, runs, and hikes that our sedentary peers can't understand and will never have the pleasure of experiencing. To deny yourself those epic, affirming, and deeply satisfying experiences would defeat the purpose of working so hard to fit training into your busy lifestyle. At the same time, just realize that you're not going to be superfast during all-day outings. You're not likely to ride a 100 mile century in 5 hours or less, nor are you likely to run a marathon in 3 hours. And you're going to feel the sting of fatigue in the second half of epic rides and hikes where you might not have in years past. Year in and year out, however, athletes using time-crunched training programs respond to this reality by taking pride in the fact they are competitive in the events they choose, and are still able to enjoy big adventures, even if those adventures are a bit slower than before.

Time-Crunched Training Leads to Time-Crunched Fitness

The Time-Crunched Triathlete Program is designed to maximize the effectiveness of the training you can complete in the limited time you have available. When you complete this program, you'll be fitter, faster, and more competitive than you would otherwise have been. On the flip side, I can't tell you that you'll be able to do everything that triathletes can who train twice the hours and twice as many workouts as you. CTS coaches use some of the principles described in this book in their work with pros—mostly the heightened focus on specificity and speed—but the training programs in this book would not prepare a pro for Ironman Hawaii. Nor would they prepare any other professional triathlete for a *full season* of Ironman, Ironman 70.3, or even Olympic-distance competitions. Not only are these programs not designed for Ironman competitors, but they're also not designed to produce race fitness for a competition season lasting year-round.

One of the key differences between professional and age-group athletes is the way they race. Pros need a series of top-level competitions in order to build fitness for a primary season goal. They are also paid to represent sponsors, and the more you race the more exposure you garner for your sponsors. Age-group triathletes, like amateur competitors in most sports, pick and choose their events differently from the pros. Your annual travel budget for getting to races is likely part of your overall family budget, which often translates into one big trip (airplanes, hotels, rental cars, food) to your primary goal event. Beyond that trip, you're sticking to races you can drive to within a few hours. That means you need to be prepared to race when there are races nearby to compete in!

Every region of the country has a racing season, or a period of time when the weather conditions and the circumstances are optimal for triathlon competitions. During this time, whether it's a few weeks or a few months, there's a concentration of events from which you can choose. Depending on the area, there may be more than one competition season each year. For instance, here in Colorado you have to wait until about June before you can start competing in triathlons with open-water swims. The off-road triathlons tend to start even later in the summer because they tend to be held at high-altitude resort towns where the ice-melt-fed lakes take longer to warm up and the trails are sometimes covered in snow until early July.

Race promoters in southern states take advantage of the warmer winters and attract athletes from all over the country by holding their events when it's too cold to compete up north. Ironman Florida and Ironman Arizona, for instance, are both held in November, and race calendars throughout the southern states are packed during the fall but nearly empty during the hottest months of the summer.

The point is, age-group triathletes primarily compete in regional events near where they live, and those regional events are concentrated during specific times of the year. Because of a more limited availability of events, it's unlikely that you could replicate the long-term race schedule of a pro or full-time amateur triathlete. What's more likely, and what my coaches and I see most often, are triathletes who want to ramp up and compete in a handful of events that lead up to one big regional race. After that there's a lull, and depending on the region, the athletes might ramp up again to compete in a series of events later in the year, or single-sport events in a different season. This is the way most age groupers race, and that's why the Time-Crunched Triathlete Program works. Most training programs are based on the classic top-down endurance training model that was originally designed to prepare elite athletes for a competition season that lasted several months. The Time-Crunched Triathlete Program, on the other hand, is designed to match the typical race schedules that are governed by the regional availability of triathlons.

There's no doubt you should continue training year-round, but since time-crunched athletes are primarily training for a series of seasonal events in their region, your training can be more focused on shorter build periods. In other words, because your competition seasons are more defined, the periods during which you need to focus on a structured training program are more defined as well.

The Time-Crunched Periodization Plan

If you use the events you're actually preparing for as the starting point of a time-crunched training program, it will become clear that there's a disconnect between the way you're racing and the way that a classic endurance periodization plan would prepare you to race. As I mentioned in Chapter 1, periodization has been around, at varying levels of sophistication, since the days of the ancient Greeks. The general concept of periodization is now so widespread that pretty much anyone who has prepared for an event or goal with a training plan designed by a coach or found in a book or magazine published since 1980 has trained using periodization. The general concept is to break up the training year into progressively smaller segments in order to focus the training stressors. Perhaps most important, periodization organizes the scheduling of rest days and weeks to ensure athletes get the right amount of time to adapt to their training.

The periodization plan most often used by athletes in a classic endurance training program starts with a base-building period in the winter and follows with a preparation period that focuses on improving sustainable power at lactate threshold as race season approaches. These workouts prepare the athlete for the high-intensity workouts in the specialization—or competition—period, which leads an athlete to a planned peak of conditioning and competitive readiness. Depending on the length of the athlete's season, there may be a second period of preparation training, followed by another specialization period and peak, before moving on to a transitional period of lighter, less structured training. This final period is meant to help the athlete recuperate from the cumulative mental and physical fatigue of a long season.

Just about any training book for triathlon, cycling, or distance running will include a yearlong periodization plan that looks something like what I have just described. It's what most people use, because it works very well for athletes who plan on being strong or competitive from April through October. Time-crunched athletes should definitely do their best to ride and train year-round, but the Time-Crunched Triathlete Program follows a very different periodization plan because of the nature of the workouts you'll be doing and the kind of fitness you'll be developing.

The principal reason that a yearlong periodization plan is necessary for high-volume trainers is that the volume's contribution to overall workload is so high that it takes a long time to gradually add small increments of intensity. If you try to accelerate the process by quickly ramping up the intensity while you are in a high-volume training plan, you'll soon reach the point where you can't recover and adapt quickly enough to continue making progress. Lower-volume or lower-frequency training plans can progress faster because the intensity contributes a greater percentage of the total workload, and there's plenty of built-in recovery time. At the same time, the intensity of the program leads to a lot of fatigue, which limits the length of time an athlete can successfully maintain top fitness before needing to back off and recover.

If you think of the classic endurance periodization plan as a dimmer switch (workload and fitness move up and down slowly and gradually), the Time-Crunched Triathlete Program is more like an on/off switch. When you're on, it's full on, and you go straight through until you flip the switch to off. The classic endurance periodization plan has four major periods: foundation (base aerobic training), preparation (aerobic and lactate threshold work), specialization (high-power work and event-specific training), and transition (recuperation and active recovery). The Time-Crunched Triathlete Program essentially cuts this down to two hybrid periods: preparation/specialization (on) and foundation/preparation (off).

PREPARATION/SPECIALIZATION (GO TIME)

This period is pretty much defined by the 6 weeks (sprint distance) or 8 weeks (Olympic and 70.3) that constitute the Time-Crunched Triathlete Programs included in this book (see Chapters 5 and 7). Normally, I like to follow a training pattern that features a recovery week after 3 weeks of training. There are some recovery or regeneration weeks built into this program as well, but because of the already low training volume, we're really only talking about backing off the intensity of one or two workouts, a few weeks into the program.

Although the programs in this book are 6 or 8 weeks long, some athletes may be able to stretch their fitness for up to an additional month. Triathletes with more years of racing experience will have greater success extending the period of time they can maintain their high-performance fitness. If you are stacking your race schedule and have multiple triathlons only a few weeks apart, it is fine to continue to cycle back into the training plan. For more information on how to do this effectively, go to page 191 in Chapter 5. If you choose to use the Time-Crunched Triathlete Program a few times in succession, I would recommend cycling through it a maximum of three times before taking a more significant recovery period. People who attempt to link four, five, or even six cycles of this program together often reach a point of diminishing returns after the third cycle. Instead of getting faster and stronger the fourth time through, progress stalls or performance even starts to decline. With adequate time between build periods, however, athletes experience incremental improvements in their training and racing performances.

FOUNDATION/PREPARATION (MAINTENANCE)

Once you have finished your target race or race season, it's time to move into the foundation/preparation phase of your training to maintain much of that hard-earned fitness. For high-volume trainers, the scientifically proven recipe to prevent detraining is to decrease the volume and retain—or even increase—the intensity. This is the technique most often used to taper athletes before big events and hold on to hard-earned fitness through an end-of-season break or transition period (Mujika and Padilla 2003). In reality, the technique leverages the same science this program is based on, but for a slightly different purpose. During the Time-Crunched Triathlete Program, you're using intensity to *increase* your workload above what you'd normally be able to achieve, in order to generate enough stimulus to improve your power at VO_2max and lactate threshold. In contrast, high-volume trainers use a short period of high-intensity, low-volume training to *reduce* their overall workload while retaining just enough stimulus to keep power at VO_2max and lactate threshold from declining.

Recovery and maintenance are the goals of the periods between the times when you're using the Time-Crunched Triathlete Program, but instead of high-volume training, aerobic endurance should be your highest priority. When you're done and you flip the switch to off, you have to back off the intensity. But you can and should maintain your volume. In other words, if you're training 6 to 8 hours when you're on the program, you should continue training for 6 to 8 hours a week during the time between build periods. The intensity is what you need to recover from, not the volume. If anything, you should stick to your training schedule so the time doesn't get siphoned away to other priorities.

More details about this period, including a transition training program, can be found on pages 187 and 218 in Chapter 5.

3

CONTROL AND INSIGHT: MONITORING YOUR TRAINING

As your available training time diminishes, the value of each individual workout increases dramatically, and that means it's important to maximize the precision and effectiveness of every effort. Being a time-crunched athlete means you have a much smaller margin for error than higher-volume athletes. Every one of us is guilty of racking up thousands of junk yards in the pool and miles of junk training on the roads and trails. When you're training 12, 16, 20, or more hours a week, those wasted efforts make up only a small percentage of your total workout time for the week or month. But when you're training only four times a week, the stakes are higher. And that's where training tools and technologies become a big factor.

There's no substitute for the hard work required to gain fitness and improve performance, but without a way to measure the work you're doing and evaluate its impact on your level of fitness and fatigue, you're just exerting yourself in the blind hope that you're doing something productive. Over the years I've heard a lot of criticisms thrown at the coaching industry and manufacturers of training technologies, many of them centered on the idea that we've created all these devices to generate massive amounts of confusing data just to convince athletes that training is too complicated to figure out on their own. The "back to basics" types cling to their unplugged training methods because that's what works for them; training is their escape from the technology that often dominates the rest of their lives, and carefully considered training programs feel too much like work. It's a cultural divide more than anything else. But for athletes who want to maximize performance, for whom results are an important component of what they're seeking from being an athlete, the ability to monitor and evaluate training workload is crucial. However, numbers are only valuable if you can use them to make better decisions for future workouts, from establishing and adjusting training intensities to determining when it's in your best interest to rest instead of work out.

Gathering and using data effectively are a complicated adventure for triathletes because the information available varies from one discipline to the next. At one end of the spectrum, we can directly measure the work being done on the bike in real time using a power meter. At the other end, the only way to determine how hard you're working in the water is based on goal paces for set distances, or the number of strokes it takes to cover a given distance. Running falls somewhere in the middle because we can at least measure heart rate (HR)—an indirect observation of workload—and pace (you can measure heart rate during swimming, too, but few athletes do). Single-sport cyclists, swimmers, and runners have the benefit of utilizing one system of measurement, but as a triathlete you have to find ways to compare the impact of a swim workout and a cycling workout on your overall workload and level of fatigue. Before we can talk about how to evaluate training workload in triathlon training, we need to take a look at the individual methods of gathering training data.

Power Meters

Precision comes from having detailed, real-time performance data you can use to monitor, evaluate, and adjust your training. And by far the best piece of equipment for providing that information is a power meter, which measures the true amount of work you produce. Unfortunately, this information applies only to your cycling training.

The most accurate power meters use strain gauges located in the crank or rear wheel to directly measure the mechanical work you're producing (kilojoules) and how rapidly you're producing that work (watts). Even if you don't own a power meter, as a cyclist you have benefited, and will continue to benefit, from the fact that others do. The work coaches have done with power-equipped athletes has broadened our understanding of how the body responds to training and fatigue, and that knowledge has led to positive changes in how workouts are arranged and prescribed. So although I highly recommend investing in a power meter and using it to advance your training, I also know—from experience—that the Time-Crunched Triathlete Program works whether you're training with power or with heart rate.

Your power meter provides a detailed record of every ride, with heart rate, power output, speed, and cadence information for every effort you put forth. As you'll see in the following sections, that information is crucial during your ride, but it's also very important afterward. One of the most important things you can do with a power meter is download the data from every ride, race, or event to your computer and into software products that can log and analyze the information. Currently the best power-analysis software out there is WKO+ from Peaksware (www.trainingpeaks.com). My coaches and I use it to analyze power files from our athletes, and if you're training with power, I highly recommend that you use it as well.

If you're training with power, especially using the Time-Crunched Tri-athlete Program, you need to focus on three main pieces of information: power, kilojoules, and fatigue.

POWER

Power, expressed in watts, is derived from the following equation: Power in Watts = Torque × Angular Velocity. To generate more power, you can push harder on the pedals to generate more torque or pedal faster to create

KEEPING IT SIMPLE

DR. EDMUND BURKE WAS A GOOD FRIEND OF MINE THROUGHOUT MY CYCLING career and was one of my primary mentors as I made the transition from athlete to coach. Ed was a pioneering sports scientist, one of the first to apply individual heart rate ranges to endurance training in order to target efforts to specific energy systems. In addition to working for the U.S. Olympic Committee and USA Cycling, he was a professor at the University of Colorado at Colorado Springs, where he taught exercise physiology to undergraduate and graduate students. He was one of the smartest men I've ever known, but even more impressive than the depth and breadth of his knowledge was his ability to make complex physiological concepts accessible to athletes whose last experience with physiology was in high school biology class. When you asked him a question, you knew there was a 30-minute answer in his head, complete with graphs, diagrams, and references, but he knew how to distill that information into a 5-minute answer that an athlete could understand completely and begin using immediately.

As a coach, an educator of coaches, a public speaker, and an author, I have tried to emulate Ed in the way I explain training and nutrition. Nowhere is that more important than during discussions about training with power. There are a thousand ways to slice and dice the massive amount of data athletes generate, and some very serious minds have spent, and continue to spend, enormous amounts of time doing just that. I have a few of these people on my staff, including CTS Premier Coach Dean Golich, who for more than 15 years has been one of the leading experts on training with power. There are athletes who love numbers, too, and many spend their free time analyzing and reanalyzing data from power files. If you're one of them, I recommend *Training and Racing with a Power Meter*, second edition, by Hunter Allen and Andrew Coggan. It is the most complete resource I have seen for anyone who wants to delve into the nitty-gritty details of training with power.

Now, if you were to give me a Ferrari, I would want to know how to get the most out of it. I'd probably know how to drive it better if I understood some key principles about how the engine and suspension work, but I wouldn't necessarily need to know how to build it from scratch. Similarly, my philosophy about physiology is that an athlete doesn't need to be able to diagram the individual chemical reactions within the Krebs cycle to understand that aerobic metabolism breaks fat and carbohydrate down into usable energy. And being able to diagram the Krebs cycle doesn't make one athlete faster than another. Likewise, a power meter is a tremendous tool that can dramatically enhance the quality and effectiveness of your training, and my point is that it can do so whether you have a basic or an advanced understanding of how it works and the data it produces.

greater angular velocity, or you can do both. Power is a direct measure of the work you are doing right now, and it is unaffected by many of the factors that can distort heart rate data, including dehydration, heat, humidity, anxiety, excitement, and stimulants like caffeine. These factors can influence your motivation or ability to produce power on the bike, but they don't alter the validity of the numbers you see on the power meter readout.

The two primary uses of power are to determine the demands of the rides, events, and races you want to participate in, and to establish training intensity ranges that you can use to develop the fitness necessary to meet those demands. That is why it is very helpful to race with a power meter and examine power files from a wide variety of events. For instance, let's say your goal is to complete the 40 kilometer cycling leg of your next Olympic-distance triathlon in 60 minutes. That means you have to be able to ride at an average speed of 40 kph (25 mph). And let's say that you have to generate 275 watts of power to maintain that speed, but right now you can sustain only 275 watts for 40 minutes. Your training must therefore be designed to increase the amount of time you're able to sustain 275 watts. Another way to look at it is to use training to increase your maximum sustainable power to 285 or 300 watts so that riding at 275 watts is not as challenging.

For single-sport cyclists competing in time trial events, we try to increase both maximum sustainable power output and the amount of time they can stay at that effort level. But cyclists don't have to run after they complete their 40K time trials, so they can leave everything out on the course and cross the finish line utterly spent. Triathletes benefit from a very different strategy on the bike: We look to increase our maximum sustainable power (otherwise known as power at lactate threshold) to as high as possible, but then compete at as low a power output as necessary to maintain an optimal position relative to our competition. It's a conservation strategy based on economy. The work necessary to establish a giant lead during the bike leg typically leaves an athlete so fatigued that he or she can't maintain a running pace high enough to maintain that hard-earned lead. In contrast, riding at a lower percentage of your maximum sustainable power during the bike leg conserves energy for a ripping run.

If you need proof that a conservation strategy is effective in triathlon, just look at Craig Alexander's winning performances at the 2008 and 2009 Ironman World Championships. In training, I counseled CTS Coach Nick White to focus on pushing Craig's lactate threshold power output to as high a percentage of his VO_2max power as possible, not because we wanted Craig to ride away from the competition, but so he could stay with the leaders while riding well below his lactate threshold power. It was a giant leap of faith for Craig, because it meant resisting the urge to chase down the strongest cyclists in the race.

In 2009, Craig watched as Chris Lieto—one of the best triathletes in the world—powered to a 12-minute lead heading into T2. He gave Lieto a lead of more than 2 miles at the start of the marathon, and for the first few miles of the run, Lieto's lead wasn't falling very quickly. But Lieto's incredibly powerful performance on the bike came at a great cost in terms of energy, and his pace began to diminish. Behind him, Craig was gaining on him with every stride. Lieto's lead was around 4 minutes when Craig reached the Energy Lab and decided it was time to make his move. He increased his pace and went off in solo pursuit of Lieto. From that point, Lieto's lead dropped at a rate of about 1 minute per mile until Craig caught him. By sheer coincidence, a group of CTS coaches, including Craig's coach, Nick White, was standing on the course at the point where Craig passed Lieto. The man who had been leading the race since the latter portions of the bike leg increased his pace to match Craig's, but his ability to stay with the defending champion was short-lived and he was soon forced to watch as the gap between him and Craig widened.

The strength of the conservation strategy is not just that it allows you to maintain a faster pace on the run, but that it also gives you the ability to accelerate and *race* the run. It's hard to overstate the significance of the fact that Craig Alexander won the race by accelerating and chasing down Lieto with enough real estate left in the race to establish a lead of more than 2 minutes by the time he ran down Ali'i Drive. As an athlete you have a choice as to where you want to expend your race-winning efforts. Lieto leveraged his strength as a cyclist to build a 12-minute lead over Craig after 112 miles on the bike. Craig conserved his energy on the bike and took 14 minutes out of Lieto in 26.2 miles of running.

Many cyclists and triathletes have less specific goals for improving their power output; rather than a goal pace for a specific distance, they just want to be able to go faster in all conditions. For these athletes, and even for athletes who are trying to meet specific demands, increasing sustainable power at lactate threshold and power at VO_2max is the best way to improve cycling performance. And when you look at the best options for improving the performances of time-crunched athletes competing for 2 hours or less on the bike, increased power at lactate threshold and VO_2max are more important than increasing base aerobic endurance. To be competitive in the events you're preparing for, you don't need the endurance to ride all day; you need the power to go fast for 20 to 40 kilometers and the fitness to do it without digging deep into your energy reserves.

In order to increase the power you can produce for efforts ranging from a few seconds to several hours, you need to establish training ranges that challenge your body and lead to the adaptations you seek. I cover this subject in more detail later in this chapter.

KILOJOULES

I don't have to tell you that pedaling a bicycle is work, but the number of kilojoules you produce during a ride provides an accurate accounting of exactly *how much* work you do during each ride. A kilojoule is a unit of mechanical energy, or work produced, and 4.184 kilojoules is equal to 1 kilocalorie. You expend kilocalories to produce kilojoules, but the human body is not a perfectly efficient machine, so only a portion of the kilocalories you expend do the mechanical work of turning your pedals. In fact, cycling efficiency is about 20 to 25 percent, meaning that about 75 to 80 percent of the energy you expend is lost, mostly as heat, which is why strenuous exercise is such a sweaty affair. If every calorie you expended was used for producing kilojoules, you would be correct in dividing your kilojoule count by 4 to come up with the number of kilocalories you burned during your workout (X Kj/4.184 = Y kilocalories). However, because of the 25 percent efficiency of the system, it takes about 4 kilocalories to produce 1 kilojoule of mechanical work. That brings the ratio of energy expended to work produced back to about 1:1. In other words, when you return from a training ride, you can generally consider the number of kilojoules displayed on your power meter to be equal to the number of kilocalories you burned during your time on the bike. There is actually some error in this number, in that your efficiency may have been between 20 and 25 percent, but the error is typically so small that it's not worth worrying about.

Kilojoules can be a more accurate way of prescribing the desired workload for a ride than either time or mileage. Basing workout duration on distance is convenient but notoriously bad in terms of determining the actual work done during the ride. From downtown Colorado Springs, for instance, I can complete 30 mile rides that are either entirely flat or extremely hilly. When I return home I've completed 30 miles, but the workload and training effect of the flat ride would be completely different

POWER-TO-WEIGHT RATIO (PWR)

ALONG WITH GIVING ATHLETES AN ACCURATE WAY OF MEASURING WORKLOAD, A power meter gives us a good method for comparing the relative climbing strengths of two different athletes. Your ability to go uphill quickly depends on the amount of power you can produce and the amount of weight you need to move against gravity. With a power meter we can quantify this by determining your power-to-weight ratio (PWR).

The PWR can be used to compare your abilities as a climber before and after a period of training, or to compare your abilities as a climber against another rider who is a different size. For instance, right now you may be able to sustain 250 watts on a local climb, and if you weigh 70 kilograms (154 pounds), your PWR would be 250/70 or 3.57 watts per kilogram. After completing the Time-Crunched Triathlete Program, your sustainable power may increase to 275 watts and your weight may decrease to 68 kilograms, bringing your PWR to 275/68, or 4.04 watts per kilogram. Even without performing climbing-specific workouts, you should reach the summit of the local climb faster with a PWR of 4.04 watts per kilogram than with a PWR of 3.57.

When comparing riders of relatively equal fitness, a taller and heavier athlete will tend to have more muscle mass and longer levers with which to generate power than a smaller athlete. However, the bigger athlete also has more mass to carry uphill, so you need more than just the two athletes' sustainable power outputs to determine which one has an advantage on a climb. This is where PWR ratio comes into play. Let's say Big Boy weighs 85 kilograms and has a sustainable power output of 320 watts, and Little Guy weighs 65 kilograms and has a sustainable power output of 250 watts. Despite having the strength to sustain 320 watts, Big Boy would reach the summit of the climb behind Little Guy, because his PWR is 3.76 watts per kilogram and Little Guy's is 3.85.

CONTINUES

CONTINUED

It's important to realize that PWR is entirely dependent on time. You can't just say a rider has a PWR of 4.0 watts per kilogram. That value must have a time associated with it, like 4.0 watts per kilogram for 20 minutes. The shorter the climb, the higher your PWR will be. For instance, I've often said that I consider 6.8 watts per kilogram for 30 minutes to be a performance marker that a rider needs to accomplish to be considered a contender for overall victory at the Tour de France. That didn't mean that Lance Armstrong could ride a 45-minute climb during the Tour at 6.8 watts per kilogram. Beyond the fact that the climb is longer than the 30-minute test, climbs in the Tour are contested after many days of racing and sometimes more than 4 hours of hard riding earlier in the stage. That's why top riders average PWRs in the 4 to 5 watts per kilogram range at the Tour, even though they can hit the 6.8 watts per kilogram threshold during a pre-Tour test.

An athlete's weight and stature can make a big difference in triathlon, not only because these characteristics impact PWR, but because they also affect the relationship between aerodynamics and power production. No matter how aerodynamic you make a bicycle, the human on top of it is the biggest impediment to going faster. But as athletes get bigger, the hole they have to punch in the air doesn't grow proportionally with their height and weight. As a result, tall athletes tend to have an advantage over shorter ones when riding in an aerodynamic position; they generate more power because of longer levers and more muscle mass, but the hole they have to punch in the air isn't that much larger than that of a much shorter rider. (One instance where a shorter rider has an advantage, however, is illustrated by American cyclist Levi Leipheimer. He has tremendous power, and he is small enough that he can tuck his head behind his hands, essentially filling the gap between his upper arms in order to smooth the airflow around his body. Taller riders can't take advantage of this position as well because of the more significant distance between the top of the saddle and the top of the handlebars.)

On triathlon courses with rolling hills or more significant climbs, smaller triathletes can level the playing field by using their superior PWR to gain time on the hills. Instead of utilizing a steady effort level, you'd want to surge up and over the top of climbs, and then use your best aerodynamic position (while still pedaling) to maximize speed and minimize power output during the descents and flat portions of the course. On descents and flat ground, bigger riders can use their power advantage to go faster, but that extra speed costs them a lot of energy. When you go faster uphill, you can take significant amounts of time away from them, and the energy cost of gaining that time is lower than in trying to outride them on flat ground.

from those of the hilly ride. Similarly, basing workouts on time has some of the same problems. A 2-hour ride on a hilly route and a windy day could be far more challenging than a 2-hour ride on flat terrain on a windless day. Based on time, you'd cover more distance on the 2-hour flat ride (let's say 40 miles), but the workload could still be lower than for covering 30 miles on the hilly ride on a windy day. And if I rode really hard on the flat ride but easy on the hilly ride, the flat ride could actually end up being harder than the hilly one. With so many variables and so little objective data (even heart rate is relatively easily influenced by outside factors), it can be difficult to accurately determine the true workload of your rides.

With a power meter, however, you can make an apples-to-apples comparison of one ride with another. A 1,500-kilojoule ride is a 1,500-kilojoule ride, whether it took you 90 minutes or 2 hours to complete, and whether it was uphill into a headwind or ripping along on flat roads with a tailwind. It's important to note, however, that kilojoules provide information about the endurance component of your training, but must be considered in conjunction with time and intensity (*how* you produced those kilojoules) to evaluate the ride's impact on your fitness, performance, and fatigue.

Races and events are among the most useful places to gather kilojoule data. If you're preparing for Olympic-distance triathlons, you'd want to gather race data from previous Olympic-distance triathlon bike legs to determine how much energy you produced during those performances. For instance, you may find that, on average, it requires 800 kilojoules of work to accomplish a 1:07 bike split for a 40K ride during a triathlon. That's the total energy demand of your bike split, which means you can use that information to guide your training (you would want some of your rides to be at least 800-kilojoule sessions, for example, to develop greater endurance for your events). But since your training rides aren't as intense as your races, it may take you 75 to 80 minutes to reach 800 kilojoules in training, compared to 67 minutes during a race.

There's an inverse relationship between power output and exercise duration, meaning that your average power output—and hence the kilojoules produced per hour—will decline as the length of rides increases. Most athletes realize this without ever being told; it's called pacing. When you leave your house for a 90-minute ride, you innately know you can afford to ride more aggressively than when you roll out for a 5-hour ride.

Fortunately, you can leverage this inverse relationship between power output and exercise duration to gain the fitness necessary to go faster during your events. As you make harder efforts during shorter workouts and build a bigger aerobic engine, you're gaining the fitness necessary to produce more kilojoules per hour through primarily aerobic metabolism. Let's say that right now, 600 kilojoules an hour is a pace you can sustain for 2 hours. As I discussed in Chapter 2, riding at 600 kilojoules an hour for an additional hour isn't going to do you much good in terms of increasing your mitochondrial density, a key marker of increased oxidative capacity in skeletal muscle. However, because shorter, higher-intensity interval workouts can increase mitochondrial density and give you the tools to burn more fat and carbohydrate through aerobic channels, these workouts can increase the number of kilojoules you produce aerobically each hour. This increased fitness can be used in two ways: You can use it to ride at a higher speed and power output that may get you up to 700 kilojoules an hour, or you can keep your race pace relatively steady and continue producing 600 kilojoules an hour, all the while conserving energy (you're relying more on fat and carbohydrate through aerobic metabolism and deriving less energy from the glycolytic system).

FATIGUE

Fatigue gets a bad rap, but it is not always a bad thing; it's actually one of the most important components of an effective training program. It is always created in the process of overloading a physical system, which makes it an integral part of the stimulus your body is responding to as you adapt and grow stronger. And like any other part of training, fatigue has to be managed properly so it can enhance your performance rather than destroy it. A power meter can be a very effective tool for helping you manage fatigue, not only during individual workouts but also within entire periods of training.

Power is a direct measure of the work you're doing right now, so it provides an accurate way to tell if you're too tired to continue with effective intervals. As you fatigue, you'll see a decline in the power output you're able to sustain for interval efforts as well as endurance-pace riding. But there's a difference between knowing that you're getting tired and making the right decision on what to do about it. I will cover this in more detail in the section "Know When to Say When" in Chapter 5; for now it's important to realize that there are times when you will want to push through the fatigue and complete your intervals but also times when skipping those intervals will be the better choice.

One of the most important things coaches learned once we started training athletes with power was that there were times when athletes were less fatigued than we originally believed. Before power meters were widely used, we used heart rate and perceived exertion to judge an athlete's level of fatigue and then adjusted training accordingly. The day after a lactate threshold or VO_2max interval session, we noticed that an athlete's exercise heart rate was often suppressed (lower heart rate values at similar paces) and ratings of perceived exertion were often elevated (efforts at similar paces felt harder). This suggested that the athlete was fatigued and needed more recovery before performing another effective interval workout.

In fact, heart rate and perceived exertion were lying. Once riders started using power meters, we saw that despite the suppressed heart rates and elevated ratings of perceived exertion, athletes were often able to complete interval workouts on back-to-back days at matching—and sometimes even higher—power outputs. Yes, there was fatigue, as illustrated by heart rate and exertion, but the power meter provided context for that fatigue. In the days before power meters, we knew fatigue was present but couldn't tell how much. When a power meter reveals that an athlete can sustain efforts at outputs equal to those of the day before, despite a suppressed exercise heart rate and an elevated rating of perceived exertion, this means there's fatigue, but not enough to warrant a full recovery day. If, on the other hand, during the second consecutive day of intervals an athlete's power output is more than 10 to 15 percent lower than on the previous day, exercise heart rate is elevated more than 10 percent, and perceived exertion is also elevated, that is an indication that the athlete's level of fatigue is high enough that a rest day is a better option than another training session.

Power meters have led to an increase in the use of two-day training blocks, and they are featured in the training programs in this book. The benefit of block training is that you generate a strong training stimulus by completing the second day of interval training in a somewhat fatigued state. Put simply, you're reinforcing the training stimulus from the first day and giving your body a more urgent request for adaptation.

Training with Heart Rate

Power meters are a wonderful training tool, but they have two major drawbacks: They're expensive, and they provide training data only for cycling. Heart rate monitors are far more versatile for multisport athletes because they can provide useful training data for monitoring and adjusting cycling and running workouts. Ideally, every triathlete would have a power meter for on-bike training and a heart rate monitor for run training, but at $1,000 to $3,700, it's unrealistic to expect all cyclists or triathletes to invest in power meters. The truth is, in terms of effectiveness, the difference between training with power and with heart rate on the bike is a matter of degree. The fact that training with power is more effective doesn't mean that training with heart rate is not effective. My coaches and I have been working with heart rate for more than 20 years, and our athletes have won and continue to win races and achieve personal goals using heart rate alone.

The strength and weakness of heart rate is that it's an observation of your body's response to exercise. It's not a direct measure of the work being done, but rather the work is being done by muscles, which in turn demand more oxygen from your cardiovascular system. Since that oxygen is delivered via red blood cells, heart rate increases as your demand for oxygen rises. It's an indirect observation of what's happening at the muscular level, but in the absence of a direct way to measure workload, heart rate does provide valuable information you can use to guide your training. Research has conclusively shown that there's a strong correlation between heart rate response and changes in an athlete's workload, and that research allowed sports scientists and coaches to start creating heart rate training zones back in the 1980s. My good friend Ed Burke was one of the first to establish a five-zone system for targeting exercise bouts to specific energy systems. Over the years other scientists and coaches—myself included—have used emerging data and experience to refine heart rate training ranges to a wide variety of activities and training protocols.

Among those refinements was the establishment of heart rate ranges that are specific to either running or cycling. Because running incorporates more muscle mass and you're supporting your body weight, your body's total demand for oxygen is greater than at a similar effort level while cycling. This means the heart rate that correlates with your lactate threshold will be higher when you're running than when you're cycling. This difference can be partly accounted for by the facts that lactate threshold is a phenomenon that occurs at the muscular level—you're just observing it via the cardiovascular system—and that heart rate data also reflect the oxygen demand from other areas of the body, including muscles that are working at intensities well below threshold.

Since running and cycling elicit different responses from the body, and we use activity-specific heart rate ranges to guide your training, we also have to use activity-specific assessments to determine your current baseline and different sets of calculations to establish those heart rate training ranges. As you'll see in the description of the CTS Field Tests for running and cycling that follow, it's relatively easy to establish accurate heart rate and power training intensities for intervals that improve your sustainable cycling power and running pace at threshold.

CARDIAC DRIFT

ONE OF THE GREATEST DISADVANTAGES OF USING HEART RATE ALONE TO GAUGE training intensity is "cardiac drift." Since up to 75 percent of the energy produced in muscles is lost as heat, your body has to work to dissipate that heat in order to keep your core temperature from rising out of control. As you exercise—and especially as you exercise at higher intensities—your body uses your skin as your car uses its radiator. Heart rate increases to deliver more oxygen, glucose, and so on to working muscles, and some blood plasma becomes sweat. The sweat is released onto the skin so it can evaporate, which carries much of this excess heat away from the body. Some of the fluid that appears as sweat on your skin was most recently part of your bloodstream. As you lose blood plasma volume to produce sweat, your heart must pump even faster to continue delivering adequate oxygen to working muscles. As a result, your heart rate will increase slightly as exercise duration increases, even if you maintain the same level of effort. The impact of cardiac drift will be lower if you're better at staying hydrated; you're replacing the fluid lost by sweating and helping to maintain a higher overall blood volume. However, no matter how diligent you are about consuming fluids, some level of cardiac drift is unavoidable during intense endurance exercise.

You can see the impact of cardiac drift very clearly in Figure 3.1. In this power file from a lactate threshold interval workout on the bike, the athlete performs three intervals at roughly the same power output, but his heart rate gets progressively higher for each effort. When athletes train with heart rate alone, they are instructed to maintain the same heart rate range for each interval. Ideally this would result in efforts of equal intensity, but as a result of cardiac drift, this often means that the first interval is actually completed at a higher power output than the subsequent ones.

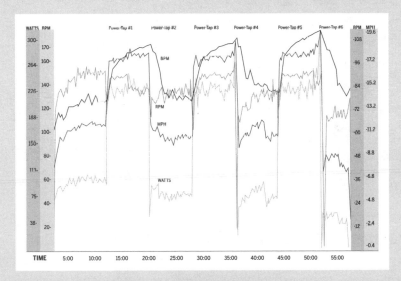

FIGURE 3.1: Cardiac Drift
You can see how the rider's heart rate increases from the first
hard effort to the third. This is a clear example of
cardiac drift, where workload remains relatively stable
(only a 2-watt difference between the first and third interval)
but heart rate increases by an average of 10 beats from
first to final interval.

CONTINUES

CONTINUED

To the athlete, heart rate and perceived exertion seem right on target, but they don't realize that power output is actually falling, and as a result, the workout loses some of its potential effectiveness. The next logical assumption is that athletes training with heart rate should adjust their heart rate ranges during interval workouts to compensate for cardiac drift. In other words, some athletes ask if they should ride their first interval at 160 to 165 beats per minute, the second one at 163 to 166, and the last one at 166 to 169. The problem with this idea is that without a power meter you can't accurately determine the extent to which your cycling performance is being affected by cardiac drift, and currently there isn't a good way to determine the real-time impact of cardiac drift on running performance. Raising your heart rate ranges during a series of intervals could either under- or overcompensate for cardiac drift, so the best option for heart rate trainers is to focus on staying hydrated and controlling core temperature (to minimize cardiac drift) and stick to the prescribed heart rate ranges for all intervals in a given workout.

The fact that the workouts in the Time-Crunched Triathlete Program are relatively short works to the advantage of athletes training with heart rate. Cardiac drift is more pronounced during workouts longer than 2 hours, so the relatively short nature of the workouts in this program helps to minimize its detrimental impact on actual interval intensities.

Training with Perceived Exertion (RPE)

As much as I embrace the role of technology in enhancing the precision of training, there's an incredibly simple measure of workload that continues to hold its own against new gadgets and software applications. Rating of perceived exertion, or RPE, is the ultimate in simplicity: It is nothing more than a scale of how hard you feel you are exercising. Not a single piece of data is collected and you don't need any special equipment. All you need is the scale.

The scale my coaches and I use in the physiology lab is the Borg Scale, which ranges from 6 to 20 (6 being no exertion at all and 20 being a maximum effort). Why 6 to 20? Well, Borg's research has shown that there's a high correlation between the number an athlete chooses during exercise, multiplied by 10, and his or her actual heart rate at that time. In other words, if you're on a cycling ergometer during a lactate threshold test and you tell me that you feel like you're at 16, there is a pretty good chance your heart rate is around 160 beats per minute. This isn't absolutely true of all athletes, but you'd be surprised how accurate the 6 to 20 scale tends to be.

Outside the lab, however, I haven't found the Borg Scale to be as helpful for athletes. Most athletes find it easier to relate to a simpler 1 to 10 scale (1 being no exertion at all and 10 being a maximum effort). Under this scale, an endurance or "cruising" pace on the bike would be 4 to 5, a challenging aerobic pace would be 6, lactate threshold work occurs at about 7 to 8, climbing and time trial efforts are a solid 8 (sometimes 9), and VO_2 intervals and all-out sprints are the only efforts that reach 10. Just as the Borg Scale multiplies the perceived exertion number by 10 to correlate with heart rate, the number chosen on the 1 to 10 scale, multiplied by 10, seems to correlate closely with the percentage of VO_2max that an athlete is currently maintaining.

With power meters providing an accurate and direct measure of workload for cyclists, and GPS-equipped heart rate monitors providing more detailed pacing information for runners, some athletes are tempted to relegate RPE to the trash bin of sports science history, but RPE remains critically important. RPE provides valuable context for the data files from your power meter or heart rate monitor, and for your paces during swim workouts. When you're fresh, riding at 200 watts may feel like a moderate spin, but when you're fatigued you may feel like you're working harder than normal for those same 200 watts (sluggish, heavy legs, pedaling through peanut butter, and similar terms may come to mind). RPE is a great early warning device for revealing fatigue; your body is telling you it can still do the job, but even though the work being done is the same, the effort to complete it is greater.

RPE can also indicate progress, even without a change in your power outputs or paces. For example, at the beginning of the season, a 5K run at an 8-minute/mile pace may feel strenuous enough to rate a 7 or even an 8. Later in the season, when your fitness has improved, running that same course at that same pace may take less out of you and feel more like a 6. To reach an RPE of 7 to 8, you may now need to hasten your pace to 7:30 minutes/mile. Similarly, RPE and pace are the primary ways you can evaluate and monitor your swim training, and as you become a more skilled swimmer you need to consider RPE as you adjust your training paces because better technique can reduce your effort level at a given pace.

I have included RPE values with each workout in this book, and I encourage you to record your RPE during each effort in your CTS Field Tests. Not only is perceived exertion important for providing context for power and heart rate files, but it also helps you learn to accurately evaluate your intensity level in the absence of all other technologies. Part of becoming a skilled endurance athlete is learning to use technology effectively while also reducing your dependence on it.

Establishing Effective Training Intensity Ranges: The CTS Field Tests

Performance testing is a crucial part of training, because it provides a snapshot of your current level of fitness and allows athletes and coaches to determine whether and how much progress has been made. As you grow stronger, testing provides a means for adjusting training intensities so you can continue to challenge yourself.

There are two primary categories of performance testing, lab and field. In the lab we put you on an ergometer or a treadmill and run you through a series of steps at ever-increasing power outputs or paces. At the same time, we have you breathing into a tube so we can analyze the composition of your inspired and expired air, and we're pricking your finger to measure the amount of lactate present in your blood. At the end of a combined lactate threshold/VO_2max test, the information is analyzed, and we can provide you with an accurate determination of your power output or pace at lactate threshold, power or pace at VO$_2$max, and blood lactate levels at all those points. Swim-specific lab testing is very difficult and the equipment necessary is generally found only in research facilities, although there are some pieces of dryland equipment (such as the Vasa Trainer) that can be used to assess performance and progress in swimming fitness. For the most part, however, swimming paces are frequently established through field testing (or pool testing, in this case).

In the field, we have the opportunity to determine the power output, heart rate, and pace you can sustain for an effort of a given duration. And although that probably sounds like a paltry amount of information compared to lab tests, the fact is that there's a strong correlation between the accuracies of lab and field testing. Having tested thousands of athletes using both methods, I generally prefer field testing because it is easier to fit into an athlete's schedule, it's cheaper and more accessible to more athletes, and it provides data that are just as useful for achieving all the aforementioned goals for performance testing. In addition, because the field test is often completed in real-world conditions out on the road, it provides athletes with greater context for their performance. They experience all the sensations (speed, wind, surface, etc.) of completing an all-out effort, which can help them better judge their efforts during events when they may not be able to see information from a power meter or heart rate monitor.

There are numerous methods for field testing, involving efforts of varying durations. Here are the two field tests I use with triathletes, which are described in greater detail in the coming pages:

1. CTS Cycling/Running Field Test: Two 8-minute all-out time trials separated by 10 minutes of easy spinning recovery. Within 10 to 15 minutes of completing the second time trial, complete an 8-minute run at the fastest pace you can sustain.
2. CTS Swimming Field Test: 400 meters as fast as you can go, 10 minutes of easy swimming for recovery, then 100 meters as fast as you can go.

The CTS Field Tests should be completed before you begin the Time-Crunched Triathlete Program the first time, and if you decide to use the program more than once in a season, you should complete the field tests again before starting the program each time. When you view the workouts and training programs (see Chapter 5), you'll notice that the CTS Field Tests are not included as workouts at the very beginning of the schedule. Rather than work them into the Time-Crunched Triathlete Program itself, I want you to complete them over the course of a few days before you begin one of the training programs. Make sure you're well rested before completing the tests, and if you decide to do the swimming and cycling/running test on the same day, it's a good idea to complete the swim test in the morning and the cycling/run test in the afternoon. Don't perform any of the tests the day after a major race or hard workout, because you won't be able to determine how fatigue affects your results.

Before I describe exactly how to perform the CTS Field Tests, I want to point out that it is important not to get too caught up in performance testing. It's a valuable component of training, but some athletes train for the tests the same way some schools teach to standardized exams. Your performance as a competitor goes beyond your ability to produce test results, and regardless of improvements in your power or pace at threshold, you'll still remain an ineffective competitor if you fail to learn how to apply your strength in real-world situations. Races are not won in the lab or on the indoor trainer, and I've yet to meet a triathlete who describes his or her best day as an athlete by talking about a performance test. Do the testing, use the results to enhance your training, but always remember that your identity as an endurance athlete is much more than a collection of testing data.

CTS CYCLING/RUNNING FIELD TEST

In a study published in the *Journal of Strength and Conditioning Research* (Klika et al. 2007), the CTS Cycling Field Test (two 8-minute cycling time trials separated by 10 minutes of recovery spinning; see Figure 3.2) was shown to be an effective method for establishing cycling training

...me high-cadence and
...rts. Power and cadence
...minutes also show a
...cating that the athlete
...e field test was run
...l effort.

...lactate threshold test
...trainer before a CTS-
...gram. At the end of
...d, on average, expe-
...reshold. There was
...mprovement in the
...the field test. The study con-
...TS Field Test is "a valid measure of fitness and changes
in fitness, and provided data for the establishment of training ranges."

For a triathlon-specific field test, I start with the CTS Cycling Field Test
and add one 8-minute run time trial afterward. As I covered in Chapter
2, there is a difference between running after cycling and running as an
isolated exercise, and since most of the workouts in the Time-Crunched

Triathlete Program are two-discipline brick workouts, it makes the most sense to establish your running training intensities from a field test that also incorporates cycling before running.

A question I often get about the CTS Cycling/Running Field Test concerns the addition of recovery time between the end of the second cycling effort and the beginning of the run time trial. If it's supposed to be triathlon-specific, they say, then why not perform a cycling-to-running transition and perform the 8-minute run immediately after the ride?

After testing many athletes using different variations of this test, and then observing the effectiveness of the resulting training intensity ranges, I've learned that giving athletes some recovery between the cycling and running portions of the test improves the quality of their efforts in both. In other words, knowing there will be time to recover following the cycling portion helps prevent athletes from holding something back, from pacing themselves conservatively, during the two 8-minute cycling time trials (especially the second one). In terms of the running portion of the test, following 10 minutes of recovery after the end of the cycling effort, the unique physiological response to running off the bike may not be as pronounced as when you transition directly from bike to run, but there is still an impact on your run pace and heart rate, and that impact will be reflected in your training intensity ranges. However, when I ask athletes to perform a race-simulation transition from bike to run during a field test, what I've seen is that they dial down their cycling effort—often in both 8-minute time trials—to preserve their run performance. And many athletes, especially experienced triathletes, end up diminishing their cycling results so effectively that they go as fast or faster in the run portion, despite the lack of recovery time between the two activities. What I'm looking for, though, is a series of three complete efforts, where you're not pacing any one of them in consideration of the others. The training intensity ranges that result from this combined test (8 minutes of all-out cycling, 10 minutes of spinning recovery, 8 minutes of all-out cycling, 10 minutes of recovery, 8 minutes of all-out running) tend to be a little bit higher and faster than ranges established from a test without recovery

WHY 8 MINUTES?

SOME ATHLETES AND COACHES ASK ME ABOUT THE RATIONALE BEHIND THE TWO 8-minute efforts that make up the CTS Cycling Field Test. My field test is unique in its brevity; it's not a 60-minute or even a 20-minute time trial because I've found that I don't need to put athletes through such an effort to gather the necessary data. It's not that a 60- or 20-minute time trial effort wouldn't work; in fact, those tests work quite well. However, my coaches and I work with a very broad spectrum of athletes, and a field test of two 8-minute efforts can be performed well by novices as well as experienced age-group competitors and even pros.

I prefer two 8-minute efforts over one longer effort because I believe there's valuable information to be gained from observing your ability to recover from and repeat a hard effort. With a 10-minute recovery period between efforts, an athlete with a well-developed aerobic engine will be able to complete the second effort with an average power output within 5 percent of the first effort. If the average power from your second effort is more than 10 percent lower than your first effort, that doesn't change your training prescription, but it gives you one more marker by which you can evaluate progress the next time you complete the test. For example, as the average power outputs for your two field test efforts become more equal, that is a sign that your training has improved your ability to buffer lactic acid and process lactate. The first effort took less out of you, and you were able to recover from the effort more quickly, leading to the ability to perform a second effort at an equal power output after just 10 minutes of easy spinning recovery.

Sometimes an athlete has a higher average power on the second effort of the CTS Field Test, and this can often be attributed to one of two factors: You were cautious on the first effort and held back, or you didn't warm up well enough before the field test (the first effort, then, was in essence the end of your warm-up). In either case, since your training ranges are

CONTINUES

CONTINUED

established from the higher of your two average power outputs or heart rates, the fact that the CTS Cycling Field Test consists of two efforts allows you to establish accurate training ranges despite performing poorly on one part of the test. In a test that consists of one longer effort, either the learning curve of the test or a poor warm-up is more likely to result in training intensities that are lower than they should be. In the long run, this isn't all that harmful to an athlete's training, because training intensities will most likely be corrected by subsequent tests, and most athletes make performance gains even if their training intensities are a little lower than they could be. Nevertheless, through testing thousands of athletes with the CTS Cycling Field Test, I have found that it provides greater accuracy the first time around as well as in subsequent tests. Similarly, people have

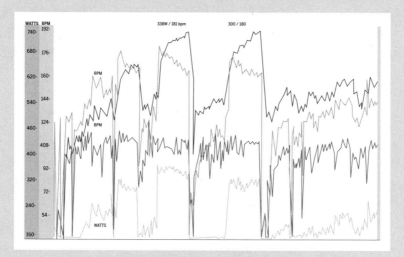

FIGURE 3.3: Inexperienced Field Test
In contrast to the steady effort in Figure 3.2, this graph shows a strong first field test followed by a significant drop in power (watts) for the second test. This indicates that the rider, although strong, lacks endurance and the ability to hold high power for repeatable efforts. This is not a "bad" field test; in fact, it reveals a tremendous amount about the athlete's specific need to develop his aerobic energy system.

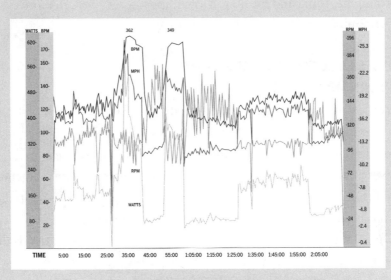

FIGURE 3.4: Bad Field Test
You can see from the sharp spike in power at the start
of the field test and the rapid decline that this athlete
did not pace himself well for the entire 8-minute effort.
He went out too hard, had to slow down, and then
pushed himself again at the end of the effort (indicated
by the sharp upward slope of the wattage data).
To achieve a better field test result, you want to use the
first 45–60 seconds of each effort to gradually get
up to speed.

asked about the addition of an 8-minute run to the existing CTS Cycling
Field Test to create a triathlon-specific test. Why not two or three 1 mile
repeats, or a 5K at race pace? My rationale is similar to the reason that the
cycling test is shorter than some others: It's a duration that's appropriate
for the majority of the athletes my coaches and I work with, a test they can
complete successfully and can integrate into training easily, and provides
the data necessary to establish effective training intensities. Longer tests,
be they mile repeats, a 5K, or even a 10K, can be very effective for some
athletes, but if at all possible, I prefer to obtain the data I need from the
shortest, least invasive test possible.

between the riding and running. More importantly, they are more effective for improving fitness and performance.

THE CTS FIELD TESTS VERSUS OTHER PERFORMANCE TESTS

The other major question my coaches and I are asked about field testing is whether the power output or heart rate we use to establish training ranges is equal to an athlete's power output or heart rate at lactate threshold. The answer is no, but the results from the CTS Field Test correlate predictably with results from laboratory testing, so a conversion factor can be applied to your numbers to establish accurate training ranges.

One of the reasons some coaches prefer longer field test efforts is that longer tests result in average power/HR/pace values that are closer to actual lab-tested lactate threshold values. The reason for this is that you can maintain an effort well above your lactate threshold for a short period of time, but because lactate threshold pretty much defines the upper limit of your sustainable effort, if you go long enough you'll settle into a pace that's very close to—and most likely below—your lactate threshold power/HR/pace. But this is another situation in which sports science doesn't necessarily work to an athlete's benefit. Yes, a 60-minute cycling time trial could provide a relatively accurate estimation of your lactate threshold power output, but only if you can stay motivated to ride all-out for a full hour. If you can't—and there's no shame in that; most age groupers struggle with such a long, intense effort—your numbers are going to be low, and you'll establish training intensities that are lower than they should be. And even if you could stay motivated enough to complete a great 60-minute time trial, it would be difficult to integrate that into your training program on a regular basis because it's such a demanding workout in and of itself.

After thousands of tests, my coaches and I have found that the CTS Cycling Field Test generates average power outputs that are about 10 percent above an athlete's lab-tested lactate threshold power output. In the calculations that I present for establishing your own training intensity ranges, this 10 percent is already factored into the equations. In other words, you'll take your actual power output or heart rate from the field test and plug it directly into the equation. Similarly, you will take your actual pace or heart rate from the running portion of the test and plug it directly into the equations—or use the pace tables provided. We have been using the CTS Cycling Field Test and the corresponding training intensity calculations for many years, and the accuracy of this method was proven in the Klika et al. study (2007), which was conducted in Aspen, Colorado. The study found that participants' maximum sustainable power outputs, as measured by the CTS Cycling Field Test on an indoor trainer, were 7.5 percent higher than their lab-tested power at lactate threshold. However, it is important to remember that the study was conducted at an elevation of 9,000 feet, where not only is power at lactate threshold lower than at sea level, but the ability to sustain efforts above threshold is even more limited. Therefore, I have continued to use the 10 percent conversion factor for calculating training intensity ranges from CTS Cycling Field Test data.

One popular cycling field test, published in *Training and Racing with a Power Meter* by Hunter Allen and Andrew Coggan (2010), is a 20-minute time trial. This test is a good one; it's short enough that many athletes can complete a high-quality effort. Allen and Coggan also use a conversion factor to account for the difference between an athlete's field test power and his or her predicted lactate threshold power. In their system, athletes record their average power output from a 20-minute time trial, multiply this number by 0.95, and then apply a series of percentages to the resulting power output to establish power training intensities. They multiply by 0.95 initially because an athlete's 20-minute power output will be about 5 percent higher than his or her power output in a 60-minute effort—which is also about equal to an athlete's lab-tested lactate threshold power output. Essentially, if you consider a 60-minute test to be roughly equal to power at lactate threshold, then a 20-minute test will give you a power output 5 percent higher than that, and the CTS Field Test will give you a power output another 5 percent above that.

CTS Cycling/Running Field Test

The field test itself is two 8-minute cycling efforts followed by one 8-minute running effort. It's important to be properly fueled and warmed up before beginning the first time trial. Refer to the preworkout nutrition tips in Chapter 4 for more information on optimal preworkout meals and snacks. When planning your field test, think about where you're going to end your ride so that you can start the run portion about 10 to 15 minutes after the second cycling effort. Many athletes find it most convenient to do the cycling portion on an indoor trainer, in a business park, or on a lightly trafficked bike path. Keep in mind that you'll want to record the distance covered during the 8-minute run, so use a course of a known distance, a path with distance markers, a track, or a GPS-enabled watch.

When you get on the bike, you'll need time to complete the warm-up, the field test, and a good cool-down, so budget a total of 75 minutes for the entire field test workout. The warm-up prior to the field test incorporates two CTS intervals, FastPedal and PowerInterval. For FastPedal, shift into a light gear and bring your cadence up as high as you can without bouncing in the saddle. There is no power or heart rate range for FastPedal, as it's a cadence-driven drill more than an exercise for energy system development. The PowerInterval is a maximum-intensity interval at 100+ rpm; bring the intensity up gradually over the first 30 seconds and hold that effort level through the end of the interval. A more detailed description of PowerIntervals can be found on pages 167–168 of Chapter 5. Start with 10 minutes of easy- to moderate-intensity riding and then complete the following warm-up routine.

Pre–Field Test Warm-up

1 minute FastPedal
1 minute easy spinning recovery
2 minutes FastPedal

> *1 minute easy spinning recovery*
> *1 minute PowerInterval*
> *2 minutes easy spinning recovery*
> *1 minute PowerInterval*
> *4 minutes easy spinning recovery*
> *Begin CTS Field Test*

FIELD TEST INSTRUCTIONS, CYCLING PORTION

Make sure to record and collect the following data:

- Average heart rate for each effort
- Maximum heart rate for each effort
- Average power for each effort
- Average cadence for each effort
- Weather conditions (warm or cold, windy or calm, etc.)
- Course conditions (indoors or outdoors, flat or hilly, point-to-point or out-and-back, etc.)
- Rating of Perceived Exertion (RPE) for each effort (how hard you felt you were working)

Step 1: Find a Suitable Course

You want a relatively flat course or a sustained climb, but rolling hills are not a great option. Avoid traffic lights and stop signs if at all possible. You can also use an indoor trainer.

Step 2: Complete Effort No. 1

Start gradually so you build up to your maximum sustainable power/effort over the course of the first 45 to 60 seconds. Aim to maintain a cadence of 90 to 100 rpm throughout the entire test (85-plus rpm if testing on a climb); mashing too big a gear at a low cadence will cause your leg muscles to fatigue quickly and diminish your power in the latter portion of the effort. Push all the way through to the end of the 8 minutes.

Step 3: Recover for 10 Minutes

When you reach the end of Effort No. 1, you should be completely drained. But don't stop pedaling. Shift into an easy gear and keep turning the pedals over. Active recovery spinning helps your body circulate oxygenated blood to your tired muscles and flush away waste products. Take a drink of water, sit up with your hands on the tops of the bars, and relax as you spin. If you're completing the test outdoors, return to the same starting point you used for the first effort, even if it takes you a little more than 10 minutes to get back there.

Step 4: Complete Effort No. 2

Slow to a near standstill and then accelerate into your second effort just as you did into your first. Avoid the temptation to pace your second effort off the first; there's a good chance this one will be even better.

Step 5: Recover, Record Your Data, and Get Ready to Run

Once you finish Effort No. 2, you're done with the cycling portion of the CTS Cycling/Running Field Test. The run portion should commence 10 minutes after the end of the final cycling effort. Spin easy for a few minutes before getting off the bike. You don't want to sit down and stop moving for prolonged periods between the cycling and running portions of the test, so how long you spin is somewhat dependent upon how much time you need to get into running shoes and to the starting point for the running portion of the test. If it's as simple as hopping off the bike, slipping into your shoes, and hitting the pavement/trail/treadmill, then you may want to spin for almost the entire 10 minutes on the bike.

When you get out on your run, take a few minutes to get your running legs under you before you start the field test effort. This is not entirely race-specific, in that during competition you will have to go directly from bike to run, but for the purposes of the field test and your subsequent training paces, a little preparation is beneficial. Run easy for 1 to 2 minutes and then complete five 15-second RunningStrides. RunningStrides are short accelerations (about 20 seconds) from a light jog to maximum speed. This drill is described in more detail on pages 170–171 in Chapter 5. Walk or jog to the starting point of your 8-minute effort, and proceed.

FIELD TEST INSTRUCTIONS, RUNNING PORTION

Information you will want to record during the run portion of the test:

- Total distance of the effort (to the nearest 25 meters)
- Heart rate at finish of the effort
- Average HR for the effort
- Perceived exertion for the effort (1 to 10)
- Course conditions (road, dirt/cinder, treadmill, rubber, indoor/outdoor, 200/400 meter track, and so on)
- Split times for each 400 meters of the effort (if you're running on a track)
- Weather conditions (hot/mild/cool, rain/dry)

Step 1: Find a Test Track or Course

The crucial things about your run course are that it be easily accessible after the conclusion of the cycling portion of the test and be appropriate for testing. A generally flat course is preferable, although a loop with minor rolling hills works fine, too. A local track can be a great option, especially if it's not busy, so that there's no one in your lane when you conduct the test. And you can complete the test on a treadmill as well. If you're using a treadmill, set it for a 1 to 2 percent grade. Try to perform each test at the same time of day to ensure consistency. Repeatability is always important for testing!

Step 2: Start the 8-Minute Effort

Start your run at a specific mark. You want to run the fastest pace you can sustain for the full 8 minutes, but take the first 30 to 45 seconds to build up to that pace. Avoid the impulse to overstride or sprint, and instead focus on finding your rhythm and pace. The secret is to use a turnover and stride length that is most efficient for your personal running style. It will take some experimentation to find your optimal stride rate and your most efficient arm carriage. The key is to stay relaxed. If you're using a tread-mill, start at about your 5K race pace or just below that, and manually in-crease the belt speed until you reach the highest speed you can maintain.

Step 3: Find Control

Settle into a steady rhythm of breathing. From here on, you are going to struggle to maintain control. You don't want your pace to steadily become slower and slower. You want to remain in control of the pace and effort. If you're using a treadmill, realize that you may need to adjust the speed of the belt in order to either surge for the end of the test or slow down to maintain your effort.

Step 4: Time Yourself

Measure your exact final distance to within 25 meters. This information will be valuable as a marker for improvement when you take subsequent field tests.

Step 5: Cool Down; Record Your Data

All that's left is to cool down with some walking/jogging for 10 to 15 min-utes, or you can get back on the bike and spin easy for 15 to 30 minutes. When you're done, make sure to consume carbohydrates and fluids per the postworkout recommendations in Chapter 4, and record your CTS Field Test data in a training log or software program. You can also use the tables on pages 104 and 105 in this chapter to record your data.

CTS Swimming Field Test

Where the CTS Cycling/Running Field Test seeks to establish training ranges based on power, heart rate and pace, the swimming field test, which consists of a 400 meter time trial followed by 5 minutes of recov-ery, and then a 100 meter sprint, is used only to establish goal paces for swim workouts. Although it's possible to use heart rate training in the pool, my coaches and I have generally found that pace—sustainable and sprint—provides the information we need in order to establish training intensities.

WHY 400/100?

The 400/100 format of the CTS Swimming Field Test is designed to both establish goal paces for your training sessions and evaluate the relative contributions of technique and aerobic capability to your swimming speed. A 400 meter swim will take a relatively slow swimmer about 8 minutes (2:00 per 100 meters) and a fast swimmer about 4 minutes (1:00 per 100 meters), and your pace over this distance is typically equivalent to your lactate threshold (or maximum sustainable) swim pace. But for a 100 meter sprint, a technically proficient swimmer should be able to go considerably faster than his or her average 100 meter split during the 400 meter portion of the test. If your 100 meter sprint time is within 4 percent of your average 100 meter split time for the 400, then technique is more of a limiting factor for your swimming speed than is your aerobic system. This doesn't necessarily change the calculations you will use to establish goal paces for your swim training sessions, but it does indicate that you would benefit from some specific work on your swimming technique. By comparison, triathletes with very good technique in the water will more often see about an 8 percent difference between their fast 100 meter sprint time and their slower 100 meter split times during the 400.

Just as I am not covering cycling or running technique heavily in this book, I am not going to include a section designed to improve your technique in the water. This is something best accomplished through one-on-one instruction at the pool. For relative novices and people who truly struggle in the water, I would recommend Terry Laughlin's Total Immersion clinics and techniques. Laughlin's method dovetails nicely with my philosophy for optimizing the swim portion of your triathlon performance; he focuses on minimizing the energy you expend in the water by streamlining your position in the water and maximizing distance per stroke. I'd also recommend local masters swim classes (I'll explain more about integrating masters swim classes into these programs in

VO$_2$MAX TESTING

AN ATHLETE'S VO$_2$MAX IS DEFINED AS THE MAXIMUM AMOUNT OF OXYGEN THE BODY can take in and use per minute, and it's often expressed relative to body weight. Lance Armstrong's VO$_2$max, for example, has been measured as high as 83 milliliters per kilogram per minute (ml/kg/min.). The average sedentary human has a VO$_2$max of about 40, and a well-trained endurance athlete will often have values from 55 to 65 ml/kg/min. Genetics plays a pivotal role in determining your VO$_2$max, but it also responds to training. You can increase your absolute VO$_2$max, the power you can produce at VO$_2$max, and how long you can sustain efforts at this maximal intensity. However, on a percentage basis, sustainable power at lactate threshold responds to training better than VO$_2$max does. An untrained athlete could conceivably double his or her power at lactate threshold but would not be able to raise a starting VO$_2$max of 40 ml/kg/min. all the way to 80 unless he or she was born with the genetics to have a VO$_2$max of 80 ml/kg/min. In other words, you can improve your power at threshold to a greater extent than you can your power at VO$_2$max. On the other hand, a relatively small improvement in power at VO$_2$max—and the amount of time you can sustain that power—can have a significant impact on performance at lower intensities.

A scenario we often aim for in training is to improve both power at VO$_2$max and power at lactate threshold, with the overall goal of getting an athlete's lactate threshold power to be a higher percentage of his or her VO$_2$max power. For example, when CTS Premier Coach Nick White was coaching triathlete Craig Alexander in preparation for the 2008 Ironman World Championships, he found that Craig's LT (lactate threshold) power was only 77 percent of his power at VO$_2$max. Through training, Craig's power at VO$_2$max increased, but perhaps more important, his power at threshold increased to about 85 percent of his VO$_2$max power. That meant he was able to use a greater percentage of his aerobic capacity for sustained efforts. In Kona he stayed near the leaders in the swim, rode conservatively on the bike to save energy, and came from minutes behind during the marathon to win his first Ironman World Championship.

Because VO_2max intervals are included in the Time-Crunched Triathlete Program (CTS PowerIntervals, VO_2Sets, and Fartlek Intervals are VO_2max efforts), many athletes want to know whether they should have a VO_2max test done. There's certainly no harm in getting a VO_2max test, especially because it can often be tacked on to the end of a lactate threshold test. However, some performance labs only have the equipment to perform the LT test, which requires small blood samples to be tested for lactate. The VO_2max test requires analysis of inspired and expired gases, and that equipment is much more expensive. Labs that have the equipment to perform VO_2max tests, like the CTS lab in Colorado Springs, can analyze inspired and expired gases during the LT portion of the test as well, which is useful for determining an athlete's VO_2 at LT as well as VO_2max.

If you can't get your VO_2max tested, don't worry about it. The reason that LT testing or field testing is so important is that we need to establish an accurate training range for efforts that are somewhere between moderately challenging and very strenuous. Accuracy counts because training too easy won't provide the necessary stimulus, and training too hard means you'll fatigue before you accumulate enough interval time. With VO_2max intervals, the intensity is as hard as you can go, which simplifies matters greatly because it means the intervals will be effective whether you've had a VO_2max test or not.

Chapter 5). For most triathletes, and especially time-crunched triathletes, it's difficult to make massive improvements in swimming speed; you can do a tremendous amount of work and end up cutting 1 to 2 minutes off your 1,500 meter swim split. Although that is beneficial, given the amount of time you have to devote to training, you can take much bigger chunks of time off your overall triathlon performance by focusing more on your cycling and running training. As a result, a better overall strategy would be to improve your technique in the water so that you exit having expended less energy, even if you have made only minimal improvements in swimming speed.

FIELD TEST INSTRUCTIONS, SWIMMING

The Swimming Field Test consists of a 400 meter time trial followed by 10 minutes of rest and then a 100 meter time trial. You swim as hard as you possibly can for each time trial with recovery time between the efforts. It is best if you get someone on deck to time your efforts so that you can concentrate on swimming as fast as possible. Do not eat for at least two hours before your test. During the 40 minutes prior to your test, drink a sports drink that is high in carbohydrates to help aid hydration and fuel replacement. Record what you eat and drink before the test so you can have the same items before your next swimming field test.

Record the following data from the swimming field test:

- Total time of each effort
- Average 100 meter split for the 400
- Split times for each 100 of the 400
- Heart rate at finish of each effort
- Average stroke rate for each effort
- Perceived exertion for each effort (1 to 10)
- Pool type (short course/long course, yards/meters, indoor/outdoor)
- Water conditions (hot/mild/cool)

Pre–Swimming Field Test Warm-up

400 meters easy swimming.

200 meters KickSwimSet (see Chapter 5).

4 × 50 meters Drill of choice (drill 25 meters, then swim easy for 25 meters while focusing on that drill's corresponding skill), with 10 seconds of rest between 50s.

4 × 50 meters Building Pace (start at 50 percent effort, gradually build to 100 percent effort in the final 25 meters) with 10 seconds of rest between 50s.

Novice swimmers should shorten this warm-up by about 25 percent, which means a 300 meter easy swim, 150 meter KSS, 3 x 50 meter Drill, 3 x 50 meter Build.

Step 1: Start the 400 Meter Effort

Have your timer start you in the water. Start with a push, and stay stream-lined off your turns. Pace yourself properly at the start and avoid the impulse to churn your arms around as fast as possible. Instead, focus on finding water. The secret is to use the stroke rate that is most efficient for your personal swim style. Settle into a steady rhythm of breathing. From here on, it's going to hurt. If it isn't hard and painful at this point, you're not working hard enough. Swim harder and faster.

Step 2: Recover Between Efforts

Take 10 minutes of recovery time before starting the 100 meter swim. Rather than just stand around on deck or in the lane during this recovery period, swim an easy 200 meters to help keep blood circulating to work-ing muscles and get them ready and warm for the next effort. Have your timer notify you when you have 1 minute left in your recovery time, and then get mentally prepared for the 100 meter effort.

Step 3: Sprint

After exactly 10 of minutes of recovery, start your 100 meter sprint. Go as hard as you can the whole time, all the way to the wall. This will hurt, but it will be over a lot sooner than the 400!

Step 4: Get Your Times and Cool Down

Have your swims timed to the nearest second. Record all the data listed above. Finish the CTS Swimming Field Test with 15–30 minutes of easy swimming to cool down after the challenge.

RECORDING CTS FIELD TEST DATA

For easy reference, you can use Tables 3.1, 3.2, and 3.3 to record your data from the CTS Field Tests.

TABLE 3.1: Field Test Data, Cycling

VALUE	FIELD TEST CYCLING EFFORT 1	FIELD TEST CYCLING EFFORT 2
Average Heart Rate		
Maximum Heart Rate		
Average Power Output		
Average Cadence		
Weather Conditions		
Course Conditions		
Rating of Perceived Exertion (RPE)		

TABLE 3.2: Field Test Data, Running

VALUE	FIELD TEST 8-MINUTE EFFORT
Total Distance	
Heart Rate at Finish	
Average Heart Rate for Effort	
Split Times Each 400 meters (if track)	
Weather Conditions	
Course Conditions	
Rating of Perceived Exertion (RPE)	

Calculating Training Intensities for CTS Workouts

In the spirit of keeping things simple, I use a relatively small number of training intensity ranges. The whole idea of intensity ranges is to focus your efforts on specific regions of the energy system continuum. As

TABLE 3.3: Field Test Data, Swimming

VALUE	400 METER EFFORT	100 METER EFFORT
Total Time		
Actual 100 m Split Times (if recorded)		NA
Average 100 m Split		NA
Heart Rate at Finish		
Average Stroke Rate		
Rating of Perceived Exertion (RPE)		
Pool Type		
Water Conditions		

I mentioned in Chapter 2, you're always using all your energy systems, but the percentage of energy coming from each system changes as you move from lower to higher intensities. One of the key principles of interval training is that by spending focused time at specific points along this curve, you can stimulate greater training adaptations than by training at self-selected speeds.

CALCULATING CYCLING TRAINING INTENSITIES

To calculate your individual training intensities for CTS Cycling Workouts, you need to know either the highest of the two average power outputs or the highest of the two average heart rates from your CTS Cycling Field Test. If you have both pieces of information, you should calculate both power and heart rate training intensities, but use the power ranges to gauge your interval efforts whenever possible.

1. Find the higher of the two average power outputs and/or the higher of the two average heart rates from your CTS Cycling Field Test.
2. Multiply this power output and/or heart rate by the percentages listed in Table 3.4 to establish the upper and lower limits of your training ranges.

TABLE 3.4: Establishing Training Intensities for Cycling

WORKOUT NAME	PRIMARY TRAINING GOAL	PERCENTAGE OF CTS FIELD TEST POWER	PERCENTAGE OF CTS FIELD TEST HEART RATE
EnduranceMiles	Basic aerobic development	45–73	50–91
Tempo	Improved aerobic endurance	80–85	88–90
SteadyState	Increased power at lactate threshold	86–90	92–94
ClimbingRepeat	Increased power at lactate threshold	95–100	95–97
PowerInterval	Increased power at VO$_2$max	Max effort (101 at absolute minimum)	100–max

Training Intensities for Joe Athlete

Let's say Joe Athlete completed the CTS Cycling Field Test and recorded average power outputs of 300 watts and 296 watts. During the same efforts, his average heart rates were 172 and 175, respectively. He would use the 300 watts and the 175 heart rate for calculating his training intensities, even though they came from different efforts during the CTS Cycling Field Test.

The lower limit of Joe Athlete's SteadyState intensity ranges would come out to 300 × 0.86 = 258 watts. The upper limit of his SteadyState intensity range would come out to 300 × 0.90 = 270 watts. So Joe Athlete should complete SteadyState intervals at a power output between 258 and 270 watts. Table 3.5 has been filled out with all of Joe Athlete's intensity ranges.

Your CTS Cycling Training Intensities

After completing the CTS Field Test, use Table 3.6 to record your cycling intensity outputs and to calculate your CTS training intensities. You should also record your data in a training log or software program, whichever you use.

TABLE 3.5: Cycling Intensity Ranges for Joe Athlete

WORKOUT NAME	PRIMARY TRAINING GOAL	PERCENTAGE OF CTS FIELD TEST POWER	CTS POWER INTENSITY RANGE (WATTS)	PERCENTAGE OF CTS FIELD TEST HEART RATE	CTS HEART RATE INTENSITY RANGE (BPM)
Endurance Miles	Basic aerobic development	45–73	135–219	50–91	88–159
Tempo	Improved aerobic endurance	80–85	240–255	88–90	154–158
Steady State	Increased power at lactate threshold	86–90	258–270	92–94	161–165
Climbing Repeat	Increased power at lactate threshold	95–100	285–300	95–97	166–170
Power Interval	Increased power at VO$_2$max	Max effort (101 at absolute minimum)	300+	100–max	175–max

CALCULATING RUNNING WORKOUT INTENSITIES

Since there was only one effort in the running portion of the CTS Cycling/ Running Field Test, we need to know only the average heart rate from that effort, as well as the time (8 minutes) and the distance you covered. We will use this information to calculate both heart rate intensities and goal paces for your interval workouts. As with the relationship between power and heart rate in cycling, you should conduct your running efforts based on pace first and monitor your heart rate and perceived exertion to provide context.

CTS Running Paces

Use Appendix A to determine your running pace ranges for the CTS Running Workouts featured in the Time-Crunched Triathlete Programs. This is not a comprehensive list of the workouts my coaches and I use, but in the interest of brevity, only the workouts utilized in the programs

TABLE 3.6: Recording Your Cycling CTS Intensities

DATE OF FIELD TEST:

WORKOUT NAME	PRIMARY TRAINING GOAL	PERCENTAGE OF CTS FIELD TEST POWER	CTS POWER INTENSITY RANGE (WATTS)	PERCENTAGE OF CTS FIELD TEST HEART RATE	CTS HEART RATE INTENSITY RANGE (BPM)
Endurance Miles	Basic aerobic development	45–73		50–91	
Tempo	Improved aerobic endurance	80–85		88–90	
Steady State	Increased power at lactate threshold	86–90		92–94	
Climbing Repeat	Increased power at lactate threshold	95–100		95–97	
Power Interval	Increased power at VO_2max	Max effort (101 at absolute minimum)		100–max	

in this book are presented here. In the left-hand column, find your minute/mile pace from the 8-minute field test effort. If you're using a GPS-enabled watch, this may be as simple as calling up the data. If you were running on a track or a course of known distance, then you need to first calculate your field test pace. To save yourself the effort of remembering conversion tables and high school algebra (Distance = Rate × Time), go online and enter your data into an online pace calculator to determine your minute-per-mile pace from the distance you covered during your 8-minute effort. Once you have your field test pace, find the appropriate pace ranges for CTS Running Workouts in Appendix A.

If your field test pace is not exactly represented in the chart provided in Appendix A, round to the nearest row, or you can calculate your exact paces using the percentages in Table 3.7.

TABLE 3.7: Using Field Test Pace to Calculate CTS Running Pace Ranges

WORKOUT NAME	PRIMARY TRAINING GOAL	PERCENTAGE OF CTS RUNNING FIELD TEST PACE	YOUR CTS RUNNING PACE RANGES
EnduranceRun	Basic aerobic development	<97	
SteadyStateRun	Improved aerobic endurance	92–98	
TempoRun	Increased pace at lactate threshold	98–102	
Fartlek Intervals	Increased speed at VO$_2$ max	102–108	

Instructions for Calculating CTS Running Heart Rate Intensities

Multiply the average heart rate from your running effort by the percentages listed in Table 3.8 to establish the upper and lower limits of your training ranges. You may notice that the percentages for establishing heart rate ranges and pace ranges are identical. That's not a misprint; with the exception of the very slow and the very fast—in other words, the extremes—these percentages yield accurate training ranges for both pace and heart rate.

TABLE 3.8: Heart Rate Percentages for CTS Running Field Test

WORKOUT NAME	PRIMARY TRAINING GOAL	PERCENTAGE OF CTS RUNNING FIELD TEST HEART RATE
EnduranceRun	Basic aerobic development	<97
SteadyStateRun	Improved aerobic endurance	92–98
TempoRun	Increased pace at lactate threshold	98–102
Fartlek Intervals	Increased speed at VO$_2$max	102–108

Training Intensities for Joe Athlete

Going back to Joe Athlete, let's now say he completed the running portion of the CTS Cycling/Running Field Test and recorded an average heart rate of 180. The lower limit of Joe Athlete's SteadyStateRun intensity ranges would come out to 180 × 0.92 = 166 beats per minute. The upper limit of his SteadyStateRun intensity range would come out to 180 × 0.98 = 176 bpm. So Joe Athlete should complete SteadyStateRun intervals at a heart rate between 166 and 176 bpm. Table 3.9 has been filled out with all of Joe Athlete's intensity ranges.

TABLE 3.9: Running Intensity Ranges for Joe Athlete

WORKOUT NAME	PRIMARY TRAINING GOAL	PERCENTAGE OF CTS RUNNING FIELD TEST HEART RATE	CTS RUNNING INTENSITY RANGE (BPM)
EnduranceRun	Basic aerobic development	<97	<175
SteadyStateRun	Improved aerobic endurance	92–98	166–176
TempoRun	Increased pace at lactate threshold	98–102	176–184
Fartlek Intervals	Increased speed at VO_2max	102–108	184–194

Your CTS Running Training Intensities

After completing the CTS Field Test for running, use Table 3.10 to record your running intensity outputs and to calculate your CTS training intensities. You should also record your data in a training log or software program, whichever you use.

CALCULATING SWIMMING WORKOUT INTENSITIES/PACES

For your swimming workouts, you'll be using a relatively small number of intensity ranges, and those ranges will be based on your average 100 meter split time from the 400 meter portion of the CTS Swimming Field Test. In Appendix B, find your 400 meter time and 100 meter split time in the left-hand columns, and follow the row across to the right to find

TABLE 3.10: Recording Your CTS Running Intensities

DATE OF FIELD TEST:

WORKOUT NAME	PRIMARY TRAINING GOAL	PERCENTAGE OF CTS RUNNING FIELD TEST HEART RATE	CTS RUNNING INTENSITY RANGE (BPM)
EnduranceRun	Basic aerobic development	<97	
SteadyStateRun	Improved aerobic endurance	92–98	
TempoRun	Increased pace at lactate threshold	98–102	
Fartlek Intervals	Increased speed at VO$_2$max	102–108	

TABLE 3.11: Using Field Test Pace to Calculate CTS Swimming Pace Ranges

WORKOUT NAME	PRIMARY TRAINING GOAL	PERCENTAGE OF CTS SWIMMING FIELD TEST PACE	CTS SWIMMING PACE RANGE (PER 100 METERS)
BaseIntervalSet	Basic aerobic development	102–120	
PaceIntervalSet	Improved aerobic endurance	100–109	
LactateThresholdSet	Increased pace at lactate threshold	94–103	
VO$_2$Set (VOS)	Increased speed at VO$_2$max	75–93	

your pace ranges for the swimming workouts utilized in this program. If your 400 meter split time is not represented exactly in the table, either round to the nearest row or use the calculations in Table 3.11 to calculate your swimming paces.

Swimming Intensities for Joe Athlete

Once again, let's use Joe Athlete's performance as an example, and let's say he completed the 400 meter portion of the CTS Swimming Field Test in 6:00. Dividing that time by 4 gives us his average 100 meter split time, which would be 1:30. We can either locate his 400 meter time in Appendix B or multiply his average 100 meter split time by the percentages in Table 3.11. For instance, the lower end of Joe's pace range for a Lactate Threshold Set would be 94 percent of 1:30, or 1:25. The upper end of his pace range would be 103 percent of 1:30, or 1:33.

Your CTS Swimming Pace Intensities

To calculate your own swimming pace ranges, apply the percentages in Table 3.11 to the average 100 meter split time from your field test. Similarly, if you performed the test in a yard pool and you want to calculate your paces in minutes per 100 yards, use these percentages.

4

INTEGRATED NUTRITION FOR SUPERIOR PERFORMANCE

In the spirit of respecting the demands on your time and the knowledge many of you already have regarding sports nutrition, I'm going to keep this chapter short by focusing on the specific topics that are essential for optimizing your fitness and body weight for triathlon competitions. After publishing an entire book on sports nutrition and nutrition periodization (*Chris Carmichael's Food for Fitness*) and writing extensively on the importance of proper nutrition in optimizing health and fitness (*5 Essentials for a Winning Life*), it's difficult for me to resist the temptation to write an exhaustive treatise on sports nutrition for this book as well. But since this is a book for athletes who are short on time, I'm going to do my best to cut to the chase.

Key Concepts in Sports Nutrition

Just to make sure we're all on the same page, let's quickly review the basics. First of all, all the calories you consume come from three macronutrients: carbohydrate (4 calories per gram), protein (4 calories per gram), and fat

(9 calories per gram). (Note: To avoid confusion, I use the more common spelling of food calories with a lowercase "c," even though the scientifically accurate terminology would be either kilocalories or Calories with a capital "C." This usage conforms with what you will find in most cookbooks and nutrition guides, so I hope you'll overlook the simplification.) These macronutrients directly and indirectly provide all the energy you use to build and maintain your body, perform all your normal bodily functions, and complete all your voluntary tasks, including exercise.

On top of these macronutrients, there are three other items you need to consume to stay alive and healthy: water, vitamins, and minerals. Despite delivering zero calories, water is sometimes referred to as a fourth macronutrient because of its overwhelming importance. In fact, water is probably more important than anything else you consume, because dehydration can kill you in days, whereas you can survive without food for much longer. Vitamins and minerals, known as micronutrients, also deliver zero calories but are necessary in varying amounts for completing the biochemical reactions that keep your body functioning properly.

Your body burns calories every minute of every day, and you are constantly deriving that energy from a mixture of carbohydrate, protein, and fat. The relative percentage of energy coming from each depends on many factors, but for the purposes of this book, I will concentrate most on how exercise intensity affects the way you use fuel. Of the three macronutrients, you rely on protein for a relatively low and constant amount of energy during exercise. Protein is an important component of an athlete's nutrition program and performance, but under normal conditions a healthy individual derives 10 to 15 percent of his or her exercise calories from protein, regardless of exercise intensity. As a result, and for the sake of simplicity, I will remove protein from the equation and focus on the relative contributions from carbohydrate and fat during exercise.

As I explained in Chapter 2, during exercise your muscles process carbohydrate and fat to produce energy using aerobic metabolism and glycolysis. Your exercise intensity and fitness directly affect the relative amount of energy being produced by each method. At rest, your body relies on fat for 80 to 90 percent of its energy needs (breathing, digestion, pumping blood, etc.). At very low exercise intensities (20 to 25 percent of VO_2max), you're still relying on fat for about 70 percent of your energy. As you reach 40 to 60 percent of VO_2max, your fuel utilization reaches about a 50-50 balance between fat and carbohydrate. Athletes with greater aerobic fitness will reach and maintain this 50–50 balance at a higher relative workload than will athletes who are less fit. As your exercise intensity increases from 60 percent of VO_2max, the relative contribution from carbohydrate increases dramatically because of the increased reliance on glycolysis. But remember, even when you're burning a lot of carbohydrate at higher exercise intensities (glycolysis burns carbohydrates exclusively), you are still processing fat and carbohydrate using aerobic metabolism. Once you exceed your lactate threshold intensity (70 to 90 percent of VO_2max, depending on your fitness level), more than 80 percent of your energy is being derived from carbohydrate.

To put this in perspective, at 90 to 100 percent of VO_2max, a 160-pound athlete's caloric burn rate may reach 20 to 24 calories per minute, which means you could burn up to 5 grams of carbohydrate per minute. That might not sound like much, but if you could maintain that intensity for an hour, you would burn close to 300 grams of carbohydrate. If you were on a bicycle, your power meter would show that you produced around 1,200 to 1,400 kilojoules (Kj) of work. At a challenging pace below lactate threshold, you would burn 9 to 10 calories per minute and produce 550 to 600 Kj/hr. Even during a 1-hour hard interval workout, that number would only increase to 750 or 850 because of the increased energy expenditure during the intervals. The point is, high-intensity exercise burns a lot of carbohydrate very quickly, meaning there are significant nutritional implications to training programs that incorporate high-intensity interval sessions.

High-Intensity Training Calls for High-Octane Fuel

I often listen to National Public Radio, and that means I've learned a lot from Click and Clack (Tom and Ray Magliozzi, the hosts of *Car Talk*).

Over the years, they have answered many questions about the difference between regular and premium gasoline, particularly concerning who needs it and who's wasting money purchasing it. My interpretation of their advice is that it basically comes down to the engine in your car. High-performance cars are built with engines that create higher levels of compression in the cylinders, which produce a bigger bang (literally) every time the cylinder fires. That in turn leads to greater horsepower and more speeding tickets. High-compression engines perform better on high-octane fuel because the fuel burns better at higher temperatures and pressures. Most cars, though, are designed with lower-compression engines that run well on regular gas and don't really benefit from premium fuel.

In some ways, you can look at your body as having two engines that power your training. Your aerobic engine is the smooth and steady automatic you'd find in the family minivan, and your glycolytic system is the turbocharged, smoke-the-tires, 500-horsepower motor in your sports car. Ideally, you'd take great care of both, but the minivan will be more forgiving of poor fuel, while the sports car needs premium fuel to deliver top performance. Intervals that call for intensities at or above lactate threshold rely heavily on the glycolytic system, and the glycolytic system operates best with a steady supply of clean-burning, high-octane fuel.

Carbohydrate is your body's high-performance fuel. There are some people who push protein as the preferred fuel, because high school biology taught us that muscle is made of protein, and therefore you must need to eat protein if you want to use your muscles. Protein is indeed necessary for building and maintaining muscle tissue, but it's not a very good fuel for intense exercise. For the most part, it has to be transported to the liver and converted into carbohydrate (a process called *gluconeogenesis*, literally "creating new glucose") so it can be transported back to muscles and be burned as fuel. Protein plays important roles in sports nutrition (muscle maintenance, immune function, enzymes, etc.), but those roles don't include being a primary fuel source for high-intensity, high-performance efforts.

Some people say fat is the best fuel for endurance performance, and they'd be correct if your goal were to swim, ride, or run very slowly all the time. Fat is a great fuel for steady, low- to moderate-intensity exercise, but if you were to take this idea to its extreme and rely solely on fat for energy, the hardest efforts you'd be able to sustain would be at about 60 percent of your VO_2max. Because fat can only be burned through the aerobic system, relying entirely on fat would mean that you wouldn't be able to take advantage of the glycolytic system's tremendous capacity for producing energy that contributes to higher speeds. In fact, the aerobic system requires a small amount of carbohydrate to burn fat in the first place, so you really wouldn't be able to fuel exercise entirely with fat anyway. From a nutritional standpoint, even the leanest endurance athlete has fat stores that are sufficient to supply the aerobic engine with the fuel it needs, so although some fat is essential in an athlete's diet, a high-fat diet is not a high-performance nutrition program.

Carbohydrate is your high-performance fuel because it can be used to power aerobic metabolism and is the primary fuel for high-intensity efforts. When you hit the throttle and demand energy for accelerations and surges, you call on the glycolytic system for a little or a lot of that energy. The glycolytic system only burns carbohydrate, which means you'd better have it onboard if you want to continue pushing the pace. In general, an endurance athlete's diet should be rich in carbohydrate and moderate in protein and fat. I wrote extensively about "nutrition periodization" in *Food for Fitness*; it's the process of matching your nutrition program to the energy demands of your training. Rather than rehash that information here, I'll just say that for the Time-Crunched Triathlete Program, endurance athletes need to get 60 to 65 percent of their total calories from carbohydrate, 13 to 15 percent from protein, and 20 to 25 percent from fat.

Your overall carbohydrate intake should be relatively high so that you can replenish the carbohydrate you burn during your workouts. This is crucial because you want to begin each training session with full stores of glycogen (the storage form of carbohydrate in muscles and your liver).

Starting training sessions with full glycogen stores increases your time to exhaustion, which is to say that you'll be able to exercise longer before fatigue significantly hurts your performance. Within the context of the workouts in the Time-Crunched Triathlete Program (see Chapter 5), this means you'll be able to complete more high-quality efforts before you fatigue to the point that you should stop. Completing more efforts at the right intensity levels leads to a greater training stimulus and bigger performance gains.

ADJUSTING CALORIC COMPOSITION

MY AFFINITY FOR CARBOHYDRATE IN NUTRITION PROGRAMS FOR ENDURANCE athletes is based on the nutrient's proven ability to improve workout quality and race-day performance. But there can be a downside to consuming 60 to 65 percent of your calories as carbohydrate; many sources of carbohydrate are not very filling or satisfying, so some athletes end up feeling hungry quite frequently. Choosing low-glycemic carbohydrate sources (carbohydrates that lead to smaller increases in blood glucose or insulin production, like those found in fiber-rich vegetables and fruits, whole-grain breads and cereals, nuts, and some dairy products) can go a long way to solving this problem, but some athletes benefit from taking steps to change the overall composition of their diet.

If you're consuming 60–65 percent of your calories as carbohydrate and you're experiencing frequent hunger between workouts, increased irritability, and notable sleepiness well before bedtime, you may benefit from reducing your carbohydrate intake and increasing the amount of protein you consume. Another sign to watch out for is regularly feeling like you're coming down with a cold the day after a hard workout, even if that feeling goes away later in the day or by the following morning.

It's important to both reduce your carbohydrate intake and increase your protein intake; don't just add more protein to the diet you're already consuming, because you will end up with a cumulative increase in total daily calories. Aim to bring your carbohydrate consumption down to about 50–55 percent of your total calories while bringing your protein intake up to between 20 and 25 percent. Fat intake should remain around 20–25 percent of your total caloric intake. For most athletes, a shift like this is only a matter of increasing protein intake by 3 to 5 ounces of protein per day (with a relatively equal reduction in carbohydrate intake), but the impact on your lifestyle can be much more significant. And as long as you make sure to follow the carbohydrate recommendations for before-, during-, and postworkout nutrition, training performance typically remains high and physiological adaptations progress normally.

Optimizing Nutritional Support for Training

In addition to a diet that's rich in carbohydrate, your nutritional habits directly before, during, and after your training sessions will have a significant impact on the quality of your training sessions, and hence your success with the Time-Crunched Triathlete Program.

PREWORKOUT NUTRITION

If you're getting ready to complete an interval workout that's going to include 16 to 20 minutes of effort at and above your lactate threshold power output or pace, you will want to make sure you're properly fueled up. There are two steps: your preworkout meal and your preworkout snack. The differences between the two are how big they are and when they're consumed.

Preworkout Meal

The most important thing about the last full meal you eat before a training session is that it be out of your stomach and digested before you start training. This is especially important for interval workouts, because

TABLE 4.1: Choosing the Right Preworkout Food

GOOD FOODS FOR PRE-EXERCISE MEALS	LESS DESIRABLE FOODS FOR PRE-EXERCISE MEALS
High carbohydrate, moderate protein, low fat: rice, cereal, pasta, sandwiches (roast beef, turkey, peanut butter and jelly), oatmeal, breakfast burrito with eggs and potatoes, whole-grain bagel and cream cheese/peanut butter/ almond butter, fruit	High fat and/or protein, low carbohydrate: steak, bacon, sausage, ice cream, chili dogs, cream sauces Low carbohydrate, low calorie: salads (garden, tuna, or chicken), diet soft drinks

high-intensity efforts tend to be downright unpleasant on a full stomach. A relatively light meal that's rich in carbohydrate (preferably about 70 percent of total calories) is a good choice, because meals that contain a lot of fat or protein stay in the stomach longer and are digested more slowly. That's a good thing if you're trying to feel full longer, but not good if you're about to go out for a hard workout. Table 4.1 lists examples of good foods to choose before a workout.

A good rule of thumb is to consume 0.5 to 2 grams of carbohydrate per pound (g/lb.) of body weight about 2 to 3 hours before your ride (see Table 4.2). More specifically, you want to be closer to 2 g/lb. if you're

TABLE 4.2: Recommended Grams of Carbohydrate in Pre-exercise Meals

BODY WEIGHT (LB.)	3–4 HOURS PRIOR (1.5–2 G/LB.)	2–3 HOURS PRIOR (1–1.5 G/LB.)	1–2 HOURS PRIOR (0.5–1 G/LB.)	0–60 MINUTES PRIOR (0.25–0.5 G/LB.)
110	165–220	110–165	55–110	30–55
120	180–240	120–180	60–120	30–60
135	200–270	135–200	65–135	30–65
150	225–300	150–225	75–150	35–75
165	250–330	165–250	80–165	40–80
180	270–360	180–270	90–180	45–90
195	290–390	195–290	95–195	50–95

eating 3 hours before training, and closer to 0.5 g/lb. if you're going to train within 2 hours of your last significant meal. And just as this isn't the time for a high-fat or high-protein meal, you shouldn't use this time to focus on fulfilling your fiber requirement for the day. The American Heart Association recommends 25 to 30 grams of fiber a day to help reduce levels of LDL cholesterol (the bad kind) and reduce the risk of developing heart disease, but fiber also slows digestion, so it's better saved for other meals.

Preworkout Snack

There may be nothing more important to the quality of your training sessions than what you eat and drink in the hour immediately prior to working out. Eat the right things, and you'll feel strong, invigorated, and energized. Eat the wrong things, and you'll feel bloated, sluggish, and nauseated. It's difficult to have a great workout when you feel like you're carrying a bowling ball in your gut.

CAFFEINE AND STIMULANTS

ANY DISCUSSION OF PREWORKOUT AND DURING-WORKOUT SPORTS NUTRITION generates questions about using caffeine and other stimulants as ergogenic aids. I'll keep this simple: Caffeine, in amounts normally found in foods, coffee, and tea, is fine and effective. Furthermore, I haven't seen any markedly better stimulant that's not on the World Anti-Doping Agency's list of banned substances or that doesn't come with a federal prison term for possession. In other words, caffeine works. It's generally safe in reasonable quantities (200 milligrams or less per dose), and its effects and side effects are well-known and predictable. People keep coming out with new additives and claim all manner of performance enhancements for them, but the truth is, plain old caffeine is hard to beat.

CONTINUES

CONTINUED

The impact of caffeine on athletic performance is twofold. The more important effect is that it improves motivation, alertness, concentration, and enthusiasm. Considering that the workouts in this program are challenging, adding a little caffeine to your preworkout snack wouldn't hurt. This is especially true if you find yourself struggling to generate the enthusiasm necessary to start a hard workout after 8 to 10 hours at your day job. Caffeine's second impact on performance is that it may help your body liberate more fat for use as energy during exercise. This isn't a bad thing, but it's also not going to have a very significant influence on the effectiveness of your workout.

Interestingly, there's some evidence that caffeine may help accelerate glycogen replenishment when it's consumed immediately after a workout. This opens up the possibility of caffeinated recovery drinks, but also means you may have a good excuse to stop at the coffee shop on your way home.

The key here is to choose foods that will get out of your gut and into your blood quickly. There are many choices available, and it's important to experiment with various combinations until you find a solution that doesn't come back up halfway through your workout. And keep in mind that what works best before a cycling session might not be the best choice before a run or swim. Nutrition is pretty easy to deal with when cycling; you can exercise while carrying a large amount of food, and you can eat regularly during the workout without feeling like you're going to throw up. But the jostling that occurs during a running workout means that you'll feel better starting with less or no food in your stomach, and that you're likely to have a better run if you consume small amounts of fluid and gels for hydration and nutrition, rather than significant amounts of solid foods. Similarly, the prone position of swimming means that training with a full or even partially full stomach increases the chances you'll experience regurgitation.

Across all three sports, your best options, from both the sports nutrition and practical standpoints, are carbohydrate-rich gels and sports drinks. That's not to say you can't have a great workout on a peanut butter and jelly sandwich or a granola bar, but you're more likely to fully digest the carbohydrates in a gel or sports drink and have all that energy available for your muscles. These products are simply easier to digest; they get out of the stomach and gut faster than conventional foods, which both makes the energy available faster and helps prevent stomach upset. To aid in the digestion and absorption process, make sure you consume at least 8 ounces of fluid anytime you eat a gel or bar. If I'm headed out for a workout that's going to contain intervals, I consume a bottle of sports drink 30 to 60 minutes before training and a gel 10 to 15 minutes before I get on my bike. With a bottle of GU Electrolyte Brew and one GU packet, that adds up to about 50 grams (g) of carbohydrate, or 0.29 g of carbohydrate per pound (I weigh about 170 pounds, or 77 kilograms).

As you can see in the following list, many other snack combinations provide 50 to 75 g of carbohydrate and would work in the hour leading up to training, and you can easily bring this down to 40 to 60 g by consuming smaller portions. Regardless of the option you choose, it's imperative that you consume 16 to 24 ounces of fluid in the hour before training, be it water, fruit juice, or a sports drink.

- 1 cup vanilla yogurt + ½ cup grape nuts
  + 2 tablespoons raisins
- 1 cup vanilla yogurt + 1 cup fresh fruit
- 1 cup juice + 1 banana
- 1 slice banana nut bread + 1 cup skim milk
- 1 energy bar + 8 ounces sports drink
- Smoothie: 2 cups skim or soy milk + 1½ cups mango
  or berries + 2 tablespoons soy protein
- 1½ cups multigrain cereal + 1½ cups skim milk
- 1 bagel + 1 banana + 1 tablespoon nut butter
- 1 cup cottage cheese + 8 whole wheat crackers + 1 apple

FUELING EARLY-MORNING WORKOUTS

EARLY MORNING IS A GREAT TIME FOR BUSY PROFESSIONALS TO SQUEEZE IN A workout. You can be up, on your way, done with your workout, and showered before your kids wake up or your BlackBerry starts buzzing. A lot of people prefer to start their day with a workout because it's their time for themselves and allows them to begin the day with a positive accomplishment. You may not be able to control much of what happens in the hours afterward, but at least you can go into the day having already checked something valuable off your list.

Fueling early-morning workouts is a challenge, because you haven't eaten for 8 to 10 hours and you burned through about 80 percent of your liver glycogen overnight. All the same, you don't have time to eat and wait around for an hour or more before starting your workout. So, what can you do to ensure you have a great morning workout?

1. **Keep it simple and small:** Your muscles are full of glycogen and ready to go; it's your blood sugar that's low because your liver glycogen stores are mostly depleted. Low blood sugar means less fuel for your brain, and a hungry brain has trouble staying focused on completing high-quality efforts. You just need something light that delivers simple and complex carbohydrates, and maybe a little protein to make it more satiating. A sports drink or a gel would work, as would any of the aforementioned preworkout snacks. If you normally drink caffeine, a shot of espresso or a small cup of coffee isn't a bad idea, but make sure you also consume about 16 ounces of plain water or fruit juice.

2. **Eat first:** It always takes a little time to get dressed and out the door, so eat before you start that process. This means eating as soon as you get out of bed, and then going about the business of getting ready to train. This is especially important if you're getting ready for a bike-run workout from your house. You'll have a little more time to fit

in a snack if you have to get up and go to the pool for an early-morning swim workout.

3. **Get started:** Early-morning workout time disappears fast, so get started even if it means doing a slightly longer warm-up to let your food settle. If you find you really need a little more time to digest your snack before you work out, be careful not to get too engaged in something like reading the paper or checking your e-mail. One athlete I talked to had a good solution: To ensure that he wouldn't get sucked into reading the newspaper, he brought only the first section into the house, leaving the rest of it on the porch for later.

NUTRITION DURING WORKOUTS

Interval workouts can have a significant impact on your willingness, ability, and need to consume food and fluids while you're exercising. In particular, hard workouts inhibit your desire and your opportunities to consume either food or fluids, which is part of the reason that your pre-workout snack is so important. But when you have fewer opportunities each week to create the stimulus necessary for positive training adaptations, it's critically important for each workout to be of the highest quality. That means you're going to need to find a sports nutrition strategy that you can use effectively during higher-intensity training sessions.

One benefit to shorter workouts is that, between the amount of glycogen you can store in your muscles and the fact that you can only process and utilize about 1 gram of ingested carbohydrate per minute anyway, there is little need to consume any calories during a 1-hour workout.

Before you call or e-mail me to point out the discrepancy between that last sentence and long-held recommendations (my own included) to eat early and often during any exercise session, let me make an important distinction: If you're planning on having a good workout that lasts more than about 75 minutes, you need to consume carbohydrate within the first

30 minutes after you start training. If you're going to be done with your hard efforts and either in the shower or into your cool-down within 60 to 75 minutes, you can complete a high-quality training session without consuming a single calorie. Will your 1-hour workout be even better if you use a sports drink or a gel? Maybe, but it depends less on the calories themselves and more on what you can tolerate.

However, the majority of the workouts in the Time-Crunched Triathlete Program range from 1:15 to 2:00 hours, with a few reaching 2:30 to 3:00 hours in select schedules. For best results, especially in the latter portions of a two-discipline workout, it will be crucial to consume carbohydrate during your training sessions.

When you're going to be training for 75 minutes or longer (and include transition time between the pool and bike, or bike and run, when you think about nutrition for training), it's important to start consuming carbohydrates, electrolytes, and fluid early on and continue to do so all the way through the end of the workout. The standard guidelines for carbohydrate consumption during endurance exercise call for 30 to 60 grams of carbohydrate per hour, more toward the high end of the range as intensity increases. From watching athletes train for more than 20 years, I can tell you that 50 to 60 grams of carbohydrate in an hour is good for bike racing, but riders on moderate-intensity group rides and centuries tend to gravitate more toward 35 to 50 grams per hour. During running workouts, 30 to 40 grams per hour is more common, again because of the jostling effect that running has on the gut. For some people, even 30 to 40 grams (one gel and some sports drink) is more than they can tolerate. Similarly, during swim workouts, athletes tend to consume very few calories and any that they do consume are almost always in the form of a sports drink. Some of you may perform well consuming a gel during a swim workout, but it's rare to see anyone consume solid food while swimming (plus, your grandma wouldn't approve of eating solid foods and then swimming anyway).

And if you're wondering if body weight has an impact on the guidelines, the answer is yes and no. The 30- to 60-gram range is pretty large, and both small and large athletes tend to fit within it, but smaller athletes often do well at the lower end, and larger riders sometimes need to be at the higher end. That said, on the bike a smaller athlete who is working hard may need to consume 50–60 grams of carbohydrate an hour, while a bigger rider who is just cruising along may only need 30–40 grams.

What do numbers like 35 grams of carbohydrate per hour mean in terms of items you can hold in your hand? Most energy gels, including GU, contain about 25 grams of carbohydrate per packet. There's more variation in the amounts of carbohydrate found in sports drinks per serving. GU Electrolyte Brew, for instance, contains 26 grams of carbohydrate in a 16-ounce serving, or 39 grams in a 24-ounce serving (equivalent to a large water bottle). Across other brands, you can consume anywhere from the high 30s to nearly 60 grams of carbohydrate in a 24-ounce serving. When it comes to energy bars, most bars targeted at endurance athletes contain 30 to 45 grams of carbohydrate per bar. Throughout your training, it's best to diversify your sports nutrition, in terms of type and texture, so you can fuel yourself properly as product availability and your taste preferences change.

Here's a tip for anyone who prefers energy gels: You must drink about 6 to 8 ounces of water with the gel for it to work properly. You're consuming a concentrated, viscous source of carbohydrate, and a few slugs of water will help your body break it down, get it out of the stomach, and absorb it from the gut more quickly. A gel plus water means you'll get to use more of the carbohydrate you just consumed. If you just down the gel and skip the water, you'll absorb most of the carbohydrate, but you'll absorb it slowly, and some will just keep going toward the other end of the system without any benefit.

HYDRATION DURING WORKOUTS

Water is the one thing you can't do without, even during a 1-hour training session. Depending on the temperature, humidity, and your personal sweat rate, you can lose up to 1.5 liters of fluid in a 1-hour workout. To make matters worse, high-intensity workouts increase core temperature more than low- to moderate-intensity rides, especially if you're riding or running indoors, and sweat evaporating off your skin is your body's primary cooling system. Sweating out up to 1.5 liters of fluid and failing to drink will absolutely hinder your performance, resulting in lower power outputs for your intervals and a shortened time to exhaustion.

You also lose electrolytes as you sweat (primarily sodium, but also some potassium and traces of other minerals), so ideally you should consume a sports drink during all workouts—but again we need to go back to the concept of tolerance. As exercise intensity and core temperature increase, athletes gradually lose their drive to drink and eat. Many also experience an upset stomach when they consume calories during hard workouts. At the same time, adding carbohydrate and sodium to the fluid increases an athlete's motivation to drink and increases the amount of fluid you consume every time you lift your bottle to your lips. The American College of Sports Medicine recommends consuming 500 to 700 milligrams of sodium per hour of aerobic exercise.

During your workouts, it's not essential that you replenish every milliliter of fluid you lose as sweat. In moderate-intensity sessions completed in cooler weather, you may be able to take in as much fluid as you lose each hour. But that can be a tall order when it's hot because of your increased sweat rate. Fortunately, during relatively short, higher-intensity workouts you can afford to replenish less fluid because the fluids (and electrolytes) you consumed beforehand will help ward off dehydration and you'll be done soon enough to replenish lost fluids rapidly. With these considerations in mind, during workouts lasting less than 2 hours you should aim to consume enough liquid to replace at least 80 percent of the fluid you're losing from sweat. The longer the workout, the closer you want to get to consuming fluid at a rate pretty much equal to the rate at which you're losing it. This also gets easier to accomplish because of that inverse relationship between exercise duration and intensity.

The bare minimum for hydration during exercise is one standard bottle (16 ounces or 500 milliliters) per hour, but that will be adequate only for low-intensity rides or runs on cool days. In warmer conditions, or for any moderate- to high-intensity workout, shoot for two bottles an hour on the bike and at least one full bottle per hour for runs. And if it's a particularly hot day, you may need to add a third bottle on the bike and a second for runs. During swim sessions, a standard bottle per hour should be adequate. I recommend consuming a carbohydrate-rich sports drink like GU Electrolyte Brew in at least half the bottles you drink during workouts longer than an hour. Not only will the taste and sodium increase your drive to drink and the amount of fluid you consume, but sports drinks are an easy way for athletes to get three items necessary for top performance—fluid, electrolytes, and carbohydrates—all in one place.

The perfect during-workout nutrition and hydration strategy varies from athlete to athlete, but as long as your combination of foods and fluids satisfies the basic requirements, the compromise that works for you is the right way to go. During interval workouts, many athletes can tolerate electrolyte solutions and lightly flavored carbohydrate/electrolyte sports drinks, but you shouldn't dilute sports drinks, because that changes the carefully designed concentrations and negatively affects absorption rates.

The bottom line is that failing to provide your body with adequate calories and fluids during exercise will result in lower-quality efforts and ineffective training sessions. As a time-crunched athlete relying on fewer workouts than your competitors, you can't afford to waste a workout due to low energy levels or dehydration. Every effort and every training session counts.

SAVING YOURSELF

EVERY ENDURANCE ATHLETE HAS FELT IT—A SUDDEN EMPTINESS IN THE GUT, a twitch in a calf or hamstring muscle, or a momentary bout of light-headedness. You didn't eat enough or drink enough, and now you're about to bonk, cramp, or both. Your body is telling you it needs food and/or fluids right now, and if you refuse to listen, your body will begin to shut down.

CONTINUES

CONTINUED

You screwed up and you know it, but it's still possible to save yourself and continue to have a good workout or race.

Time is of the essence, and desperate times call for—or at least excuse—desperate measures. If you're bonking, you need carbohydrate fast. That means simple sugars and a lot of them. Down two energy gels right away (with at least half a bottle of water), or try to consume a full bottle of carbohydrate-rich sports drink. If you're out of sports drink or you've already eaten all the food you have, it's time to hit the vending machines or the candy aisle of the convenience store. Everyone has favorite emergency foods; some go for chocolate chip cookies and Mountain Dew, while others go for Little Debbie Oatmeal Cream cookies and Coke. My personal favorites are a Snickers bar and a Lipton Iced Tea (sugar and caffeine equal to a Coke but no carbonation). Obviously, these options are not the preferred choices for sports nutrition—they almost always put too much sugar into your belly—but they'll do the trick in a pinch. You'll get a boost from the sodium, sugar, and caffeine, and buy yourself enough time to get back on track with your nutrition.

If you're starting to cramp, you need to look for electrolytes, primarily sodium and potassium. Not all cramps are caused by a lack of electrolytes, but it's very difficult to pinpoint exactly what's causing the situation in your calf while it's happening, and there's an above-average chance that consuming electrolytes will help solve the problem. If it works, you get to keep going. If it doesn't, you'll still have to deal with the cramp, but at least you'll have more electrolytes onboard. In other words, as soon as you feel a precramp twinge in your calf, hamstring, or quadriceps, try to consume 200 to 400 milligrams of electrolytes. Depending on the products available, this can mean one or two energy gels and/or a full bottle of sports drink. Often this will mean consuming more carbohydrate than you ideally want at one time, but without the electrolytes you will cramp, and right now that will harm your performance a lot more than overconsuming carbohydrate.

Even with a ton of athletic experience and plenty of education as a CTS coach, Patrick Valentine got himself into some trouble at the Ironman 70.3 New Orleans in 2010. He knew that going from the dry conditions of Colorado Springs to the humidity of the Gulf Coast would lead to some challenges in terms of hydration and core temperature regulation, and he developed a solid nutrition and hydration strategy prior to the event, but race day didn't go quite as planned. Just a few miles into the run, he started feeling a twitch in his left hamstring and he immediately realized that his entire race was in danger. If he started cramping now, he'd most likely have to walk most of the remaining 10 miles of the race, and if the cramps got really bad they could prevent him from finishing at all. He was carrying two GU Energy Gels and he downed them one right after the other, and he also drank a bottle of water—somewhere between 12 and 16 ounces—to help his body digest the carbohydrates and get the electrolytes into his system. At the next aid station he slowed down and drank what he estimated to be four cups of electrolyte drink. In total, over a 10-minute period he consumed way more carbohydrate and sodium than I or any sports dietitian would recommend. But the reasons we don't recommend such rapid consumption are that absorption rates slow down and there's a significant risk you'll end up with an upset stomach.

In my opinion, when the building is on fire you dump as much water on it as you need to put the fire out, and you worry about the possibility of water damage later. Patrick needed sodium, and he managed to get it despite the fact that he took in more fluid than he wanted to, and more carbohydrate than his body should have been able to handle. If you cramp or bonk, it's all over, so if you screwed up and put yourself in a bad nutritional position, eat and drink a lot in an attempt to bring yourself back from the brink. You might have to deal with an upset stomach later (Patrick was able to bounce back without any stomach issues), but the alternative is cramping or bonking right then and there. In other words, you're avoiding an immediate certainty in exchange for a future possibility.

POSTWORKOUT NUTRITION

Your nutrition and hydration choices immediately following your workouts play important roles in preparing you for successful training sessions in the following days. This is true whether you're on a high-volume, moderate-intensity training program or a higher-intensity, lower-volume plan, but lower-volume trainers have some additional challenges to overcome.

It's likely that you will finish your interval workouts having consumed only one bottle of plain water. I am guessing some of you will have chosen an electrolyte drink instead, fewer will consume a carbohydrate-rich sports drink, and very few will have eaten a gel or any solid food. We can talk about guidelines and recommendations all we want, but the reality is that athletes consume fewer calories during high-intensity interval sessions. You can compensate for this somewhat with your preworkout snack, but after your training session is done, it's very important to focus on nutrition and hydration so you can replenish what you've depleted and give your body the nutrients it needs to recover and adapt.

Start with a carbohydrate-rich recovery drink. These specially formulated mixtures contain the three components you need most: carbohydrate, sodium, and fluid. Perhaps most important, these drinks are easy to consume so that you start getting nutrients into the system faster. Your body is primed to replenish muscle glycogen stores most rapidly within the first 30 to 60 minutes following exercise, and the sooner the better. This period is known as the "glycogen window," and quite literally there are more gates or "windows" open to allow sugar to enter muscle cells during this time. Sodium helps replenish the sodium lost in sweat, but it also plays an important role in transporting carbohydrate out of the gut and into the bloodstream (part of the reason you rarely see sodium-free sports nutrition products). And of course, fluid is important for replacing the water that evaporated off your skin to keep you from overheating.

In terms of total amounts, your goal within the first 2 hours after exercising should be to consume 500 to 700 milligrams of sodium and enough water to equal 1.5 times the water weight you lost during the exercise session. In other words, if you lost 2 pounds (32 ounces) during your workout, you should drink 48 ounces of fluid in the 2 hours after you get back. Within 4 hours after training, you should consume 1.5 grams of carbohydrate per kilogram (g/kg) of body weight. For a 170-pound (77 kg) athlete, 1.5 g/kg means 115 g of carbohydrate. That can be quite a challenge, especially when you add in the protein and fat calories that come with that carbohydrate, and obviously it becomes even more challenging for heavier athletes. That's why this recommendation is for over a 4-hour period. Ideally you should consume the first 50 to 60 g of that carbohydrate within the first 30 to 60 minutes so you can take advantage of the glycogen window, but the rate of glycogen replenishment doesn't magically go to zero after 60 minutes. Stuffing your face to eat 115 to 135 g of carbohydrate in an hour isn't fun, nor is it necessary to fully replenish your glycogen stores in time for tomorrow's training session.

Managing Your Total Caloric Intake

One of the greatest aspects of being an athlete is being able to eat like one. When you were on a high-volume training program, you may have burned an average of 600 calories an hour for 12 to 14 hours, meaning you churned through approximately 7,200 to 8,400 calories each week. When you dropped down to 7 hours a week of training without increasing its intensity, your weekly caloric expenditure declined by more than 3,000 calories. More than likely that led to some weight gain, because most athletes are relatively slow to reduce their caloric intake as their training level diminishes.

So although your primary goal in starting the Time-Crunched Triathlete Program may be to improve your triathlon performance, you probably wouldn't mind losing a few pounds in the process. That's where your total caloric intake comes into play. The math is simple: You will lose weight if you expend more calories than you consume. However, if you consume too few calories, you will fail to provide your body with the fuel necessary to complete high-quality workouts, recover from them, and adapt to them.

CALCULATING CALORIES

Endurance athletes place a particular premium on being lean, but this goal can present a significant challenge to coaches and athletes because it can be difficult to consume enough calories to support training while simultaneously attempting to create a caloric deficit that leads to weight loss. Although I don't recommend attempting to exactly match your caloric intake and expenditure on a daily basis, there are tools and calculations you can use to obtain a reasonably accurate view of how training affects your total daily caloric expenditure. For the running and swimming components of the training, we still need to rely on calculations that produce calorie estimates that are pretty close but have some percentage of error. Athletes working with power meters for cycling can use the kilojoule information from their workouts to replace an estimate with an actual measurement. The kilojoules of work you perform during a cycling workout are approximately equal to the number of calories you burned during that time, and when incorporated into the overall picture of a triathlete's energy expenditure, kilojoule data from a power meter can dramatically improve accuracy.

Your total caloric expenditure for a day has three main components: resting metabolic rate (RMR), lifestyle, and exercise. Your RMR can be measured directly in a lab, but is more often derived from one of several calculations. The energy requirement of your lifestyle (work, daily activities) is incorporated by multiplying your RMR by a lifestyle factor, and the calories you expend during voluntary exercise can be either estimated or measured directly, depending on the exercise and the equipment available.

You can use the following steps and equations to calculate your total daily caloric expenditure.

1. Resting Metabolic Rate

Resting metabolic rate (RMR, sometimes called basal metabolic rate) represents the number of calories your body needs every 24 hours to complete basic bodily functions and keep you alive. At CTS we prefer the Mifflin–St. Jeor equation, which is a little complicated to use but has been shown to be more accurate than other equations. To find your RMR using this equation you will need to know your weight in kilograms (1 kilogram = 2.2 pounds), your height in centimeters (1 inch = 2.54 centimeters), and your age in years. Input your data into the appropriate equation below:

$$\text{Male: RMR} = 10 \times \text{weight} + 6.25 \times \text{height} - 5 \times \text{age} + 5$$
$$\text{Female: RMR} = 10 \times \text{weight} + 6.25 \times \text{height} - 5 \times \text{age} - 161$$

2. Lifestyle Factor

Take the number from your RMR above and multiply it by the appropriate lifestyle factor taken from Table 4.3. For example: A 37-year-old, 5-foot 10-inch, 150-pound male has an RMR of 1,612 calories. He works at a desk all day and drives to and from the office, so his lifestyle factor is 1.25. Thus his minimum daily calorie needs are 2,015 (1,612 × 1.25).

TABLE 4.3: Lifestyle Factors

ACTIVITY FACTOR	DESCRIPTION	MULTIPLY RMR BY
Very light	Most of workday is sitting or with some standing—relatively little physical activity.	1.25
Light	Work involves some sitting, mostly standing and walking, for example retail sales—light recreational activity.	1.55
Moderate	Work involves sustained physical activity with little sitting, for example UPS or mail delivery—active recreational pursuits. Walk or bike to work.	1.65
Heavy	Occupation is physical labor—very active recreationally. Few jobs fall into this category.	2.0

3. Exercise Calories

a. *Cycling expenditure:* This is where you get to apply the kilojoules displayed on your power meter. If you're not using a power meter, you can use Table 4.4 to estimate how many calories you burn during your cycling workouts.

b. *Running expenditure:* In the spirit of keeping things simple, I use an equation straight from a physiology textbook, *Essentials of Exercise Physiology*, second edition, by McArdle, Katch, and Katch (2000). The equation is simply this: 1 kilocalorie per kilogram of body weight per kilometer (1 kcal/kg/km). It doesn't matter how fast you go, the total energy cost of covering that kilometer remains pretty much the same; the rate of energy expenditure increases the faster you run, but since you cover ground more quickly, you reach the end of the kilometer having burned about the same number of calories as if you'd gone half as fast. What does matter, however, is grade. Running uphill is more costly than 1 kcal/kg/km, and running downhill is less costly. There are several complicated equations that you can use to estimate the energy cost of running specific grades, but even after spending the time to make all the calculations, what most athletes find out is that a loop or route with rolling hills adds between 100 and 300 calories to the earlier, simpler equation. The 1 kcal/kg/km equation won't work for extreme climbs, like running up Barr Trail here in Colorado Springs (13 mile trail to the 14,000 foot summit of Pikes Peak), but it works well for the vast majority of flat to rolling hill training runs that athletes complete on a day-to-day basis.

c. *Swimming expenditure:* Of the three disciplines within triathlon, swimming is the most difficult one to nail down in terms of caloric expenditure. The problem is that economy in the water and stroke technique can dramatically change the workload necessary for covering a given distance. A very skilled swimmer can complete 500 meters faster than a less skilled swimmer and use the same or less energy to cover the distance. Fortunately, during swimming workouts (as opposed to recreational swimming), the range for caloric expenditure is not that broad, about 9 to 13 kilocalories per minute. So if you take 10 kcal/min. (for the sake of easy arithmetic) and multiply by the length of your swim, you get a decent ballpark estimate of the caloric expenditure of your swim workout. As you can see, if you play with the numbers, the difference between burning 9 kcal/

min. and 13 kcal/min. during a 45-minute swim workout is only 180 calories, so the 10 kcal/min. estimate is perfectly reasonable.

Once you determine your caloric expenditure from exercise, add that number to the total of your RMR multiplied by your lifestyle factor to determine your caloric expenditure for the day.

It is important to realize that the process of calculating total daily caloric expenditure is not perfect. The Mifflin–St. Jeor equation is more accurate than others, but there's always a chance that a calculation will be less accurate than a direct measurement. The lifestyle factor provides a good way to account for the energy demands of your lifestyle, but it's a multiplier and not a direct measurement. Two of three values you're using for determining exercise calories are estimates, and even the one direct measurement you have—kilojoules, in cycling, if you have a power meter—doesn't provide a truly accurate accounting of the number of calories you burned because, as I explained previously, the conversion between kilojoules and calories is close but not perfect. Nevertheless, the process described here is a good way to get a reasonably accurate look at your total daily caloric expenditure while training.

KEEPING TOTAL CALORIC EXPENDITURE IN PERSPECTIVE

Total daily caloric expenditure calculations are most helpful for making sure an athlete's caloric intake is in the right ballpark. The calculations

TABLE 4.4: Calories Burned During Workouts

FEMALE BODY WEIGHT (LB.)	CALORIES BURNED PER HOUR OF AEROBIC EXERCISE	MALE BODY WEIGHT (LB.)	CALORIES BURNED PER HOUR OF AEROBIC EXERCISE
120	572	140	731
140	668	160	835
160	762	180	940
180	857	200	1,044
200	953	220	1,148

are usually accurate to within a few hundred calories, and an athlete's recollection or tracking of caloric intake is often off by a similar amount. As a result, it's difficult—and typically unproductive—to consider either number exact. Rather, these calculations are best used to reveal and correct major disparities between an athlete's perceived caloric expenditure or intake and his or her actual expenditure or intake.

As described in the preceding pages, between technologies and calculations, you can get a reasonably good estimate of the calories you burn during workouts. Now, does that mean you should attempt to match your caloric intake to your training session every day? No. First of all, you'd drive yourself—and your spouse and kids—crazy in the process. Second, your body doesn't have a counter that resets to zero at midnight, so there isn't a useful way to match caloric intake and expenditure on a strictly daily basis.

It's better to think about balancing average caloric expenditures and intakes over a three-day period. The information from your power meter may tell you that right now you're burning 750 calories during your hard 45-minute running workouts and 1,500 calories during your longer weekend rides. After you've gained fitness, these numbers may go up to 900 and 1,800, which may mean a slight adjustment to your caloric intake.

WEIGHT MANAGEMENT

Even among endurance athletes, triathletes have some interesting nutritional habits. This is especially true of triathletes who follow traditional training programs that call for 10 or more workouts per week. With days that often include more than one training session, the energy expenditure for an athlete in a traditional triathlon program can be significantly higher than it is for a single-sport athlete at a similar competition level. As a result, triathletes have become very adept at the "grazing" method of eating, constantly consuming small amounts of food throughout the day. Overall, this is a good adaptation; it's better to eat smaller meals more frequently than to consume the standard American diet of three large meals a day. But as a time-crunched triathlete, you will be following a training program that more closely resembles a single-sport program, at least insofar as your training schedule includes fewer workouts per week. As a result, there are some important modifications you need to make to your nutrition program so it supplies the energy you need for high-quality training sessions without leading to unwanted weight gain.

For endurance athletes, the desire to become and remain lean sometimes approaches the level of obsession, and it's not uncommon for athletes to extend workouts or add training sessions in order to burn more calories. But as I've already documented, adding workload can do you more harm than good if it throws off the balance of your structured training program. And while my coaches and I have had great success with the training and performance-enhancement aspects of the Time-Crunched Triathlete Program, some triathletes on the program have really struggled with weight management. The fact is, if you fail to modify your dietary habits as you transition from a traditional triathlon training program to the Time-Crunched Triathlete Program, there's a significant chance you will gain weight. With fewer workouts each week, your energy expenditure is likely to decrease, despite the increased intensity in the individual training sessions. If you continue to eat as if you're fueling for and recovering from 10 workouts when you're actually doing half that many, you'll most likely gain weight.

In order to get or stay lean—and improve your fitness—as a time-crunched triathlete, there are two main concepts you need to keep in mind: focused fueling and caloric overcompensation.

Focused Fueling

The vast majority of the workouts in the Time-Crunched Triathlete Program are 2 hours or shorter, which means you can be optimally fueled by focusing primarily on good nutrition habits in the hour before, during, and the hour after training. When athletes in high-volume training programs are preparing for rides and runs of 3-plus hours, those training sessions impact the size and composition of several meals before and after the workout. On the other hand, one benefit to keeping your workouts somewhat shorter is that you can fuel high-quality training sessions with foods and drinks consumed immediately before and during the workout itself. For many athletes, this may mean consuming more sports nutrition products than you do right now. Many athletes resist using gels and bars in workouts shorter than 2 hours, partly because of expense and partly because there's a perception that they don't really need that much fuel for a 60- to 90-minute workout. But from both a weight-management and a performance perspective, and specifically for workouts lasting 2 hours or less, it's better to consume calories you specifically want to use for training, as close as possible to the times when you will need them. In other words, a 100-calorie GU Energy Gel eaten 15 minutes into your workout will enhance the quality of the efforts you perform as little as 10 minutes after that. Your preworkout snack and the calories you ingest during exercise have a direct and acute impact on the quality of your training session.

When you focus on fueling immediately before and during your workouts, you can avoid consuming more calories than you need. In thousands of dietary analyses, one pattern that emerges is that many athletes consume more food than necessary prior to relatively short workouts. They increase the size of their meals and the frequency of snacks in anticipation of a workout, but the total caloric increase over a nontraining day can easily be out of proportion to the actual demands of the day's exercise session. Focused fueling helps eliminate this problem for time-crunched athletes by reinforcing the notion that you don't need to change your baseline eating habits; just add training-specific calories in the hour before training and fuel up early in workouts with high-carbohydrate gels and sports drinks. Since gels are typically only about 100 calories, it's difficult to gorge yourself on them, and you'll be in better shape than if you had downed a 600-calorie treat at a coffee shop.

Caloric Overcompensation

When you're in the Time-Crunched Triathlete Program, one thing to watch is the difference between perceived exertion and actual caloric expenditure. Depending on the training you were doing before you started this program, you may experience a significant change in your total weekly caloric expenditure. If you are coming down off a higher-volume program, you may experience a decrease in your weekly energy expenditure from training. However, if you are transitioning from a training program of relatively equal hours each week, you may experience an increase in caloric expenditure due to the increased intensity found in this program.

As a starting point, I recommend using the calculations listed earlier in this chapter to evaluate your caloric needs on typical training days. Many athletes find they can arrive at some broad generalizations about the caloric demands of different types of training. For instance, after making the calculations several times for lactate threshold workouts, you may find that the numbers always fall within a 50 to 75 calorie range (like 700–750 calories/hour). Going forward, you can then use that range as a general guideline for at least a few weeks, rather than making the calculations day after day.

But regardless of your actual caloric expenditure, you must be careful to avoid a particular trick of the mind that is especially troublesome for endurance athletes: caloric overcompensation. The previous discussion of focused fueling touches on the problem of caloric overcompensation, in that it sometimes manifests as eating too many calories in anticipation of an upcoming workout. But the more insidious aspect of caloric overcompensation occurs after workouts, particularly after training sessions that are difficult. An interval workout that felt really hard may not have cost you as many calories as you think, and the harder the workout, the greater this discrepancy between perceived and actual caloric expenditure.

In interval workouts you work hard during the efforts, but you also recover at low-intensity levels between efforts. The cumulative time at high intensity may be only 16 to 24 minutes out of an hour on the bike. The workout will feel very difficult and will provide the stimulus necessary to improve your fitness, but the actual total caloric expenditure may be relatively low. If you base the size of your postworkout meals on the perceived exertion from your workout, you may very well consume a lot more calories than you need.

Caloric overcompensation is common following strenuous runs, and it may be even more of a problem following swimming. Hunger is one response to a low core temperature, and it's not uncommon for athletes to get pretty cold—and hungry—following the cool-down portion of the swim workout, the trip through the locker room, and the walk outside into a cool morning. Your body craves calories when you're cold because breaking food down into usable energy creates heat. You may notice the same phenomenon after runs or rides in cold weather, and there can be a real and additive effect from your body working to stay warm (actually burning more calories) as you're exercising in really cold conditions. As simple as it sounds, a hot shower and getting into warm clothes after your swimming sessions can help to reduce this core-temperature-driven desire to overeat.

Overall, I'm not recommending that you match your postworkout meal to the kilojoule number on your power meter or the calorie count of each individual run or swim session; I am only saying that you want to use the data to get a sense of how many calories you're actually burning during workouts.

In my experience, the best way for time-crunched athletes to manage caloric intake, make great training progress, and lose some weight at the same time is to eat as you normally do during most of the day and only make small adjustments to your nutritional habits immediately before, during, and immediately after your training sessions. So, although you certainly want to consume sufficient calories to support your training, when you're on a low-volume or lower-frequency training program, it's best to let your pre-, during-, and postworkout sports nutrition habits take care of a significant portion of the calories you burned during your exercise session.

Being an athlete should have a positive impact on your diet, and everything in your diet affects the quality of your training and recovery, so don't take the recommendations above to mean you can gorge on greasy fast food for breakfast and dinner as long as you consume high-quality fuel before, during, and after your training sessions. I'm trusting you to eat a diet that's suitable for an athlete, one that's rich in whole grains, lean proteins, and fresh fruits and vegetables, and relatively low in both total and saturated fat. And if you do that, you'll need to make only minor adjustments to optimally support your training in the Time-Crunched Triathlete Program.

Nutrition Strategy for Racing the Run

The basic premise of the Time-Crunched Triathlete Program is that by increasing the intensity of workouts and focusing on triathlon specificity, you will have the strength and fitness to race the run instead of merely completing it. In order to take advantage of the fitness this program will provide, it's important that you also execute a well-planned nutrition strategy during the race. Having the fitness to race the run will mean nothing if you don't have the fuel available to maintain an intensity high enough to run fast.

The greatest nutrition challenge presented by triathlon is the combination of disciplines. You can't really consume food or fluids during the swim (unless you drink the water you're swimming in). Once on the bike, you can absolutely consume calories, but since you're going to be racing primarily sprint and Olympic-distance events, your pace on the bike will be quite fast. When you're racing 20 to 40 kilometers and you're on the bike for between 30 and 75 minutes, you can hold a pace that's close to or even above lactate threshold, and that makes taking in calories challenging. In half- and full-Ironman-distance events, on the other hand, the pace during the bike leg is generally below lactate threshold, and at that intensity level it is relatively easy to consume the maximum number of calories your body can take in and process (about 60 grams of carbohydrate per hour, or 250–400 calories per hour depending on the foods you choose).

But by far the biggest fueling challenge in triathlon involves the run. Starting the run with too much food or fluid in your gut can lead to gastric distress very rapidly. Within a mile or two of leaving T2, you could be walking or retching, despite having the fitness to continue running a fast pace. And even if your nutrition strategy avoids gastric distress in the opening miles of the run, the jostling that occurs in running makes it difficult to take in large amounts of calories. If you go into the run low on energy, it is very difficult to get back on top of your nutrition because you simply can't tolerate the amount of food it would require to do so.

For athletes competing in sprint and Olympic-distance events, there are two places where you need to stock up on energy: before the swim and during the bike leg. By focusing the majority of your caloric intake during these two periods, you will have the energy onboard to sustain your fastest pace and you will minimize the chances of gastric distress. Here's how to get it done.

PRECOMPETITION

The shorter the race, the more important your prerace meal becomes, simply because there won't be time during the event to make up for nutritional deficiencies. For sprint and Olympic-distance events, it is good to leave the start line fully fueled but feeling a little bit hungry. The alternative—starting the race fueled and feeling full—is more likely to lead to feeling sluggish, bloated, or close to vomiting during the early going.

To reach the start line fueled but with a generally empty stomach, you need to consume your final full meal about 2 to 3 hours before the gun goes off. The exact composition of this meal varies from person to person and requires some experimentation during training, but generally it should be a meal that is rich in carbohydrate and moderate in both protein and fat. The carbohydrates you choose should be low to medium on the glycemic index, but this far out from competition you don't need to stock up on the simplest of sugars. Whole-grain breads and cereals, oatmeal, whole-grain pancakes or waffles, fruit, and vegetables are good carbohydrate sources. In terms of protein, yogurt (dairy or soy), eggs, or even sliced chicken or turkey in a sandwich can work well. But remember that protein shouldn't be the primary focus of the meal. Fat is generally not a nutrient you have to be proactive about including in a prerace meal; sticking with healthy sources of carbohydrate and protein will keep your fat intake low to moderate. To increase the fat content of the meal, which can be important for athletes who find they are excruciatingly hungry by the time they reach the starting line, try adding avocado, peanut butter, or almond butter to your prerace meal.

In terms of how much to eat, refer back to page 120–121. Your optimal prerace and pretraining meal should be very similar, especially since your race nutrition strategy and food choices should be tested ahead of time in training.

ONE TO TWO HOURS BEFORE COMPETITION

As you're going through your final race preparations, you should be sipping water and sports drinks, and gradually nibbling away at light carbohydrate snacks. Once you reach about 1 hour before start time, stop eating solid foods and aim to consume one bottle of sports drink 30 to 60 minutes prior to the start of the swim leg. For some athletes, especially athletes who are prone to prerace jitters, this may be too much fluid or too many calories. If that describes you, and you're more likely to feel nauseated as a result of consuming a bottle of sports drink so close to competition, try reducing the amount of fluid or perhaps using an energy gel and half a bottle of water rather than a sports drink.

Overeating before a race can be just as bad as failing to eat enough. Your nutrition strategy should never place too high a priority on consuming calories in the hour before competition. The vast majority of your prerace fuel should already be onboard, thanks to good meals on the day leading up to the race and a well-timed, well-structured prerace meal. Between the prerace meal and the start of the race, fluids and electrolytes take priority over energy. Calories in the final hour before a race are a bonus; they're great if you can get them, but if consuming energy is going to upset your stomach and ruin your swim, then stick with fluids and electrolyte drinks.

DURING THE BIKE LEG

I didn't forget about the swim leg; there's just not a lot of choice about nutrition and hydration during the swim portion of a sprint or

Olympic-distance triathlon. The next place you can realistically expect to be able to eat is on the bike.

Transition is not a great place to eat, especially if you're competing (as opposed to participating), because you need to get in, get your wetsuit off, put your helmet on, and get out on the course as rapidly as possible. The exception to this occurs when conditions are very hot. At most your bike will have space for two bottles of fluid, but competitors in sprint and Olympic-distance events rarely carry more than one. If it's hot and you're able to carry only one bottle for a 40K bike leg (60 to 70 minutes of ride time) that leads to a 10K run (35 to 50 minutes of run time), consuming additional fluids in T1 can help stave off the detrimental effects of dehydration.

For a sprint triathlon, I recommend taking one GU for the bike leg, and for an Olympic-distance race I recommend taking two. In either race, consume a gel about 10 to 15 minutes into the bike leg, and remember to wash it down with about 8 ounces of fluid. Preferably, you should drink plain water with energy gels, but if you have only one bottle and that bottle contains sports drink, then drink that; you need to take in some fluid with a gel. Using a sports drink to wash down a gel is not ideal from an absorption standpoint, but it's better than consuming a gel with no fluid at all.

In the middle third of a 40K bike leg, up until about 15 to 20 minutes from T2, consume a sports drink so that you're supplying your body with a steady stream of carbohydrate. The idea here is to spare as much of your muscle glycogen as possible for use during the run. About 15 minutes before reaching T2, eat your second gel, and from this point to the end of the bike leg, consume only small amounts of plain water or sports drink (but preferably water at this stage).

For a sprint triathlon, you're not on the bike long enough to need a second gel, and as I'll explain soon, slamming a gel too close to T2 can lead to significant stomach problems. Instead, after taking one gel about 15 minutes into the cycling leg, consume a sports drink or water during the rest of the bike leg. Taper your fluid intake down to small sips in the final 10 minutes on the bike, especially if you're having a sports drink.

DURING THE RUN

The reason you want to be specific about when and where you consume calories during the cycling leg is that those calories can make or break your run. On the bike, athletes can generally tolerate eating and can comfortably consume a lot of calories. The prone position of swimming and the jostling that occurs in running make it more difficult to tolerate eating as you swim and run. And, as many athletes have learned the hard way, starting the run with too much food or fluid in the stomach can be a painful and debilitating experience.

If you make the mistake of eating or drinking too much in the last 10 to 15 minutes of the bike leg, you'll know it within the first mile of the run. Instead of feeling strong and fast, you'll feel like you're running with a bowling ball in your gut. Worse yet, there's a decent chance you'll deposit the contents of your stomach at the side of the road.

The problem of having gastric distress early in the run is actually twofold. Obviously, the bloated, nauseated feeling is a problem, but so too is the fact that a distressed gut doesn't process food and fluids appropriately. In order to get your system back to functioning normally, you must slow down, which often means walking or stopping altogether. Trying to push through the nausea can make the situation worse; now you're burning energy and sweating, but the food and fluid meant to replenish what you're losing is stuck in your dysfunctional gut. Before long you bonk, despite having consumed an appropriate amount of energy.

Preventing gastric distress in the beginning of the run is the reason I recommend consuming your last energy gel about 15 minutes before T2 during an Olympic-distance triathlon, and not consuming a second gel during the bike leg of a sprint triathlon. You want to arrive at T2 with a largely empty stomach, and 15 minutes should be long enough for a gel or several ounces of sports drink to be out of your stomach. In fact, 15 minutes should be enough time to get the carbohydrate from either a drink or gel all the way to your working muscles.

Once you get past the first mile of the run, you'll know whether you have successfully managed the bike-run transition from a nutritional standpoint. You'll also know that there's nothing standing between you and ripping a fast run! I recommend that sprint and Olympic-distance triathletes take one gel with them for the run leg. Sprint triathletes rarely need or want it during a 5K, but I encourage you to look at it as an insurance policy. It weighs next to nothing, and if you do end up needing it, you will be incredibly relieved to have it with you.

Some athletes have more trouble eating on the run than others, but nearly every athlete has more trouble eating on the run than eating on the bike. If you can manage to get down 30 to 40 grams of carbohydrate per hour, that's doing quite well (comparatively, cyclists can easily consume 60 to 90 grams per hour, even when they don't need that much). Olympic-distance triathletes should aim to consume a gel 2 to 4 kilometers into the run (with some water for easier digestion), and sports drink as tolerated after that. Depending on how fast you're running and how hard you're pushing yourself, you may want/need to transition to plain water in the final few kilometers of the run.

AFTER THE FINISH

Once you cross the finish line and get over the initial breathlessness of your final (and perhaps winning) kick, continue walking/jogging for 5 to 10 minutes to cool down. Grab a recovery drink that's rich in carbohydrate and electrolytes and contains a small amount of protein. The protein will help accelerate the transport of carbohydrate into muscles that are eager to accept it. Few athletes can tolerate large volumes of fluid immediately following hard running efforts, especially when it's hot out, so don't rush it. You have 30 to 60 minutes following exercise during which your body is primed to replenish depleted energy stores most quickly. Cool down, get some dry clothes on, have your recovery drink, and continue drinking fluids. And within about an hour after your event, you should aim to sit down for a meal.

5

WORKOUTS AND
TRAINING PROGRAMS

The fitness industry offers literally thousands of workout options to willing athletes, partly because creating new types of workout routines helps to keep people engaged (and they are a great way to sell DVDs during late-night infomercials). But when it comes to improving race-day performance for endurance athletes, you don't need gimmicks; you only need fundamental workouts that are proven to develop your energy systems. You need to increase your ability to take in, absorb, deliver, and utilize oxygen to power your working muscles. Energy system development isn't always sexy—some of the intervals are long and steady efforts—but they get the job done very well.

Before reading about the specifics of each workout included in the Time-Crunched Triathlete Training Programs, it's important to understand that all workouts are governed by five critical workout components. By manipulating these parameters, you can create a workout to target just about any physiological demand found in sport.

The Five Workout Components

When you get ready to head out for training sessions, you can use these variables to address the principles of training discussed in Chapter 3:

Intensity
Volume
Frequency or repetition
Environment (pool/open water, surface, terrain)
Turnover (stroke, cadence, stride)

You can completely change the goal of a workout by changing one of its components. On the bike for instance, climbing intervals that are 10 minutes long can target two completely different energy systems if you simply change the cadence. Climbing at a cadence of 70 revolutions per minute (rpm) will tend to push an athlete to his or her climbing lactate threshold, which is slightly higher than flat-ground lactate threshold due to an increase in muscle recruitment. I prescribe such workouts to develop an athlete's ability to sustain prolonged climbing efforts in races. But if the same climbing workout is done at a cadence of 50 rpm, the tension applied to the leg muscles increases greatly, and the stress on the cardio-vascular system decreases. I use slow-cadence climbing efforts to increase leg strength and muscular power development. In this case, varying the cadence of an effort transforms a lactate threshold workout into an on-the-bike, resistance-training workout.

INTENSITY

Intensity is a measure of how hard you are working, and it should be clear by now that you will be working quite hard in this training program. The impact of a workout is directly related to the intensity at which you are working, and over the years, we have become increasingly precise in the methods we use to measure intensity.

Precision is important for success with the Time-Crunched Triathlete Program, so I strongly encourage you to use a power meter on the bike and a GPS-enabled watch for running, or at the very least a heart rate monitor that records average heart rates for individual intervals. Training with power and heart rate is covered in more detail in Chapter 3.

VOLUME

Volume is the total amount of exercise you're doing in a single workout. By definition, *time-crunched* means lower volume, at least in terms of the hours you spend training. But there's another concept here that makes up for some of that reduction in volume, called *volume-at-intensity*. Classic endurance training programs contain many hours of training at moderate intensity, but relatively little time training at higher intensity. The Time-Crunched Triathlete Program strips out most of the moderate-intensity volume of those programs, but retains and may even increase the volume-at-intensity, especially volume-at-high-intensity. In a given week in this program, you're most likely going to spend more time training at and above your lactate threshold power output than you have during any portion of your previous training programs.

FREQUENCY/REPETITION

Frequency is the number of times a workout is performed in a given period of training, whereas repetition is the number of times an exercise is repeated in a single session. Riding 3 PowerInterval workouts in a week is frequency; riding 12 PowerIntervals in a single workout is repetition (see the cycling workouts on pages 167–169 for a definition of PowerIntervals). Frequency and repetition are used to ensure the quality of your training sessions. In the Time-Crunched Triathlete Program your goal is to accumulate time at high workloads, because that's the driving force behind the adaptations you're seeking. PowerIntervals are maximum-intensity intervals, and their effectiveness is based on sustaining your highest possible power output for a given period of time.

Let's say you have a lactate threshold power of 250 watts, and that you can sustain that output for 20 minutes. You might be able to average 300 watts for 3 minutes during a PowerInterval. There's no point in trying to complete a 20-minute PowerInterval, because your output will fall so dramatically after the first 3 to 5 minutes that the rest of the effort will no longer be useful as a PowerInterval. It would feel ridiculously difficult, and your heart rate would stay elevated, but once your power output drops, that effort is no longer addressing the goal of a PowerInterval. On the other hand, if you do seven 3-minute PowerIntervals at 300 watts each, separated by recovery periods, you'll accumulate 21 minutes at 300 watts. That's why interval training is so much more effective for improving performance (and burning calories) than exercising at a steady pace or level of effort.

Frequency gives you another way to accumulate workload, by repeating individual interval sessions during a given week, month, or even year. For instance, a week with two PowerInterval workouts like the one above means 42 minutes at 300 watts. The harder the intervals, the more recovery you need before you'll be ready to complete another high-quality training session. Fortunately, this works in favor of the time-crunched athlete, because reducing the number of workouts in your schedule leaves plenty of time for recovery during the week. Three of the five programs in this book have four workouts per week, and the Experienced Olympic and Ironman 70.3 programs have five workouts per week. In all of the programs, the workouts are spaced out in order to provide adequate recovery between sessions. I will discuss ways you can adjust the programs to fit your personal and professional schedule later in this chapter. For now, realize that you will have some latitude to move the workouts around without much risk of diminishing the quality of your training. In other words, if you have to pile three hard days of intervals back-to-back in one week, that's not ideal, but it's probably better than skipping them because you couldn't do them on the days they were originally planned.

ENVIRONMENT

You can use environmental factors to manipulate your workouts. In some cases you can increase or decrease the workload of particular efforts, as with performing cycling intervals while going uphill.

When training with power, cycling workload is most accurately expressed as the number of kilojoules—the amount of mechanical work—you produce during a training session. (How rapidly you produce those kilojoules determines your power output.) You can use terrain to manipulate your workload, and this is especially good for time-crunched athletes, who need to get as much as possible done in 60 to 90 minutes. Riding uphill and performing efforts on hills can significantly increase the overall workload for your intervals, even though it can sometimes decrease the overall workload for the session (depending on the difference between the time spent at higher power outputs going uphill and the time spent going downhill at much lower power outputs).

Cycling intervals on hills can also be useful for overcoming lagging motivation. Sometimes it can be difficult to push yourself through maximum-intensity intervals on flat ground, but a hill adds resistance and a visible challenge, and sometimes that's the little something extra you need to make your workout more effective. Of course, training on hills is also important from a specificity standpoint. If you want to go faster on climbs, it helps to train on them. If you live in Kansas or some other pancake-flat location, increasing your sustainable power at lactate threshold is the number-one thing you can do to help you go faster uphill (when you finally encounter one). Riding into the wind can be a useful strategy for flatlanders who are training for hills; your power output and effort level will be high as you push against a significant resistance, which will likely bring your cadence down to levels similar to what you would use on a climb (80 to 85 rpm instead of 90 to 100).

Environment has a big impact on specificity in all sports. The surface you run on can make a difference in your pace and in the amount of stress you put on your body. Running on the road is harder on your legs and feet than running on a softer surface, but if you're going to be running a 10K on the road at the end of an Olympic-distance triathlon, then a good portion of your training runs should be done on the road. Training is not just about developing energy systems; it's also about preparing the joints, bones, and connective tissues for the challenges of competition.

Running on a treadmill is quite different from running outdoors, and you can use treadmills to your advantage in training. The suspension found in treadmills (some absorb more shock than others) means that treadmill running typically has less impact on your feet and legs than running outdoors—even on a trail. If you have a history of foot and knee problems, running on a treadmill may enable you to complete more running time without pain. Running on the treadmill can also make interval training more convenient because you can program in the appropriate paces and durations and let the treadmill adjust your pace and hold it steady for the duration of the interval. This is often helpful for athletes who find they have trouble motivating themselves to maintain a fast enough pace on their own for difficult intervals. In the end, you'll have to find that motivation to push yourself if you want to succeed on race day, but if you need the treadmill to provide that motivation sometimes, that's OK. If you're going to use a treadmill for running interval workouts, set the incline to a grade of 1 to 2 percent to better simulate outdoor conditions (wind, surface, and so on).

In the water, the environment can also make a big difference. Ideally you'd be able to train extensively in open water in order to prepare for an open-water swim in competition. If there's any place in triathlon where training energy systems can provide insufficient preparation for competition, it's in swimming. That's because swimming in a lake, bay, or ocean is very different from swimming in a clear, relatively shallow pool. There are no lane lines in open water, you often can't see the bottom, and there are no walls or clocks with which to gauge your pace. I have not specifically written open-water swim workouts into the programs in this book, but with whichever program you choose, I strongly suggest that you perform at least four to six of the swim workouts in open water. Of course, if open water isn't available, you need to focus on developing your energy systems and try to get a little open-water practice when you get to the race site. Cyclists and runners living in the flatlands have a similar challenge when training for hilly races, although theirs is more of a physiological challenge (lifting their bodies against gravity) instead of a skills challenge (sighting buoys, swimming straight, gauging pace).

TURNOVER

It's difficult to find one word that covers this workout component accurately across multiple sports. What I'm talking about is actually stroke/kick rate in swimming, cadence in cycling, and stride rate (turnover) in running.

Stroke Rate/Kick Rate

Stroke rate, or the number of strokes you take per minute (not strokes per length, and not distance per stroke) in steady swimming remains relatively constant even as athletes become faster swimmers. Even when you are accelerating to get around a swimmer or latch on to the tail of a faster group during the swim portion of a triathlon, your stroke rate should not increase dramatically. And while there is definitely a lot of variability in terms of stroke rates from athlete to athlete, a good benchmark for a proficient swimmer would be about 45 to 50 strokes per minute. What will change as you become a stronger swimmer is the force you can exert during the pulling segment of your stroke and, as your technique improves, the amount of water you catch with each pull. The latter may be the more important of the two, because water is a thick and viscous medium. It's not nearly as forgiving of poor technique as cycling or running.

The kicking component of swimming plays an important role in triathlon performance. As you'll see in the Time-Crunched Triathlete Programs, the swims frequently end with a KickSwimSet. It is there for two reasons. First, it's important, in training and during your race, to engage the legs more significantly as you reach the end of your swim so that your leg muscles are ready to get you through the transition to the bike, and then off to a good start on the bike. Second, there's a training component to the KickSwimSet as well. Being a proficient kicker in the water can make you a faster swimmer with only a small increase in workload.

For a long time, there's been a trend in triathlon to diminish the role of kicking during the swim. Certainly you don't want to kick with the same force and purpose used by single-sport competitive swimmers, but you also don't want to minimize kicking and just drag yourself through the water. A steady kick helps maintain a streamlined body position in the water by keeping your legs closer to the surface. A forceful kick can help to maintain your forward momentum (which the water is constantly working against) during the short portions of your stroke where your pulling force diminishes. In cycling we know that very little positive force is applied when the pedals are straight up and down, and that the downstroke is where the vast majority of a cyclist's power is generated. Similarly, there is a point in the swim stroke where your pulling arm is reaching the very end of the stroke and your recovering arm is about to contact or just barely beginning the next pull. This is where a steady and purposeful kick can make you faster, not by actually increasing your speed, but by keeping you from slowing down. You can tell when an athlete is not using a purposeful kick; his or her progress through the water is jerky instead of steady and smooth.

Some triathletes don't want to kick during the swim any more than they absolutely have to because they want to save their legs for the cycling and running portions of the event. Indeed, there's evidence that swimming at a time trial pace during a triathlon, including a forceful and rapid kick, leads to diminished performance in subsequent cycling and running performances and an overall decline in triathlon results (Peeling et al. 2005). However, there's a huge difference between kicking as if your life depended on it and merely dragging your legs through the water. Somewhere in the middle, a purposeful and moderately forceful kick is beneficial to your swimming performance without hindering your subsequent cycling and running performances.

Cadence

I have been a proponent of high-cadence cycling ever since we used it during Lance Armstrong's comeback from cancer to improve his performance for sustained climbs and time trials, and the basic premise behind high-cadence cycling makes the technique advantageous for triathletes as well. We found that Lance could maintain high-power efforts longer by pedaling faster in a lighter gear. You can produce 250 watts at 80 rpm or 100 rpm, but your leg muscles will fatigue faster riding at 80 rpm than at 100 rpm. Power is a measure of how rapidly you can do work. Think in terms of moving a pile of 250 bricks in a minute. When you divide the work into smaller portions but get it done in the same amount of time, each load is lighter and you can move faster. If you double the number of bricks you carry in each load, you'll move the pile in half as many loads, but you'll have to work harder to move each load, and each trip will take longer. As an endurance athlete, your training optimizes your muscles' ability to work continuously and contract frequently. High-cadence cycling takes advantage of the adaptations already provided by aerobic training, not only muscular adaptations but also cardiovascular ones. Your heart and lungs don't fatigue the same way skeletal muscles do, and maintaining higher cadences helps shift stress from easily fatigued skeletal muscles to the fatigue-resistant cardiovascular system.

The issue of optimal cadence in triathlon has been debated and researched for a long time, but the research is still equivocal. In a 2009 review of relevant research, Millett et al. (2009) presented compelling evidence for both high-cadence (90-plus rpm) and low-cadence (less than 80 rpm) cycling during the bike portion of a triathlon. Proponents of low-cadence pedaling in triathlon point to studies like the one from Vercruyssen (2005) that showed a longer time to exhaustion in a run following a cycling bout at 90 percent of lactate threshold (or maximum sustainable) power, with the final 10 minutes of the bout performed at a lower cadence, than the time to exhaustion following a high-cadence or freely chosen cadence cycling bout of the same structure. On the other side, proponents of high-cadence cycling can point to Gottschall and Palmer's 2002 paper, which showed that pedaling at a higher cadence for a 30-minute cycling bout translated to a 3K running time that was 1 minute faster than the same run after a 30-minute cycling bout at a lower cadence and at a freely chosen cadence.

Reading between the lines, the research community seems to acknowledge that there are many factors involved in the bike-to-run transition, and cadence is only one of them. But researchers have the luxury of being equivocal; they don't have to apply their results to real athletes getting ready for competitions. Based on both available research and the experience my coaches and I have accumulated with real athletes, I recommend a relatively high cadence for the cycling portion of a triathlon. By "relatively high," I mean 90 to 100 rpm through the entire duration of the cycling leg. Lower cadences (65 to 80 rpm) lead to muscle fatigue, especially in fast-twitch fibers that are not as fatigue-resistant as slow-twitch fibers. Higher cadences (110 to 120 rpm) work well for some single-sport cyclists, but are often difficult to maintain in an aerodynamic or semiaero position. And such high cadences seem to require much more specificity of training in order to get to the point where a cyclist can produce adequate power at such high cadences.

Keep in mind, however, that there's no magical cadence that everyone should shoot for. Rather than aim for a specific number, I recommend that athletes try to increase their normal cruising cadence and race pace cadence by 10 percent in a year (with the understanding that very few athletes can ride effectively at sustained cadences above 120 to 125 rpm on flat ground).

Stride Rate/Length

Although there are compelling reasons to proactively alter your cycling cadence, research does not support the proactive alteration of running stride in either length or rate. Nearly 20 years ago Cavanaugh and Williams (1982) showed that runners naturally gravitate to the stride length that is most economical for them in terms of oxygen consumption. Numerous other investigations on running economy have reached similar conclusions. Over time, however, your running stride will most likely get longer as you become a more experienced endurance athlete. Your muscles and joints adapt to a greater range of motion for running faster (assuming you promote joint mobility with strengthening exercises like those found in Chapter 8), and you gain the muscle power and aerobic capacity to propel yourself farther with each stride.

Interestingly, once you're a reasonably proficient runner, your biomechanics don't change all that much as you get progressively faster. The maximum angle between your front and back leg doesn't increase much in order to produce a longer stride; the fact that you're propelling yourself forward with more force and have greater forward momentum means that you travel farther during the airborne portion of your stride. Some elite marathoners are able to maintain a stride rate of nearly 100 strides per minute, but like professional cyclists, this high turnover rate may require the specialization found in single-sport training. For experienced amateur triathletes, a running stride rate of about 90 to 95 strides per minute is within the normal range, and that rate doesn't necessarily change whether you're running a 10K at the end of an Olympic-distance triathlon, doing a moderate-paced EnduranceRun, or completing a Fartlek Interval (see below).

But just because there's no reason to force the issue of stride length and frequency for sustained runs, these variables can be manipulated for training purposes. For instance, during a warm-up prior to a running workout or triathlon, a series of 20-second RunningStrides (drills from a standing start, focusing on a constant 20-second acceleration) help to develop the neuromuscular pattern for higher-speed running, before you have the fitness necessary to maintain those higher speeds. Similarly, when done during a warm-up before a hard interval workout, RunningStrides get your body ready for the neuromuscular pattern and force production you'll be using during the intervals.

Workouts and Training Programs

Over the years, I have developed an extensive list of workouts for improving performance. The following is the selection of those workouts that are featured in the training programs that appear at the end of this chapter. Training intensities are included for every workout in terms of power output (cycling only), heart rate, and pace (running and swimming only) wherever applicable. All of these intensities are based on your performances in the CTS Field Tests. Rating of perceived exertion (RPE) is also included for each workout, using the 1 to 10 scale described in Chapter 3.

Regarding the structure of workouts, you will see in the programs that there is a total time for each ride and run (example: 60 minutes EM, or EnduranceMiles) as well as interval sets that are to be completed (example: 3 × 8 min. SS, or SteadyState Intervals). All intervals are to be completed within the total workout time, not in addition to it. In other words, within your 60 minutes on the bike, you should complete three 8-minute SteadyState Intervals.

SWIMMING DRILLS

The swimming workouts in the Time-Crunched Triathlete Program almost always start out with a set of swimming drills. These drills are just some of the many technique-oriented drill options out there, and as you use the program more than once, feel free to substitute drills that you prefer or drills that address a skill or technique that you need more specific work on.

RIGHT ARM/LEFT ARM This is essentially one-arm freestyle swimming. Keep one arm at your side in line with your shoulder and hip while the other arm follows through with a complete stroke. During this drill, focus on the stroking arm's entry, noticing how your hand and forearm enter the water (your elbow should be higher than your wrist and hand). The arm that is at your side should follow the same plane as your shoulders and hips. In other words, if you are pulling with your right arm, your left arm should be at your side. As you stroke, your left shoulder should come out of the water as your right arm is pointing toward the bottom of the pool.

DISTANCE PER STROKE This drill is a normal freestyle stroke, but with the specific goal of taking fewer strokes per lap. For example, while swimming with your normal stroke you may take 20 strokes per lap, but during this drill the goal would be to take 18 strokes (without just pushing off the wall further). In order to accomplish this, focus on pulling more water with each stroke by extending your reach as far as possible and bringing your hand all the way through the end of the stroke before bringing it out of the water. Kick with purpose and focus on the push and pull of the water and the rotation of your body.

FINGERTIP DRAG Body rotation during swimming is crucial to achieving a full and powerful stroke. The alternative is a flat stroke where your arms just swing around to the sides. The fingertip drill helps promote proper body rotation because in order to lightly drag your fingertips along the surface of the water, you need to get your shoulder and elbow up. To complete the fingertip drill, lightly drag your fingers along the surface of the water during the recovery phase of your freestyle swim stroke. As your body rolls more to the side with the dragging fingertips, you'll notice you can extend into a longer pulling phase with your stroking arm.

CATCH-UP Catch-up drills help you develop the pulling component of your stroke as well as work on correct body position during the roll phase. One hand should always be out in front at full extension while you take a full stroke with the other hand, focusing on proper pulling position and body roll. As you complete the stroke and return the hand to the reentry portion of the stroke, the stroking hand will touch the already extended hand, at which point you start a complete stroke with that hand.

CLOSED FISTS The Closed Fists drill is great for illustrating how important the forearm is in your swim stroke. To do this drill, swim a normal freestyle stroke, but close your hands into fists. Swimming this way will obviously reduce the amount of water you can pull with your hands, and with practice you will notice how much water you can pull with your forearms. Once you go back to swimming with both forearms and open hands, you'll feel as if you are swimming with paddles!

SWIMMING WORKOUTS

KICKSWIMSETS (KSS) A forceful and purposeful kick can help you become a faster swimmer, and specific kick training can enhance your swimming performance without hindering your subsequent cycling or running performances. In the final 100 to 300 meters before the end of the swimming leg of a triathlon or brick workout, an increased focus on kicking can also help prepare your legs for the transition out of the water. Focus on kicking from your core and hips, rather than from the knees. Keep your toes pointed, and to increase the forcefulness of your kick, don't just think of pushing down harder and faster with your feet, but also think about accelerating the change of direction (down to up and up to down) to get more snap into your kick. These sets can be varied in many ways. I recommend the following two variations for triathletes:

Training Intensities for KickSwimSets
RPE: 5
HR: NA
Pace: NA

- Kicking with a kick board
- Kicking with fins—to focus on leg strength and give the swimmer a chance to get a feel for moving fast through the water

BASEINTERVALSETS (BIS) This workout is your moderate-intensity swim pace for building greater endurance and a stronger aerobic engine. Since the intensity is not very high, it is also a good time to focus on form and technique, as there is not much pressure to maintain fast 100 meter splits. This intensity is

Training Intensities for BaseIntervalSets
RPE: 5–6
HR: NA
Pace: 104–120 percent of CTS Field Test pace per 100 meters

most often used in conjunction with other, more difficult, swimming intervals. Many of the other intervals involve swimming at or above lactate threshold.

Continuing to swim at an endurance pace after harder intervals helps to teach your body how to process and use accumulated lactate for fuel. During BIS, you should be kicking steadily at about 3 beats per stroke.

PACESWIMSETS (PSS) Your 100 meter split pace for the PaceSwimSet is just a little bit slower than your average 100 meter split for the 400 meter portion of the CTS Field Test, and as such, it is right about the maximum pace you might want to attempt during competition. As I'll explain in more detail in Chapter 6, swimming too fast in a triathlon can do you more harm than good. The PaceSwimSet workout is typically longer than LactateThresholdSwim (LTS) and definitely longer than the VO$_2$Set (VOS; see page 164). It is used to build your endurance and confidence for swimming your race distance at race pace and without stopping. You should be kicking steadily at about 3 beats per stroke.

Training Intensities for PaceSwimSets
RPE: 8
HR: NA
Pace: 100–109 percent of CTS Field Test pace per 100 meters

LACTATETHRESHOLDSWIM (LTS) The Lactate ThresholdSwim workout targets your pace at lactate threshold. The workout pace range starts out slightly slower than your average 100 meter split from the 400 meter portion of the CTS Field Test, but goes up to include paces slightly faster than your field test splits. As with the cycling and running workouts designed to target glycolytic energy system development, this workout accumulates training time at and slightly above your maximum sustainable pace. As you try to go faster to stay within your pace ranges, don't just try to churn your arms and legs faster. Instead, focus on "lengthening" your stroke by extending your arm far in front of you and keeping your elbow high as you begin the pulling portion of your stroke. Imagine you are reaching over a barrel to get your hand back into the water. Similarly, focus on catching as much water

Training Intensities for LactateThresholdSwim
RPE: 9
HR: NA
Pace: 94–103 percent of CTS Field Test pace per 100 meters

as you can and pushing all the way through the stroke so your hand exits the water by your hip. "Lengthening" the stroke is similar to the strategy cyclists use to apply productive force to a greater portion of the pedal stroke. We tell cyclists to push across the top and pull through the bottom of the pedal stroke in order to add productive force to a few more degrees of the crank's rotation. In the water, you can go faster by extending the effective range of each pull through the water. You should be kicking steadily at about 3 beats per stroke.

VO₂SETS (VOS) By their very nature, intervals designed to enhance speed and capacity at VO_2max must be short. These swimming intervals are only about 1 to 2 minutes in length at the longest, but they generate a great deal of lactate. As a result, your body adapts to cope better with lactate accumulation, tolerance, and utilization while swimming. As with the LTS, it's important to focus on maximizing the speed you generate from your stroke, as opposed to merely churning your arms and legs faster. In racing conditions, the gains you make from these intervals come in handy during the initial flurry at the start and during any surges you need to make to either pass a competitor or bridge across open water to get into the draft of a faster group. You may also find that these intervals give you the reserves to surge in the final 150 meters of the swim leg so you can get out of the water ahead of the competition.

Training Intensities for VO₂Sets
RPE: 10
HR: NA
Pace: 75–93 percent of CTS Field Test pace per 100 meters

SWIMPULLSETS (SPS) SwimPullSets can be completed in a few different ways, depending on the equipment you have available, but the goal is always to focus on the pulling phase of your swim stroke. There are three common variations for SPS.

Training Intensities for SwimPullSets
RPE: 5
HR: NA
Pace: NA

With paddles and pull-buoy: The paddles add resistance for your upper body, and the pull-buoy keeps your legs from sinking but eliminates the need to kick. Remember to focus on maintaining a good body roll as you transition from side to side.

Without paddles and with pull-buoy: Without the paddles you won't experience the extra resistance they provide, but since you're not kicking due to the pull-buoy you still have the opportunity to focus on proper stroke technique in the pull phase. Remember to extend into a complete stroke and maintain good body roll.

With paddles and without pull-buoy: The paddles will add resistance for your upper body, but you'll have to kick to maintain proper body position in the water. Your kick, however, should be just forceful enough to keep your body in a streamlined position in the water; virtually all the power for moving forward should come from your upper body.

A good body roll during SPS helps to eliminate excessive shoulder stress. If using paddles, start off with small ones (to help curb any shoulder problems that could occur due to overstressing the shoulder joint too quickly) before progressing to larger paddles. If using the pull-buoy, you need to be sure to place it above the knees where it comfortably rides between your thighs.

CYCLING WORKOUTS

ENDURANCEMILES (EM) This workout is your moderate-paced endurance intensity. The point is to stay at an intensity below lactate threshold for the vast majority of any time you're riding at EM pace. The heart rate and power ranges for this intensity are very wide to allow for widely varying conditions. It is OK for your power to dip on descents or in tailwinds,

Training Intensities for EnduranceMiles
RPE: 7
HR: 50–91 percent of highest CTS Field Test average
Power: 45–73 percent of highest CTS Field Test average

just as it is expected that your power will increase when you climb small hills. One mistake some athletes make is to stay at the high end of their EM range for their entire ride. As you'll see from the intensity ranges for Tempo (T) workouts, the upper end of EM overlaps with Tempo. If you constantly ride in your Tempo range instead of using that as a distinct interval intensity, you may not have the power to complete high-quality intervals when the time comes.

You're better off keeping your power and/or heart rate in the middle portion of your EM range and allowing it to fluctuate up and down from there as the terrain and wind dictate. Use your gearing as you hit the hills to remain in the saddle as you climb. Expect to keep your pedal speed up into the 85 to 95 rpm range.

TEMPO (T) Tempo is an excellent workout for developing aerobic power and endurance. The intensity is well below lactate threshold, but hard enough that you are generating a significant amount of lactate and forcing your body to buffer and process it. The intervals are long (they can be as long as 2 hours for pros), and your gearing should be relatively large so that your cadence comes down to about 70 to 75 rpm. This helps increase pedal resistance and strengthens leg muscles. Also, try to stay in the saddle when you hit hills during your T workouts. It is important that you try to ride the entire length of the T workout with as few interruptions as possible—T workouts should consist of consecutive riding at the prescribed intensity to achieve maximum benefit.

Training Intensities for Tempo

RPE: 6

HR: 88–90 percent of highest CTS Field Test average

Power: 80–85 percent of highest CTS Field Test average

STEADYSTATE INTERVALS (SS) These intervals are great for increasing your maximum sustainable power because the intensity is close to lactate threshold. As you accumulate time at this intensity, you are forcing your body to deal with a lot of lactate for a relatively prolonged period of time. These intervals are best performed on flat roads or small, rolling hills. If you end up doing them on a sustained climb, you should really bump the intensity up to ClimbingRepeat (CR) range, which reflects the grade's added contribution to your effort. Do your best to complete these intervals without interruptions from stoplights and so on, and

Training Intensities for SteadyState Intervals

RPE: 7

HR: 92–94 percent of highest CTS Field Test average

Power: 86–90 percent of highest CTS Field Test average

maintain a cadence of 85 to 95 rpm. Maintaining the training zone intensity is the most important factor, not pedal cadence. Recovery time between SS Intervals is typically about half the length of the interval itself.

CLIMBINGREPEATS (CR) This workout should be performed on a road with a long steady climb. The training intensity is designed to be similar to that of an SS Interval but reflect the additional workload necessary to ride uphill. The intensity is just below your lactate threshold power and/or heart rate, and it is critical that you maintain this intensity for the length of the CR. Pedal cadence for CR intervals while

Training Intensities for ClimbingRepeats
RPE: 8
HR: 95–97 percent of highest CTS Field Test average
Power: 95–100 percent of highest CTS Field Test average

climbing should be 70 to 85 rpm. Maintaining the training intensity is the most important factor, not pedal cadence. It is very important to avoid interruptions while doing these intervals. Recovery time between intervals is typically about half the length of the interval itself. This interval intensity is also used as a component of OverUnder Intervals.

POWERINTERVALS (PI) PowerIntervals may be short, but they are strenuous and great for developing speed on the bike. These short efforts are a big part of the way you will apply the concepts of high-intensity training to your program to make big aerobic gains in a small amount of time. These intervals are maximal efforts and can be performed on any terrain

Training Intensities for PowerIntervals
RPE: 10
HR: 100–max
Power: At least 101 percent of highest CTS Field Test average

except sustained descents. Your gearing should be moderate so you can maintain a relatively high pedal cadence (100 or higher is best). For athletes who are familiar with *The Time-Crunched Cyclist*, there were two types of PI in that program, Steady Effort and Peak-and-Fade PowerIntervals. Due to the different demands of bike racing and triathlon, I use only the Steady Effort PI in the programs in this book.

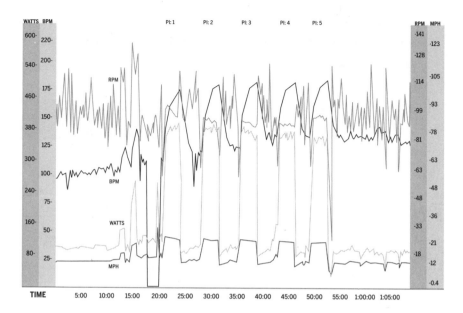

FIGURE 5.1: Steady Effort PowerInterval
This athlete completed five relatively consistent power intervals.
Notice that wattage data from each interval forms a mostly stable horizontal
line, while heart rate lags behind and continues to rise throughout.
This is a good example of why training with power is so useful in providing
a picture of actual workload.

Try to reach and maintain as high a power output as possible for the duration of these intervals. Ideally, these efforts should look like flat plateaus when
you view your power files (see Figure 5.1). Take the first 30 to 45 seconds to
gradually bring your power up and then hold on for the rest of the interval. The
point here is to accumulate as much time as possible at a relatively constant
and extremely high output.

Aim for your intervals to be well above 101 percent of your CTS Field Test
power. Many athletes will consistently hit 110 to 130 percent of CTS Field Test
power, and some may go higher. The 101 percent level marks the bare minimum. If you can't consistently exceed this level, you're too tired to complete
an effective PI workout.

The rest periods between PIs are purposely too short to provide complete
recovery, and completing subsequent intervals in a partially recovered state

is a key part of what makes these efforts effective. Typically, recovery times are equal to the interval work time, which is sometimes referred to as a 1:1 work-to-recovery ratio.

OverUnder Intervals (OU) OverUnder Intervals are a more advanced form of SS Intervals. The "Under" intensity is your SS range, and the "Over" intensity is your CR range. By alternating between these two intensity levels during a sustained interval, you develop the "agility" to handle changes in pace during hard, sustained efforts. More specifically, the harder surges within the interval generate more lactate in your muscles, and then you force your body to process this lactate while you're still riding at a relatively high intensity. This workout can be performed on a flat road, rolling hills, or a sustained climb that's relatively gradual (3 to 6 percent grade). It is difficult to accomplish this workout on a steep climb, because the pitch often makes it difficult to control your effort level. Your gearing should be moderate, and pedal cadence should be high (100 rpm or higher) if you're riding on flat ground or small rollers. Pedal cadence should be above 85 rpm if you're completing the intervals on a gradual climb.

To complete the interval, bring your intensity up to your SS range during the first 45 to 60 seconds. Maintain this heart rate intensity for the prescribed Under time and then increase intensity to your Over intensity for the prescribed time. At the end of this Over time, return to your Under intensity range and continue riding at this level of effort until it's once again time to return to your Over intensity. Continue alternating this way until the end of the interval. OverUnder Intervals always end with a period at Over intensity. This workout builds up high levels of lactic acid. Working in this way trains your body to dissipate and buffer lactate, also known as increasing your lactate tolerance. Recovery periods between intervals are typically about half the length of the

Training Intensities for OverUnders
RPE: 9
HR. 92–94 percent of highest CTS Field Test average (Under) alternating with 95–97 percent (Over)
Power: 86–90 percent of highest CTS Field Test average (Under) alternating with 95–100 percent (Over)

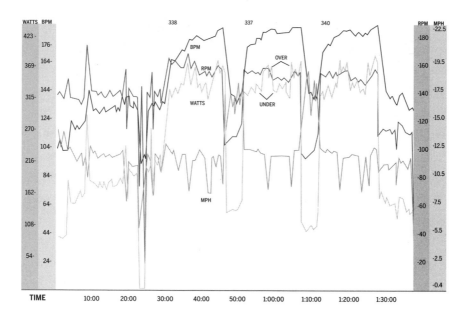

FIGURE 5.2: OverUnder

In this particular power file the athlete performed three OverUnder intervals, alternating between Over and Under twice per interval. Note the high-higher-high-higher pattern in each. The athlete also did a great job riding easy during recovery periods.

work interval. A more advanced version of this interval would alternate between SS and PI intensities instead of SS and CR intensities.

Note that in the training programs, the parameters of the OU intervals are written as 3 x 12 OU (2U, 1O), 5 minutes RBI. This should be read as follows: Three intervals of 12 minutes. During the 12-minute intervals, the first 2 minutes should be at your Under intensity (2U). After 2 minutes, accelerate to your Over intensity for 1 minute (1O), before returning to your Under intensity for another 2 minutes. Continue alternating in this manner (in this example you'd complete 4 cycles of Under and Over) until the end of the interval. Spin easy for 5 minutes (rest between intervals, or RBI) and start the next interval.

RUNNING WORKOUTS

RunningStrides (RS) RunningStrides are a great drill to incorporate into a warm-up prior to a training run and can be a component of a triathlon warm-up as well. These accelerations help to develop the neuromuscular adaptations necessary for higher-speed and higher-intensity running. They are also very useful as a component of your warm-up prior to difficult training efforts. Although you can perform RunningStrides on any surface, it's best to find a flat area, prefer-ably grassy (the infield of a running track or

Training Intensities for RunningStrides
RPE: 9
HR: NA
Pace: Above 5K race pace, but not an all-out sprint

the grassy area of a local park works well). From a standing start, accelerate into a run of approximately 100 meters (about 20 seconds at a pace faster than your 5K race pace). Your exact pacing is not crucial; you want to go sub-stantially faster than you could sustain for a 5K, but this is not a 100 meter all-out sprint. Focus on your mechanics, including foot strike, knee drive, and arm swing. You will have from 4 to 12 RunningStrides in a session. Recovery is easy jogging back to your starting point. HR zones are not prescribed for this workout because the interval is too short to see a heart rate response.

ENDURANCERUN (ER) You're going to spend much of your running time in the Endurance-Run intensity range. This is the moderate-intensity running time surrounding your fo-cused interval sets, as well as the intensity for your endurance runs that contain no specific intervals. The upper intensity range for an En-duranceRun is really just a ceiling; you should

Training Intensities for EnduranceRun
RPE: 6–7
HR: 50–97 percent of CTS Field Test average
Pace: 50–97 percent of CTS Field Test pace

stay under 97 percent of your CTS Field Test heart rate and pace for the vast majority of the run. The lower limit of 50 percent of your field test heart rate/pace allows for lower effort levels due to pauses in ERs (street crossings, etc.). Rather than worry about the lower limit, the larger concern is that you don't push too hard during ERs and inadvertently turn a moderate-intensity endurance-building effort into an interval workout. A good rule of thumb is to run ER at about 75 percent of your CTS Field Test average heart rate, which gives you room for harder efforts up hills or when you need/want to pick up the pace. The pace chart in Appendix A also provides the midpoint pace within this range, which is another good starting point for pacing during ER and allows for increases or decreases based on RPE.

STEADYSTATERUN INTERVALS (SSR) These relatively long intervals push you to a challenging pace but keep you below your lactate threshold intensity and pace. Intervals like this play a very important role in developing a stronger aerobic engine because you are maintaining an effort level greater than your normal "cruising" pace. This workout can be performed on the road, trails, or treadmill. If you're outdoors, you can do these intervals on flat to rolling terrain or on a long gradual climb. Short, steep climbs aren't a great choice of terrain for SSR because the terrain itself pushes you above the recommended intensity range. SteadyStateRun Intervals should be performed after a warm-up that includes

Training Intensities for SteadyStateRun Intervals
RPE: 7
HR: 92–98 percent of CTS Field Test average
Pace: 92–98 percent of CTS Field Test pace

4 to 5 RunningStrides. SSR should be done at the prescribed pace and HR intensity, and it is important that you maintain that intensity for the duration of the interval. Do not go too hard on the first one, as each SSR will be 10 to 15 minutes in length, and there will typically be 1 to 3 intervals. The recovery between intervals is 5 to 8 minutes of easy jogging.

The pace for SSR should be slower than for TempoRun (see below). Please don't confuse the workout terminology in the cycling and running workouts. In the cycling workouts, Tempo Intervals are conducted at a lower power and heart rate intensity than SteadyState Intervals. In the running workouts, the nomenclature is reversed (TempoRuns are harder than SSR). It is an unfortunate crossover of terminology, but I've chosen to keep the SSR and TempoRun names associated with the intensities listed here because they align with the standard nomenclature used in the running literature.

TEMPORUN INTERVALS (TR) TempoRun Intervals are a crucial workout for making you a faster and stronger runner. The pace and intensity for these

intervals are strenuous, and you will be running at or even slightly above your lactate
threshold intensity. It has long been said that
you can't become a faster runner without first
running faster in training, and that's exactly
what these intervals do. They help to drive the
process of increasing the size and density of
mitochondria in your muscles, improving your

Training Intensities for TempoRun Intervals
RPE: 8–9
HR: 98–102 percent of CTS Field Test average
Pace: 98–102 percent of CTS Field Test pace

ability to process and utilize lactate and to manage core temperature. Following a warm-up that includes 6 to 8 RunningStrides, your TempoRun will last
15 to 60 minutes and should be run with minimal interruption in the prescribed
intensity. At this pace, you will be fluctuating from just below to just above
your lactate threshold intensity, and this fluctuation plays a significant role in
stimulating the adaptations you're after. These intervals are best performed on
flat to rolling terrain. Experienced athletes can often complete these intervals
on sustained climbs, but inexperienced athletes often struggle to keep the
intensity within the appropriate range on hilly terrain.

FARTLEK INTERVALS (FI) Fartlek Intervals were invented by Swedish coach
Gösta Holmér in the 1930s and are widely used for developing running speed.
There are many versions of Fartlek Intervals, and the length of the efforts deter-
mine the energy system that is being targeted.

Training Intensities for Fartlek Intervals
RPE: 10
HR: 98–108 percent of CTS Field Test average
Pace: 98–108 percent of CTS Field Test pace

In the Time-Crunched Triathlete Programs, I
use short intervals of 1 to 2 minutes because
these durations are short enough to allow you
to sustain a pace well above race pace and well
above your lactate threshold pace. These are
your VO_2max running efforts, similar in objective and execution to PowerIntervals in the
cycling workouts. Following a warm-up that
includes 6 to 8 RunningStrides, bring your pace up to the prescribed pace
and maintain this pace for the duration of the short interval. The recovery
periods between Fartlek Intervals are purposely too short to allow for full

recovery, because part of the training stimulus comes from starting the next high-intensity effort before you have completely recovered from the previous one. During the recovery periods, slow to a jog, or slow to a walk if you need to, but keep moving. These intervals can be completed on any terrain or on a treadmill, and if you're planning on competing on a hilly course, it's a good idea to do Fartlek Intervals on hills.

NEGATIVESPLITRUN (NSR) A NegativeSplit-Run is a workout during which you complete the second half of your training session at a faster pace than the first half. If you have a GPS watch, or are running on a route you know well, you can do this anywhere you can keep track of your pace. Often, however, these workouts are best performed on an out-and-back route or a loop you can repeat twice. The key is not to start out too fast. At the beginning of the run

Training Intensities for NegativeSplitRun
RPE: 7–8 for the first half, 8–9 for the second half
HR: 92–98 percent of CTS Field Test average for first half, 98–102 percent for second half
Pace: 92–98 percent of CTS Field Test pace for first half, 98–102 percent for second half

you may feel strong and excited, but if you're already running at your maximum sustainable pace, you won't be able to increase your speed in the second half. By the same token, however, you shouldn't lollygag during the first half just so you can achieve the negative split in the second half. You want to run the first half of this workout slightly below your race pace so that you can increase to race pace or faster. At the halfway point of your run, increase your pace to your goal race pace, and during the final 25 percent of your run, increase your speed to slightly (5 to 10 seconds) above race pace.

Properly Executing Brick Workouts

Most of the workouts in the Time-Crunched Triathlete Program are two-discipline brick workouts. These sessions take a bit more planning than a single-sport workout. Not only do you need to remember all the necessary gear for two sports, but you also need to consider how you're going to transition from the pool to your bike, or from your bike to your run. When brick workouts are included in traditional triathlon programs, they are most often done as race-simulation workouts, meaning athletes are encouraged to treat the transition from one activity to the next as a race-pace transition. Such transition practices are essential for gaining the skills and habits necessary to have fast and efficient transitions on race day, but I don't expect you to incorporate a transition practice into every one of the brick workouts in the Time-Crunched Triathlete Program. Instead, as a matter of convenience and logistics, try to keep the time between the first and second segments of your workouts to less than 15 minutes. This gives you enough time to pack up your swimming gear, get it into your car, get the bike off the roof, and so on. Similarly, when you finish the cycling portion of a bike-run brick, it's OK to take the time to secure your bike and find an appropriate place to change your clothes (if necessary, depending on your apparel choices).

There will be times, however, when your schedule does not allow you to complete both segments of a brick workout back-to-back. The question athletes always ask in those circumstances is, May I separate the two parts of the brick workout into two independent workouts? The answer is yes, but understand that the workouts are designed to be performed as bricks. They are not simply a cycling workout and a running workout that happen to be scheduled one right after the other. The efforts included in each portion of the workout are designed to work together to optimally enhance your performance. That said, you'd be better off completing each segment independently than skipping either one or the other, or both. If your schedule demands that you occasionally split a brick workout into two independent workouts in the same day, that's OK. Just try to minimize the number of times you split the bricks.

Choosing the Right Training Program

Every day, my coaches use the concepts discussed in this book to create custom training schedules for the athletes they work with. Obviously, we'd love to build one for you as well, but I understand that personal coaching is not economically feasible or appealing to everyone. I'm a businessman, but at my core I'm an athlete and a coach; I publish training plans in books so that more people can use them and benefit from new ideas. In an effort to address the needs of athletes with different goals and varying levels of experience, I have included four training plans at the end of this chapter and an additional bonus program in Chapter 7. The plans in this chapter are divided into sprint and Olympic-distance programs and then further divided into intermediate and advanced levels. As you may notice, there are no novice or beginner plans. This isn't a book or program for athletes who are brand new to triathlon; the workouts—especially the swims and runs—start out at durations and intensity levels that assume you are already a proficient runner and swimmer.

Detailed descriptions of each program, and the athletes they are best suited for, follow.

INTERMEDIATE SPRINT PROGRAM

Training Plan 5.1 (page 202) is the right choice for athletes who have been racing triathlons for fewer than three years and athletes who have yet to complete an Olympic-distance race. The workload in this 6-week schedule takes into consideration the fact that you may have fewer total hours of training across swimming, cycling, and running. It begins at the lowest initial workload of any of the programs in the book and builds intensity and volume—and especially time-at-intensity—more gradually than does the Advanced Sprint program. This program is also a good choice for an athlete who is coming back to triathlon after a prolonged period away from training (like six months or more) for sprint-distance triathlons or other endurance events of similar durations. The weekly commitment in terms of training time peaks at 5.5 hours in this program.

ADVANCED SPRINT PROGRAM

If you've been racing sprint-distance triathlons for more than three years, or if you've been racing longer events and are shifting back to focus on sprint-distance events, then you have the cumulative training experience necessary to handle the workload and progression in the Advanced Sprint program (Training Plan 5.2, page 204). This 6-week schedule starts off at a higher intensity level than the Intermediate Sprint program, meaning you need to be in relatively good physical condition when you start the program. If you've been away from training for a significant period of time, either spend 3 to 4 weeks regaining some base fitness before starting this program or jump into the Intermediate Sprint program. The weekly time commitment of the Advanced and Intermediate Sprint programs is essentially identical, but the interval work in this program is more strenuous and the total time-at-intensity is greater as well. The weekly commitment in terms of training time peaks at just under 8 hours in this program.

INTERMEDIATE OLYMPIC PROGRAM

Naming this 8-week program (Training Plan 5.3, page 208) was a bit tricky because it's an intermediate program from the standpoint of the fitness and proficiency level necessary to handle the workload, but it absolutely can be used by triathletes who are preparing for their first Olympic-distance race. If you've been a triathlete for fewer than three years, you'd be better off using this program than the Advanced Olympic program. If you're more experienced but still preparing for your first Olympic-distance triathlon, I would recommend taking the conservative approach and using this program instead of the Advanced Olympic program. The slightly lower intensity level and four-workouts-per-week schedule also work well for triathletes who have already completed one or more half-Ironman or Ironman events within the last two years, but who have not been involved in structured training in the past six months. Generally, if you have any doubt about whether you should use the Intermediate or Advanced Olympic program, choose the Intermediate program. See how it goes, and you can always use the Advanced program for your next goal. The weekly commitment in terms of training time peaks at 8 hours in this program.

ADVANCED OLYMPIC PROGRAM

This is the 8-week program (Training Plan 5.4, page 212) used most often by veteran triathletes who want to focus their training on being highly competitive in Olympic-distance triathlons. It's a favorite of athletes who are scaling back their time commitment to training and competing after recently competing in half- or full-Ironman-distance events. This is the only program in this chapter that includes five workouts per week, and the Ironman 70.3 program is the only other five-workouts-per-week plan in this book. Even with the five workouts, the weekly commitment in terms of training time only rises above 8 hours in weeks 6 and 7.

Knowing When to Say When

Of all the obstacles to achieving high-performance fitness, your brain is the biggest. The same commitment and determination that have propelled you to success in your career and personal life can turn against you as an athlete, blinding you to the signs of excess fatigue and diminishing returns. Listening to your body is essential for enhancing the effectiveness of your training, and even with a perfectly structured training schedule, many factors influence your ability to complete every workout exactly as it's written. A poor night's sleep, a meeting that ran long, a less-than-optimal lunch because you were busy, or just inadequate recovery from your last workout—all athletes experience a period of time when their bodies are sending them signals that the workload is too high. If you recognize these signals and adjust your workouts accordingly, it's easy to stay on track and continue making progress. On the other hand, if you ignore the signals and blindly plow forward, you'll most likely do yourself more harm than good. There are two times when you really have to know when to say when—during an interval session and between workouts.

WHEN TO STOP AN INTERVAL SESSION

Interval workouts are only effective when you can maintain an intensity level high enough to address the goal of the session. If you're supposed to be doing lactate threshold intervals but your pace or power output is too low, that workout is not going to have the desired impact on your fitness. There are many athletes who follow a well-structured program but who still don't experience positive results; many of them fail to improve because the workload of the program is too high. They accumulate more fatigue than they can recover from, and in subsequent workouts they can't achieve the intensity levels necessary to make progress. The workouts feel difficult (RPE values are high), but the actual power and pace values are too low. As an athlete, when you reach the point in a workout when you can no longer sustain the intensity necessary to achieve the goal of that training session, you're done for the day. The best thing you can do is skip the remaining intervals and focus on recovery so you can be 100 percent prepared for your next workout. Quality takes precedence over quantity, because quantity without quality generates needless fatigue. Continuing an interval session after your performance level has dropped, particularly when it's dropped so far that you're no longer addressing the appropriate energy system, doesn't add anything positive to the high-quality work you performed earlier in the day. If anything, you're actually chipping away at the potential gains that workout could produce.

But the line between effective and ineffective training isn't always clear, so it's important to have some guidelines you can use to evaluate your performance and make a good decision. It should come as no surprise that the sensations of exercising at or near lactate threshold are different from the sensations of exercising at or near VO_2max. But because there are differences between these intensities, they each have their own guidelines for stopping or continuing your workout.

VO_2MAX WORKOUTS

There are three workouts in this book that target performance at VO_2max: PowerIntervals (cycling), Fartlek Intervals (running), and VO_2Sets (swimming). The decision-making process around stopping or continuing in the face of gathering fatigue is the same across all three, so for simplicity's sake, I'll focus on PowerIntervals. To be effective, these intervals have to be maximum-intensity, high-power efforts. Ideally, the recovery periods between intervals give you the ability to complete all the efforts at consistent power outputs. However, because they are so strenuous, you're going to fatigue, and you'll be fighting harder to reach that high power output during the final intervals. The big question is, as your power outputs start dropping, how do you judge whether you should continue with the next interval or shut down and go home?

I've seen a few methods that attempt to quantify the drop in power output over a series of intervals in order to provide a clear point at which further intervals are not recommended. One of the better ones is provided by Hunter Allen and Andrew Coggan in *Training and Racing with a Power Meter*. They recommend using the third interval of a VO_2max-interval workout as your benchmark. They recommend stopping if your power output in subsequent intervals drops to more than 15 percent below that level. I think that method can work quite well, not only in cycling but also in running and swimming (using a 15 percent reduction in pace instead of power output as the guideline). But since time-crunched athletes have fewer opportunities each week to work out, it's worth trying to adjust the workout parameters a bit to see if you can get some more high-quality work done before calling it quits.

Rather than automatically cutting your workout short if your power outputs or paces are starting to fade, I recommend first adding some time to the recovery period between intervals. This means that if your power output from one PI to the next falls by 15 percent or more, add 1 minute to the recovery period immediately following that effort. For Fartlek Intervals you should also add 1 minute to the recovery period, and you should double the prescribed recovery time following a VOS in a swimming workout. If the next interval is no better than the one before it—despite the extra recovery time—then you're done for the day. Don't add even more recovery time between efforts, and don't change the recovery periods between sets. If the added recovery time allows you to get through the end of the workout—or even just a few intervals closer to the end—that's great. Completing the work will help you perform your next VO$_2$max workout without having to add recovery time.

Even if you don't spend the time or mental effort to figure out if your last interval was equal to or X percent lower than the one before it, VO$_2$max intervals are pretty much self-limiting. If you're doing them correctly, meaning that each interval is an all-out effort, then your power output or pace isn't likely to decline gradually and imperceptibly. In my experience, most athletes are pretty good at telling when the wheels fall off the wagon. Your performance won't be just a little lower than before—it will tank. On the bike, your legs will feel like bricks, your pedal mechanics will become very ugly, and you'll feel as if you're pedaling through wet concrete while breathing through a straw. During Fartlek Intervals, you'll similarly feel as if you're breathing through a straw, and it will feel as if you have weights strapped to your ankles or you're running in slow motion. And when you tire during VO$_2$Sets in the water, your arms will feel like lead and you'll feel as if you're fighting for your life. But as I said previously, there's a difference between recognizing fatigue and making the right decision. When your body tells you it's done, you're done for the day (see Figure 5.3 for an example). Grunting your way through one more interval won't make you more of a man or woman, and listening to your body now is going to prevent you from doing more damage to muscles that are already in need of recovery and replenishment.

LACTATE THRESHOLD WORKOUTS

When it comes to lactate threshold workouts (SS and OU intervals on the bike, TR and SSR workouts in running, and LTS and PSS in swimming), which target improvements in power or pace at lactate threshold, it's not uncommon for athletes to struggle in the final 1 to 3 minutes of an individual interval. After all, these efforts tend to be 5 to 15 minutes long, and they are not that far below the workload from your CTS Field Test (see Chapter 3). However, struggling in the final 1 to 3 minutes of one of these intervals is not cause to skip the next effort. More than likely, following

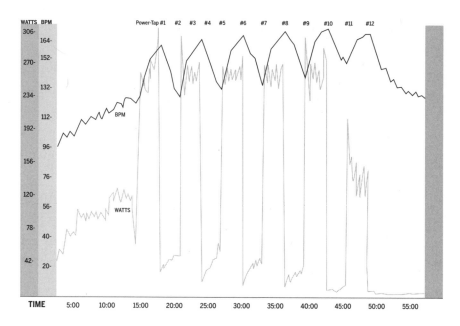

FIGURE 5.3: Reaching Overload
This rider started with five strong PI efforts but quickly ended on the sixth
interval when average power dropped by over 100 watts. It was clear to
the athlete that the workout was over. He had reached overload and wisely
chose to skip interval 7.
(Note: cadence trace removed for clarity.)

the prescribed recovery period, you'll be able to repeat or exceed your performance in the previous effort.

You'll know it's time to stop an SS or OU cycling workout when you can't reach the prescribed training intensity within the first 60 seconds of an interval, or if the perceived effort to stay at that power output makes the interval feel like an all-out, do-or-die time trial. SteadyState Intervals should feel like 7 on a 1 to 10 scale of perceived exertion, with CRs at 8 and OUs at 8 or 9. Only PIs should feel like 10, and if you're not going anywhere, on top of feeling as if your eyes will pop out of your head, then you're done for the day.

Similarly, you'll know it's time to stop an SSR or TR running workout when you can't maintain the prescribed pace past the first 90 seconds of an interval, or if the perceived effort to stay at the appropriate pace feels like an all-out effort. SteadyStateRun intervals should feel like a 7 on a 1 to 10 scale of perceived exertion, and TempoRun intervals should feel like an 8 or 9. When there's a significant mismatch between the perceived exertion and your pace, in that your RPE remains significantly higher than it should be for the pace you're actually doing, it's time to stop.

Determining when you're too tired to complete your LTS or PSS workouts is a bit more complicated, but you can get some good feedback from your breathing pattern. Typically, athletes breathe every other stroke at these paces (every time your right arm comes out of the water, for instance). Some athletes are able to breathe every fourth stroke during these intervals, but since these are a bit more intense, most people find it's more effective to switch to breathing every third stroke (if you are comfortable breathing to both sides) or every other stroke. Remember, though, that your breathing should be labored but in control during these efforts. If you feel as if you're struggling for breath, or that you want to stroke faster just so you can get to your next breath more quickly, then you're most likely working harder than prescribed intensity. When your breathing goes from controlled and labored to uncontrollable panting, that's a good sign you've crossed lactate threshold and are headed toward VO_2max.

If your breathing is out of sync with the prescribed effort level for LTS and PSS, the first step is to back off your pace until you get your breathing back under control. Continue at this reduced pace for approximately 100 meters, then return to your prescribed pace per 100 meters. If you experience the same mismatch between the breathing and RPE required to stay at the prescribed pace, bring your pace back down to the point where your breathing is labored but controlled. At this point, check your pace to see how far you are off pace. If you're more than 20 seconds slower than the prescribed pace once you've brought your breathing under control, you're done with LTS or PSS work for the day. Finish your workout with a 100 meter KickSwimSet.

When to Skip a Workout

I can't tell you the number of times I've rolled away from the CTS office in Colorado Springs completely convinced I was too tired to have a good workout, only to return 90 minutes later after hitting every single power output I was shooting for during my intervals. Fatigue can be a tricky thing to judge, especially when you're training on a lower-frequency, higher-intensity program. The individual workouts generate a lot of fatigue, but there are only four or five workouts scheduled per week, leaving two or three complete rest days. For many athletes, this is enough recovery to have consistently strong performances during their workouts. Nonetheless, the intensity in this program may be enough—especially coupled with your busy work and family schedule—to make you too tired to complete a workout here or there. The trick is understanding whether you need a kick in the butt to get you out the door or an extra day of rest so you can get back to kicking butt.

Since you have so little time each week to train anyway, your decision shouldn't be whether to train or not, but rather whether or not you should complete the scheduled workout. You should exercise regardless, if for no other reason than to ensure that your already limited training time isn't siphoned away any further. Similarly, although I understand the occasional need to move workouts around in the schedule due to business trips or family obligations, I'm not a big fan of rescheduling interval workouts that are skipped due to fatigue. If you're too tired to complete a workout on Monday and you move it to Tuesday, it's likely you'll then be too tired to have a good workout again when you try to get back on schedule during Wednesday's workout. I'd rather see you skip the interval session completely and get back on track with a series of great efforts during the next scheduled workout.

But let's get back to making the decision about whether or not to complete the day's scheduled interval session. The programs in this book are primarily brick workouts, and the vast majority are either swim-bike or bike-run bricks. If you're feeling tired when you get on your bike, it's a good idea to start with a focused warm-up and see if that kick-starts your motivation and energy systems. After 5 to 10 minutes of moderate-paced riding, complete the following:

1 minute FastPedal
1 minute easy recovery
1 minute FastPedal
1 minute easy recovery
1 minute PowerInterval

By this point, you should be about 15 minutes into your ride, and the efforts you have completed should give you enough real information to evaluate whether you're ready to have a high-quality interval session. If you were merely struggling with motivation to get out the door, your body will respond positively to these short efforts, and they will effectively "blow the crap out of the carburetor" (a reference that may be completely lost on athletes too young to remember when cars had carburetors instead of fuel injection; for them, let's just say you need to clear out the system to fire on all cylinders). If you felt as if you were really dragging in the PowerInterval, or your power output for the effort was considerably lower than normal for a 1-minute effort, I recommend skipping the scheduled interval session and instead completing a moderate-paced endurance ride before transitioning to the running portion of the workout. You should start your run with the intention of completing the prescribed workout. Even if you backed away from doing lactate threshold intervals on the bike, you should make an attempt to complete the prescribed work during the run (whether it's intervals or just a steady run). When you get into the interval portion of a run, use the guidelines on when to stop an interval session to determine whether you should continue. If it's an Endurance-Run, complete the prescribed time unless your sustainable pace is more than 45 seconds per mile slower than your "normal" ER pace. Many times, you'll be able to have a good run following a not-so-great ride, and that's OK. Some high-quality work is better than none.

If you're about to start a swim-bike brick and you're not sure if you're fatigued or just in need of a kick in the pants, get in the water and complete the following warm-up. By the end of this warm-up it should be clear if you have the stamina for a great workout or if an easier day would benefit you more. See pages 160–162 for descriptions of how to complete each drill. Take 15 seconds between drills.

100 meters easy swimming

25 meter Closed-Fists drill

25 meter Catch-up drill

25 meter Fingertip Drag drill

25 meter Distance per Stroke

4 × 50 meter Descending Intervals: 50 meter BIS, 50 meter PSS, 50 meter LTS, 50 meter LTS-plus pace. This series of 50 meter swims will get progressively faster, starting at your BIS pace, then your PSS pace, LTS pace, and finally a bit faster than LTS pace (5 to 7 seconds faster than LTS 100 meter pace). Rest 15 seconds between the 50s.

As you get to the final two 50 meter segments of the warm-up above, you'll know if you were having a motivation problem before getting in the water, or if you're truly fatigued. If your RPE and breathing for the LTS and LTS+ 50s are way out of proportion to the effort, or if you feel as if you're just dragging your body through the water, then today probably isn't going to be a good day for high-quality threshold or VO_2max swimming sets.

Rather than getting out of the water immediately, however, repeat the warm-up. This will provide some more volume, more drill work, and a few more accelerations. At the end of the second round through the warm-up, rest 15 to 30 seconds and complete a 100 meter KickSwimSet. In total, this will give you 900 meters in the water with plenty of technique work and some short efforts, all of which will likely make your next swim session more effective. Transition to the prescribed second segment of the workout and use the guidelines for stopping an interval to determine if you should complete all the intervals in that workout. Frequently, athletes who have a not-so-hot swim are still able to have an effective ride or run afterward.

Training Between Time-Crunched Triathlete Programs

As I mentioned in Chapter 2, once you have completed a race season, it's time to move into the foundation/preparation phase of your training to maintain much of that hard-earned fitness. Your training during this period should be less structured, but focused on maintaining steady intensities at about 65 to 85 percent of your maximum sustainable pace. This means maintaining a solid effort that's more challenging than an easy cruising pace during your runs, rides, and swims. If you notice a decline in your ability to push over hills at high speeds (on the bike or running), that is because these efforts call upon the VO_2max system, which you're not focusing much attention on right now. The dropoff is normal, and those performance markers respond quickly when you return to more intense training. By training at a challenging tempo, you'll still be getting a reasonable amount of energy from the glycolytic energy system, which will help prevent significant detraining of your aerobic system and power and pace at lactate threshold. Including some intense efforts and bricks once a week will further aid in preventing significant detraining, which means a masters swim workout or a hard local group ride is a good idea.

Whether you've cycled through the program once or three times, when you're done racing for a while, I recommend taking at least four weeks between completing the Time-Crunched Triathlete Program and starting it again. Or you can make the maintenance period as long as you like. At CTS we have had the most success with athletes when they use this program for two periods of racing in a year, with each competition period lasting no more than three months (two or three cycles through the program if you're doing multiple races). Depending on an athlete's goals and location, it is sometimes possible to add a third build period in one year, but this typically works only if each iteration of the program lasts the prescribed six to eight weeks and you're not cycling back through the program two or three times consecutively before taking significant recovery periods. The Time-Crunched Triathlete Program is perfect for having a great spring season and another surge in performance in the late summer or early fall. To fit in three cycles, you must start early (February) to be prepared for an early spring season, prepare again for a midsummer peak, and then prepare again for one in the fall. Although this can work for anyone, it is most often an option for athletes in warm climates because their season can start earlier and end later than the season in northern states. Training Plan 5.5 (page 218) shows the Transition schedule.

Frequently Asked Questions

Having written several training books and worked with thousands of athletes, my coaches and I have gained a sense of the questions athletes frequently ask when they are working their way through printed training programs. Here are answers to the most common questions we've received about our time-crunched programs.

> ***Can I shift the whole program so I have a day off on the weekend?***
> Yes. The workouts in the Time-Crunched Triathlete Program are written primarily for Tuesday/Thursday/Saturday/Sunday (the five-day-per-week programs include a workout on Monday as well). However, we understand that some athletes would rather have a whole weekend day for nontraining activities, like playing with the kids, going out with your spouse, or just doing nothing at all. The easiest thing to do is just shift the entire program back by one day. More often, athletes choose to shift to training on Monday/Wednesday/Friday/Saturday. This shift also works well for the five-day-a-week programs

because the Monday workout that now becomes a Sunday workout is only about an hour, and that's relatively easy to fit into a Sunday. What you don't want to do, or what you want to do as infrequently as possible, is rearrange the days of the schedule. The recovery periods between workouts are designed to allow for optimal training sessions, and the intensity levels of the sessions are reflective of the amount of recovery you're expected to have following that workout.

Is it OK to split the brick workouts into two separate workouts? The short answer is yes, but try to minimize the number of times you split the bricks.

Can I incorporate group rides/runs and masters swim classes into the Time-Crunched Triathlete Program? Yes, but it's important to keep group rides/runs and masters classes in the proper perspective. In all three cases, you're giving up some measure of specificity in order to gain convenience or motivation. There's no doubt that training with a group is enjoyable, and I've noted throughout this book that the community of triathlon is one of the sport's greatest assets. But during a group ride or "Tuesday Night World Championship" training race, it's difficult to perform the specific intervals you might have scheduled for that day. Many group runs are similarly unstructured and may be conducted at a pace that's either too easy to provide a training stimulus for you or so fast that you're adding workload to your existing program. That's not to say that using the Time-Crunched Triathlete Program means resigning yourself to training solo for the next few months. It just means that the majority of your training sessions should be conducted as prescribed, and you should incorporate group rides and runs sparingly (like once a week).

Masters swim classes are a slightly different story. There's a lot of variability between masters classes, based largely on the group of people who frequent the class and the coaching philosophy of the coach/instructor. Some are run very similarly to spin classes in the local gym; it's a series of hard workouts but there's really no structured progression. These are most often found where there's a large range of experience within the group of athletes and/or in classes led by coaches with a single-sport swimming background. When the athletes' abilities and goals are all over the map, it's difficult to create workouts that meet everyone's specific needs, so the default is often to just make the workouts hard. That's not necessarily an incorrect strategy; it's just not optimal for athletes who have a specific training goal. And in the case of the classes led by swim-specific coaches, some of them (not all, certainly, but some) still believe in using massive amounts of yardage for triathletes who only need to be able to swim a solid 750- to 1,500 meter split.

On the other hand, a masters class can be beneficial for improving your swimming technique, especially for athletes who came to triathlon from any sport other than competitive swimming. Better technique in the water will improve your swim split and reduce the energy cost of the swim more significantly than improving your swimming fitness. Energy system development is important for a faster swim, but no matter how much you improve your fitness, poor technique leads to an enormous waste of energy. It is primarily for this reason that I recommend going to a masters swim class, but do some research before you go. Find a class taught by a triathlon coach (not just someone who is or was a competitive triathlete; there's a difference), because these classes typically feature workouts that address the principles of effective triathlon training, including progression. If you're using a masters class in place of the swim portion of a swim-bike brick workout, be sure to end the swim with a KickSwimSet to improve your transition to the bike.

Can I compete before reaching the end of the program? Yes. You will not be tapered for the event as you will be for an event at the end of the programs, but that doesn't mean you can't compete in a triathlon, 5K, or 10K run as part of your training. If your race is on a Saturday, simply replace the scheduled workout with the competition and continue the training program as scheduled on Sunday. Your Sunday workout may not be great if the race was considerably more strenuous than the workout it replaced, but if that's the case, just make sure to focus more proactively on recovery activities on Sunday and Monday.

If your race is on a Sunday, you want to scale back the intensity of the scheduled Saturday workout because even though you're training through this event instead of peaking for it, you still want to be rested and ready to have a good race. Replace the scheduled Saturday workout with a 45- to 60-minute ride at EnduranceMiles pace. Include four 1-minute PowerIntervals separated by 1 minute of easy spinning recovery as well. A little intensity gets your body ready for a good warm-up and competition the next day.

It's important not to mistake this encouragement to occasionally replace workouts with competitions for a recommendation to race every weekend while using the Time-Crunched Triathlete Program. The more closely you adhere to the scheduled workouts, the better the progression within the program will work. However, you're an athlete, so you can participate in events that are fun and satisfy your desire for competition and a positive social environment. You must find the balance that works for you.

Can I cycle back through the Time-Crunched Triathlete Program if I am preparing for multiple events? Although the programs in this book are six or eight weeks long, some athletes may be able to stretch their fitness for up to an additional month. Triathletes with more years of racing experience will have greater success extending the period of time they can maintain their high-performance fitness. If you are stacking your race schedule and have multiple triathlons only a few weeks apart, it is fine to continue to cycle back into the training plan. After the final week of the training program, give yourself one week of recovery (ending on a Sunday) and then dive back into the training. For the programs in this book that list Monday as a rest day, this would mean your next training day is Tuesday; but if you're antsy to get started you can run, ride, or swim on Monday for up to an hour, with the goal of getting yourself back into the swing of training before a more purposeful workout on Tuesday. In order to determine where you should jump back in, count backward from your next race day, and pick up the program where appropriate. For example, if you are racing a triathlon once a month for three months in a row, you have four weeks between races. The first week following your race should be a recovery week. Ride easy, have fun, swim when you want, and run when you want—no structure, no sufferfests. Table 5.1 shows a sample of a post-race recovery week.

After a week of relative downtime, it's time to get back to structured training. Find your place within the program that's appropriate for your next event (see pages 175–176 in this chapter for more information on choosing the right program), so you have three weeks to your race day. For example, if you are using the Advanced Competitor Olympic program, after your rest week you'd want to start at Week 6 and progress from there to your next race.

TABLE 5.1: Sample Post-race Recovery Week

MONDAY	TUESDAY	WEDNESDAY	THURSDAY	FRIDAY	SATURDAY	SUNDAY
Rest Day	Swim: 35 min. Bike: 30 min.	Rest Day	Bike: 45 min easy Run: 15 min. off bike	Swim: 40 min., 4 x 50 sprint on 10 sec. RBI Run: 35 min. ER 4 x 30 sec. RS	Bike: 1:00 EM	Rest Day

If you choose to use the Time-Crunched Triathlete Program a few times in succession, I recommend cycling through it a maximum of three times before taking a more significant recovery period.

How often can I use the Time-Crunched Triathlete Program? Many athletes are able to use this program three times a year. If you're using an eight-week training program and then taking roughly four weeks of transitional training before getting back into the program again, three cycles of this pattern take about nine months. A lot of people prefer to use the program twice a year, especially if they are doing Olympic-distance events or if one of their events is a half-Iron-distance race. The key to using the program more than once is taking time after your goal race to recuperate—both mentally and physically—with some lower-intensity, less structured training. See page 218 in this chapter for an example of a Transition Training Plan you can use between times when you're using the Time-Crunched Triathlete Program to prepare for an event.

Should I do my workouts in the morning, afternoon, or evening? In more than 30 years as an athlete and a coach, I've yet to see any compelling evidence that one time of day is any better than another for training. However, there's no doubt that individual athletes are better off choosing times that are the least disruptive to their families and professional schedules. If early mornings work for you because you can get up and be done with your training before helping to get the kids fed and off to school, then mornings are your best training time. If you hate mornings but you're a night owl and have the energy to train after the kids go to bed, then evenings are your best training time. And if you have the opportunity to train in the middle of your workday . . . well, I'd take it. Personally, I'd rather go into the office early and train at lunchtime, because it gives me something to look forward to during the morning, and I often return from my midday workouts fired up and ready for a productive afternoon. The most important thing is to find a workout time that fits into your daily schedule and enhances what you're able to accomplish during the rest of the day. If your workout time is disruptive, you're more likely to find reasons to skip workouts. For more guidance on fitting workouts into your lifestyle, see pages 196–201.

Do I need to repeat the CTS Field Test each time I start the Time-Crunched Triathlete Program? Yes. Whether you're using the training workouts in this book or you're on a year-round coaching program, your fitness will fluctuate over the course of a year. As a result, your maximum sustainable power output on the bike and your paces in running and swimming will rise and fall, and it's important to repeat the CTS Field Tests at regular intervals to make sure your training intensities are appropriate for your current fitness level. Most often, when triathletes use the Time-Crunched Triathlete Program twice in one season (in the spring and once again in the late summer, for example), their field test results improve the second time in all three disciplines. As a result, your training intensities go up and you make greater progress. Over the winter, your fitness tends to fall more than during a recovery/maintenance period that covers a portion of the summer. (This is because you're more likely to continue riding/running/swimming during the summer, even if you're between periods of structured training.) As a result, field test results in the spring are often equal to or sometimes lower than field test results from the previous summer/fall. This is why a good winter training program is important; it's difficult to make progress from year to year if your fitness goes backward for three months over the winter.

How can I incorporate training DVDs if I'm doing the Time-Crunched Triathlete Program workouts on an indoor trainer? Many cyclists and triathletes have a library of indoor cycling DVDs and ask about substituting workouts in the program with DVD workouts when they must use an indoor trainer. This is understandable, because in addition to the workout itself, the DVDs (whether they're ones CTS has produced or someone else's) provide music and encouragement, which makes indoor trainer time more pleasant and often more productive. The answer to the question is yes, you can substitute training DVDs for individual cycling workouts in the Time-Crunched Triathlete Program if you're going to be training indoors. However, I think it's best to limit such substitutions to one workout per week, and it's important to choose DVDs that feature workouts that address the same goals—or at least similar goals—as the training session that was originally prescribed. For example, if you have a PowerInterval workout scheduled, look for a training DVD that features short, maximum-intensity intervals, even if the exact number of sets and interval durations are a little different. CTS-produced DVDs that fit this description include *Max Power, Race Power, Race Simulation, Mountain Biking, Criterium, Cycling for Power, Climbing Power,* and *Climbing Speed.* Similar workouts from other companies will often refer to being race-specific, high-intensity, or just plain hard.

If you have SteadyState or OverUnder intervals scheduled and you're looking for a training DVD to use, find one that focuses on intervals that increase maximum sustainable power or power at lactate threshold. These will likely be longer, sustainable efforts of 6 to 15 minutes, but the key is that the intervals be subthreshold or in or around your SS intensity level. CTS-produced DVDs that fit this description include *Threshold Power, Time Trial, Climbing, Climbing II,* and *Climbing Strength,* and titles from other companies will often refer to being applicable to time trials or power at lactate threshold.

Can I use the Time-Crunched Triathlete Program even if I don't have any specific racing goals? Sure. The Time-Crunched Triathlete Program will prepare triathletes to achieve greater performances in competition, but it's also an effective use of limited training time even if you're not preparing for a specific event or series of events. If you have limited time available to train, a high-intensity program is the only kind that will significantly improve your fitness. We have athletes who have used the Intermediate Olympic program two or even three times in a year simply to have some structure in their training. Their performance markers improve incrementally each time they use the program, and if and when they decide to prepare for a specific event, they start that preparation with a serious head start. As I've said all along, the purpose of training is to give you the opportunity to get greater enjoyment from being an athlete. For some people that simply means being able to ride faster rather than slower when they get a chance to go for a substantial ride on the weekends, or to run more comfortably when they get a chance to jump into a charity run. Some people view these programs as a great way to maintain a solid base of fitness, so they are more ready to jump into any activity, be it cross-country skiing, hiking, snowboarding, or mountain biking. You can absolutely use this program to accomplish those goals.

Integrating Training into Your Lifestyle

The Time-Crunched Triathlete Program is very effective for athletes who are short on time, but you still must be able to arrange your personal and professional schedule so you can balance your priorities. After meeting thousands of athletes over the years, I'm convinced that no two scenarios are entirely identical. Your personality, career choice, belief system, and even the length of your commute impact your perspective on balancing work, family, and training. I don't profess to have the answers to every challenge facing the modern triathlete/working parent/career professional, but having spent many years working with a wide range of athletes, I have found some solutions that have proven effective for a lot of the men and women my coaches and I have worked with.

CAREER PROFESSIONALS

Since Carmichael Training Systems is a company devoted to "empowering the athlete in every body," I have instituted a company policy that encourages all my employees to extend their "lunch" breaks to two hours. This free time during the day can be used around the normal lunchtime hours, but it can also be used at any other time of day. Some of my employees, therefore, train in the morning and come in at 9:00 or 10:00, or they leave a bit early in the evenings. Since we're running a business, they need to schedule these periods so they don't impede productivity, but over the years we've rarely had any problems in that regard. And I don't demand that this extended "lunch hour" be used only for athletic training; some extra time to run errands during the day is just as valuable because it can allow employees to spend their evenings with their spouses and families instead of running to the grocery store. More and more companies are adopting similar policies under the guise of "wellness programs," and if your company doesn't have anything like this in place, I highly recommend proposing one.

There's a school of thought that happy employees make great employees, and unhappy ones are poisonous to the overall working environment. As the CEO of a company with nearly 50 full-time employees, I have seen both the positive impact of policies that encourage balanced lifestyles and the detrimental impact of policies that make it harder for employees to enjoy the lifestyle they work so hard to support. We all need to work in order to pay the bills, and we all want a career that's rewarding enough that we're motivated by more than a paycheck. But whether you're an employer or an employee, I think it's important to structure the workplace environment—or the environment for your employees—in a way that allows people to be simultaneously successful at work, at home, and in training. Carmichael Training Systems has been a strong and vibrant company for more than 10 years, almost entirely because the people in the organization work hard, value the work they do, and take advantage of company policies that enable them to maintain a balanced and active lifestyle.

If your current work environment does not allow you to fit two-hour workouts into your day, one of the most successful solutions, and among the most agreeable to employers and business goals, is to shift your work-day by one hour. This can be done in either direction, shifting to an earlier start or a later one.

Shift to a Later Start Time

Instead of the standard 8-to-5 or 9-to-5 workday, try to shift your workday back one hour so that you leave work at 6:00 P.M. A one-hour shift allows you to complete two-hour workouts in the morning without waking up at 4:30 A.M., and could be less disruptive to your workday than trying to carve out a two-hour break in the middle of the day. This strategy works well for managers and directors who have a lot of meetings during the day, because a successful workday for you depends on being able to meet with colleagues during normal business hours.

Shift to an Earlier Start Time

Starting your workday an hour earlier, and hence leaving an hour early to get your workouts done, is a strategy that also works. The difficulty of using this strategy is that you must have the strength of purpose to actually leave the office earlier than your colleagues. If you're not careful, you'll end up starting your day early, getting caught up in projects and meetings, and staying in the office well past the time you originally planned to leave. Instead of getting more time for training, you'll inadvertently extend your workday and have even less time available for training, recovery, and interactions with your family

Which strategy is best for you? If you're the kind of person who can't resist the temptation to stay and do "just one more thing," you may be better off trying to train in the morning before work. Similarly, if you have a job in a creative field (graphic design, writing, programming), it's often difficult to stop working if you're in the middle of a project. My coaches and I have noticed that people in creative fields often fare better training in the morning, before starting their workdays. Many times, these athletes end up skipping or shortening afternoon workouts because they were so deeply involved in a project that they didn't want to stop. People in more management-oriented positions sometimes have an easier time breaking away for workouts in the afternoon because their workdays are often a long procession of meetings and phone calls. Your day is already segmented into 30- and 60-minute blocks in and around meetings, so ending the day early is a relatively simple matter of not scheduling meetings past 3:30 so you can walk out the door by 4:00.

WORKING PARENTS

Kids change everything, and as much as we all love our children, there's no doubt that for most of us it was easier to find time for training before we had them. Whereas the athletes who don't have children can leave home early in the morning and/or return home later in the evening, being engaged in your children's lives means being at home when they are awake and participating in their activities. This is one of the big reasons that training in the morning or during work hours appeals to parents of school-age children; it opens up late afternoons and evenings to go to sports games, recitals, and school plays. You are more likely to be around to eat dinner as a family, help out with homework, and generally be present in your kids' lives.

The scheduling arrangement that works for working parents is very individual and depends on a great number of factors, not the least of which are the ages of your children and your opportunities for sharing the responsibilities of parenting. After coaching thousands of working parents, my coaches and I have the following suggestions:

Trade Time

If you're in a two-parent household, consider trading time with your spouse or significant other. If you are going to commit to training in the morning, you will not be around to get the kids up, fed, and off to school.

But if the parenting responsibilities in the morning are not going to be yours, then you will need to commit to being present in the afternoon or evening. Similarly, if you're going to train in the evenings, commit to being the parent who handles the morning around the house. Sometimes it's not even a matter of trading and more a matter of making sure that you commit to being present and engaged in a certain timeframe to balance the time you will be away working or training. In families where both parents are athletes, trading time, especially on weekends, is essential for enabling both people to get training time and time to themselves.

Get a Babysitter

This is a remarkably simple solution, but one that many working parents are hesitant to use. Obviously there's a cost involved, which can create a barrier, but can also provide motivation. You're far more likely to stay focused on your workout when you know you're essentially paying for it. Athletes who use babysitters to help facilitate training often report that those training sessions feel even more productive, as if they are training with an added purpose—to justify the expense of paying the babysitter.

Other parents are reluctant to hire a babysitter so they can train because they perceive it as being overindulgent or even selfish. If it's the money that makes it seem excessive or frivolous, get over it. Although I'm sure some of you are very frugal, it's far more likely that you spend as much or more on other products and services that allow you to do what you want to more conveniently. Since most couples use the babysitter route so they can both get in a workout at the same time, the cost is essentially divided between two training sessions. As a result, it's far cheaper to hire a babysitter for a few hours than to purchase two personal training sessions or two massage therapy appointments. And if you and your spouse/significant other enjoy training together, a couples training session is far cheaper than going out to a movie or dinner, for which you would also have to get a babysitter.

If, on the other hand, your reluctance to hire a babysitter so you can train is based on the idea that it's inappropriate to leave your children with a caretaker just so you can exercise, it's not my place to tell you what's right for you and your family. However, I have observed that parents who are able to pursue their own goals, in addition to caring for their families, tend to be happier and more content in their relationships with both their children and life partner. Taking time for yourself and pursuing a fitness goal that has nothing to do with your children does not mean you're neglecting your family. It's a matter of balance, and the happier you are with all areas of your life, the better role model you become for your children.

Include Your Children in Your Training

This one is a bit tricky, because it is not always easy to focus on executing your workouts properly when you're pulling your kids in a trailer or pushing them in a running stroller. But you may very well be able to include your children in some of your workouts. The wife of one of my coaches is a stay-at-home mom who runs a tutoring and ACT/SAT prep business from the house. To fit a swim workout into her day, she enrolled their kids in swim lessons at a local pool, and while they are at their lessons, she goes to the lap pool and bangs out a 1,000-yard swimming workout. Eric, a CTS athlete who has an eight-year-old son named Bryce, takes his son along with him on runs, provided the run is an hour or shorter. His son rides his bike while Dad runs, and as a means of helping his father, Bryce carries his dad's water bottle on his bike.

The fact that you are an athlete can have a big impact on your children. Our children emulate what they see every day, and when they see you exercising, they perceive being active as a normal and positive component of being an adult. In the long run this increases the likelihood that they will grow to be active and healthy adults themselves.

TRAINING PLAN 5.1: Intermediate Sprint Program

	MONDAY	TUESDAY	WEDNESDAY	THURSDAY
WEEK 1	Rest Day	**Swim: 30 min. (900 m/yds.)** WU 150 Drill 6 x 50 Catch-up (20 sec. RBI) BIS 3 x 100 (15 sec. RBI) KSS 2 x 25 (15 sec. RBI) CD 100 **Bike: 45 min. EM** 3 x 6 min. SS (4 min. RBI)	Rest Day	**Bike: 45 min. EM** 4 x 6 min. SS (4 min. RBI) **Run: 15 min. ER**
WEEK 2	Rest Day	**Swim: 30 min. (1,100 m/yds.)** WU 150 Drill 6 x 50 Closed Fists (20 sec. RBI) PSS 5 x 100 (15 sec. RBI) KSS 2 x 25 (15 sec. RBI) CD 100 **Bike: 1:00 EM** ⁻ 3 x 8 SS (5 min. RBI)	Rest Day	**Bike: 45 min. EM** **Run: 15 min. ER** *Keep transition to less than 5 min.
WEEK 3	Rest Day	**Swim: 30 min. (1,200 m/yds.)** WU 150 Drill 6 x 50 Fingertip Drag (20 sec. RBI) PSS 6 x 100 (15 sec. RBI) KSS 2 x 25 (15 sec. RBI) CD 100 **Bike: 1:00 EM** 3 x 8 OU (2U, 2O) (4 min. RBI)	Rest Day	**Bike: 45 min. EM** **Run: 15 min. ER** *Keep transition to less than 5 min.
WEEK 4	Rest Day	**Swim: 45 min. (1,600 m/yds.)** WU 150 Drill 8 x 50 Distance per Stroke (20 sec. RBI) BIS 3 x 300 (20 sec. RBI) KSS 2 x 25 (20 sec. RBI) CD 100 **Bike: 1:00 EM**	Rest Day	**Run: 45 min. ER** 3 x 5 min. SSR (4 min. RBI)
WEEK 5	Rest Day	**Swim: 30 min. (1,400 m/yds.)** WU 100 Drill 4 x 75 (25 Right Arm/25 Left Arm/25 Distance per Stroke) 15 sec. RBI PSS 4 x 200 (15 sec. RBI) KSS 2 x 25 (15 sec. RBI) CD 150 **Bike: 1:00 EM** 2 x [3 x 2 min. PI] 2 min. RBI/ 8 min. RBS	Rest Day	**Run: 45 min. ER** 4 x 3 min. FI (3 min. RBI)

FRIDAY	SATURDAY	SUNDAY	TOTALS
Rest Day	Run: 25 min. ER Swim: 30 min. (1,000 m/yds.) WU 100 Drill 6 x 50 Catch-up (20 sec. RBI) PSS 6 x 75 (15 sec. RBI) CD 50	Bike: 1:00 EM	SWIM: 1:00 BIKE: 2:30 RUN: 0:35 TOTAL: 4:05
Rest Day	Run: 30 min. ER 4 x 10 sec. RS (60 sec. RBI) Swim: 30 min. (1,200 m/yds.) WU 200 Drill 6 x 50 Closed Fists (20 sec. RBI) BIS 2 x 300 (20 sec. RBI) CD 100	Bike: 1:00 EM 3 x 8 OU (2U, 2O) (4 min. RBI)	SWIM: 1:00 BIKE: 2:45 RUN: 0:45 TOTAL: 4:30
Rest Day	Run: 45 min. ER 3 x 5 min. SSR (4 min. RBI) Swim: 30 min. (1,200 m/yds.) WU 200 Drill 6 x 50 Fingertip Drag (20 sec. RBI) PSS 300-200-100 (15 sec. RBI) CD 100	Bike: 1:00 EM 3 x 10 OU (3U, 2O) (5 min. RBI) Run: 15 min. ER	SWIM: 1:00 BIKE: 2:45 RUN: 1:15 TOTAL: 5:00
Rest Day	Swim: 30 min. (1,200m/yds.) WU 200 Drill 6 x 50 Distance per Stroke (20 sec. RBI) VOS 4 x 100 (20 sec. RBI) KSS 4 x 50 (15 sec. RBI) CD 100 Bike: 1:30 EM 5 x 2 min. PI (2 min. RBI)	Run: 45 min. ER 4 x 3 min. FI (3 min. RBI)	SWIM: 1:15 BIKE: 2:30 RUN: 1:30 TOTAL: 5:15
Rest Day	Swim: 30 min. (1,300 m/yds.) WU 200 Drill 6 x 50 Distance per Stroke (20 sec. RBI) VOS 5 x 100 (20 sec. RBI) KSS 4 x 50 (15 sec. RBI) CD 100 Bike: 1:30 EM 5 x 2 min. PI (2 min. RBI)	Run: 1:00 ER 4 x 10 sec. RS (60 sec. RBI)	SWIM: 1:15 BIKE: 2:30 RUN: 1:45 TOTAL: 5:30

CONTINUES

CONTINUED

TRAINING PLAN 5.1: Intermediate Sprint Program

	MONDAY	TUESDAY	WEDNESDAY	THURSDAY
WEEK 6	Rest Day	Swim: 45 min. (1,600 m/yds.) WU 150 Drill 4 x 75 (25 Right Arm/ 25 Left Arm/25 Distance per Stroke) 15 sec. RBI PSS 2 x 400 (20 sec. RBI) PSS 2 x 100 (15 sec RBI) KSS 2 x 25 (15 sec RBI) CD 100 Bike: 1:00 EM 2 x [3 x 2 min. PI] 2 min. RBI/8 min. RBS	Rest Day	Run: 45 min. ER 4 x 10 sec. RS (60 sec. RBI)

RBI = Rest between intervals | RBS = Rest between sets | WU = Warm-up | CD = Cooldown

TRAINING PLAN 5.2: Advanced Sprint Program

	MONDAY	TUESDAY	WEDNESDAY	THURSDAY
WEEK 1	Rest Day	Swim: 30 min. (1,000 m/yds.) WU 150 Drill 6 x 50 Catch-up (20 sec. RBI) BIS 4 x 100 (15 sec. RBI) KSS 2 x 25 (15 sec. RBI) CD 100 Bike: 1:00 EM 4 x 6 min. SS (4 min. RBI)	Rest Day	Bike: 45 min. EM 3 x 8 min. SS (4 min. RBI) Run: 15 min. ER *Keep transition to less than 5 min.
WEEK 2	Rest Day	Swim: 30 min. (1,200 m/yds.) WU 150 Drill 6 x 50 Closed Fists (20 sec. RBI) PSS 6 x 100 (15 sec. RBI) KSS 2 x 25 (15 sec. RBI) CD 100 Bike: 1:00 EM 3 x 8 SS (5 min. RBI)	Rest Day	Bike: 1:00 EM Run: 15 min. ER *Keep transition to less than 5 min.
WEEK 3	Rest Day	Swim: 30 min. (1,200 m/yds.) WU 150 Drill 6 x 50 Fingertip Drag (20 sec. RBI) PSS 6 x 100 (15 sec. RBI) KSS 2 x 25 (15 sec. RBI) CD 100 Bike: 1:15 EM 3 x 8 OU (2U, 20) (4 min. RBI)	Rest Day	Bike: 1:00 EM Run (off the Bike): 20 min. ER *Keep transition to less than 5 min.

FRIDAY	SATURDAY	SUNDAY	TOTALS
Rest Day	Swim: 15 min. (800 m/yds.) WU 200 Drill 6 x 50 Distance per Stroke (20 sec. RBI) VOS 4 x 50 (10 sec. RBI) CD 100 Bike: 30 min. EM Run (off the Bike): 10 min. ER + 4 x 10 sec. RS (60 sec. RBI)	SPRINT- DISTANCE RACE	SWIM: 1:00 BIKE: 1:30 RUN: 1:00 RACE TOTAL: 3:30 + RACE

FRIDAY	SATURDAY	SUNDAY	TOTALS
Rest Day	Run: 30 min. ER Swim: 30 min. (1,200 m/yds.) WU 200 Drill 6 x 50 Catch-up (20 sec. RBI) PSS 4 x 200 (15 sec. RBI) CD 100	Bike: 1:15 EM Run: 20 min. ER	SWIM: 1:00 BIKE: 3:00 RUN: 1:05 TOTAL: 5:05
Rest Day	Swim: 30 min. (1,500 m/yds.) WU 200 Drill 6 x 50 Closed Fists (20 sec. RBI) BIS 3 x 300 (20 sec. RBI) CD 100 Run: 45 min. ER 4 x 10 sec. RS (60 sec. RBI)	Bike: 1:15 EM 3 x 8 OU (2U, 2O) (4 min. RBI) Run: 20 min. ER	SWIM: 1:00 BIKE: 3:15 RUN: 1:20 TOTAL: 5:35
Rest Day	Run: 45 min. ER 3 x 5 min. SSR (4 min. RBI) Swim: 45 min. (1,600 m/yds.) WU 300 Drill 6 x 50 Fingertip Drag (20 sec. RBI) PSS 2 x [200-100-2 x 50] (15 sec. RBI) CD 200	Bike: 1:30 EM 3 x 10 OU (3U, 2O) (5 min. RBI) Run: 15 min. ER	SWIM: 1:15 BIKE: 3:45 RUN: 1:20 TOTAL: 6:20

CONTINUES

CONTINUED

TRAINING PLAN 5.2: Advanced Sprint Program

	MONDAY	TUESDAY	WEDNESDAY	THURSDAY
WEEK 4	Rest Day	**Swim: 45 min. (1,600 m/yds.)** WU 150 Drill 8 x 50 Distance per Stroke (20 sec. RBI) BIS 3 x 300 (20 sec. RBI) KSS 2 x 25 (20 sec. RBI) CD 100 **Run: 45 min. ER** 4 x 5 min. SSR (4 min. RBI)	Rest Day	**Bike: 1:00 EM** 7 x 2 min. PI (2 min. RBI) **Run: 15 min. ER** *Keep transition to less than 5 min.
WEEK 5	Rest Day	**Swim: 45 min. (1,700 m/yds.)** WU 150 Drill 4 x 75 (25 Right Arm/25 Left Arm/25 Distance per Stroke) 15 sec. RBI PSS 5 x 200 (15 sec. RBI) KSS 2 x 25 (15 sec. RBI) CD 100 **Bike: 1:00 EM** 2 x [3 x 3 min. PI] 2 min. RBI/ 8 min. RBS	Rest Day	**Run: 1:00 ER** 5 x 3 min. FI (3 min. RBI)
WEEK 6	Rest Day	**Swim: 45 min. (1,600 m/yds.)** WU 150 Drill 4 x 75 (25 Right Arm/25 Left Arm/25 Distance per Stroke) 15 sec. RBI PSS 2 x 400 (20 sec. RBI) PSS 2 x 100 (15 sec. RBI) KSS 2 x 25 (15 sec. RBI) CD 100 **Bike: 1:15 EM** 2 x [3 x 3 min. PI] 2 min. RBI/8 min. RBS **Run: 1:00 ER 5 x 3 min. FI** (3 min. RBI)	Rest Day	**Run: 45 min. ER** 4 x 10 sec. RS (60 sec. RBI)

RBI = Rest between intervals | RBS = Rest between sets | WU = Warm-up | CD = Cooldown

FRIDAY	SATURDAY	SUNDAY	TOTALS
Rest Day	**Bike: 1:30 EM** 7 x 2 min. PI (2 min. RBI) **Run: 45 min. ER** 5 x 3 min. FI (3 min. RBI)	**Swim: 30 min.** **(1,200 m/yds.)** WU 200 Drill 6 x 50 Distance per stroke (20 sec. RBI) VOS 4 x 100 (20 sec. RBI) KSS 4 x 50 (15 sec. RBI) CD 100 **Bike: 1:30 EM**	**SWIM: 1:15** **BIKE: 4:00** **RUN: 1:45** **TOTAL: 7:00**
Rest Day	**Swim: 45 min. (1,800 m/yds.)** WU 200 Drill 6 x 50 Distance per Stroke (20 sec. RBI) VOS 7 x 100 (20 sec. RBI) VOS 6 x 50 (20 sec. RBI) KSS 4 x 50 (15 sec. RBI) CD 100 **Bike: 1:30 EM** 7 x 2 min. PI (2 min. RBI)	**Run: 1:00 ER** 4 x 10 sec. RS (60 sec. RBI) **Bike: 1:30 EM**	**SWIM: 1:30** **BIKE: 4:00** **RUN: 2:00** **TOTAL: 7:30**
Rest Day	**Swim: 20 min. (1,000 m/yds.)** WU 200 Drill 6 x 50 Distance per Stroke (20 sec. RBI) VOS 6 x 50 (10 sec. RBI) CD 200 **Bike: 30 min. EM** **Run (off the Bike): 10 min. ER +** 4 x 10 sec. RS (60 sec. RBI)	**SPRINT-DISTANCE** **RACE**	**SWIM: 1:00** **BIKE: 1:45** **RUN: 1:00** **RACE** **TOTAL:** **3:45 + RACE**

TRAINING PLAN 5.3: Intermediate Olympic Program

	MONDAY	TUESDAY	WEDNESDAY	THURSDAY
WEEK 1	Rest Day	**Swim: 30 min. (1,350 m/yds.)** WU 300 Drill 6 x 50 Catch-up (20 sec. RBI) BIS 3 x 200 (20 sec. RBI) KSS 2 x 25 (20 sec. RBI) CD 100 **Bike: 1:00 EM** 3 x 8 min. SS (4 min. RBI)	Rest Day	**Bike: 45 min. EM** 3 x 8 min. SS (4 min. RBI) **Run: 15 min. ER** *Keep transition to less than 5 min.
WEEK 2	Rest Day	**Swim: 30 min. (1,500 m/yds.)** WU 300 Drill 7 x 50 Closed Fists (20 sec. RBI) PSS 7 x 100 (15 sec. RBI) KSS 2 x 25 (15 sec. RBI) CD 100 **Bike: 1:00 EM** 3 x 10 min. SS (5 min. RBI)	Rest Day	**Bike: 45 min. EM** 3 x 8 min. SS (4 min. RBI) **Run: 15 min. ER** *Keep transition to less than 5 min.
WEEK 3	Rest Day	**Swim: 45 min. (1,800 m/yds.)** WU 300 Drill 7 x 50 Fingertip Drag (20 sec. RBI) PSS 4 x 200 (15 sec. RBI) KSS 2 x 25 (15 sec. RBI) CD 100 **Bike: 1:00 EM** 4 x 8 min. SS (4 min. RBI)	Rest Day	**Bike: 1:00 EM** 3 x 10 min. SS (4 min. RBI) **Run: 15 min. ER** *Keep transition to less than 5 min.
WEEK 4	Rest Day	**Swim: 45 min. (1,850 m/yds.)** WU 200 Drill 6 x 50 Distance per Stroke (20 sec. RBI) BIS 4 x 300 (20 sec. RBI) KSS 2 x 25 (20 sec. RBI) CD 100 **Bike: 1:00 EM**	Rest Day	**Run: 45 min. ER** 4 x 10 sec. RS (60 sec. RBI)
WEEK 5	Rest Day	**Swim: 45 min. (1,850 m/yds.)** WU 200 Drill 4 x 75 (25 Right Arm/ 25 Left Arm/25 Distance per Stroke) 15 sec. RBI PSS 4 x 300 (20 sec. RBI) KSS 2 x 25 (20 sec. RBI) CD 100 **Bike: 1:00 EM** 2 x [3 x 3 min. PI] 3 min. RBI/8 min. RBS	Rest Day	**Run: 45 min. ER** 4 x 10 sec. RS (60 sec. RBI)

FRIDAY	SATURDAY	SUNDAY	TOTALS
Rest Day	Run: 45 min. ER Swim: 30 min. (1,300 m/yds.) WU 100 Drill 6 x 50 Catch-up (20 sec. RBI) BIS 2 x 300 (20 sec. RBI) CD 100	Bike: 1:00 EM Run: 15 min. ER	SWIM: 1:00 BIKE: 2:45 RUN: 1:15 TOTAL: 5:00
Rest Day	Run: 45 min. ER 4 x 6 min. SSR (4 min. RBI) Swim. 30 min. (1,500 m/yds.) WU 200 Drill 6 x 50 Closed Fists (20 sec. RBI) BIS 2 x 400 (20 sec. RBI) CD 200	Bike: 1:30 EM 3 x 10 OU (3U, 20) (5 min. RBI) Run: 15 min. SSR	SWIM: 1:00 BIKE: 3:15 RUN: 1:15 TOTAL: 5:30
Rest Day	Run: 1:00 ER 4 x 6 min. SSR (4 min. RBI) Swim: 45 min. (1,800 m/yds.) WU 200 Drill 6 x 50 Fingertip Drag (20 sec. RBI) PSS 2 x [300-200-100] (15 sec. RBI) CD 100	Bike: 1:30 EM 3 x 10 OU (3U, 20) (5 min. RBI) Run: 15 min. ER	SWIM: 1:30 BIKE: 3:30 RUN: 1:30 TOTAL: 6:30
Rest Day	Swim: 45 min. (1,600 m/yds.) WU 400 Drill 6 x 50 Distance per Stroke (20 sec. RBI) VOS 6 x 100 (20 sec. RBI) KSS 4 x 50 (15 sec. RBI) CD 100 Bike: 2:00 EM 7 x 2 min. PI (2 min. RBI)	Run: 1:15 ER 5 x 3 min. FI (3 min. RBI)	SWIM: 1:30 BIKE: 3:00 RUN: 2:00 TOTAL: 6:30
Rest Day	Swim: 1:00 (2,000 m/yds.) WU 400 Drill 6 x 50 Distance per Stroke (20 sec. RBI) VOS 5 x 200 (20 sec. RBI) KSS 4 x 50 (15 sdec RBI) CD 100 Bike: 2:15 EM 7 x 2 min. PI (2 min. RBI)	Run: 1:15 ER 5 x 3 min. FI (3 min. RBI)	SWIM: 1:45 BIKE: 3:15 RUN: 2:00 TOTAL: 7:00

CONTINUES

CONTINUED

TRAINING PLAN 5.3: Intermediate Olympic Program

	MONDAY	TUESDAY	WEDNESDAY	THURSDAY
WEEK 6	Rest Day	**Swim: 45 min. (1,850 m/yds.)** WU 200 Drill 4 x 75 (25 Right Arm/ 25 Left Arm/25 Distance per Stroke) 15 sec. RBI PSS 3 x 400 (20 sec. RBI) KSS 2 x 25 (20 sec. RBI) CD 100 **Bike: 1:15 EM** 5 x 3 min. PI (3 min. RBI)	Rest Day	**Run: 1:00 ER** 5 x 3 min. FI (3 min. RBI)
WEEK 7	Rest Day	**Swim: 45 min. (1,850 m/yds.)** WU 200 Drill 4 x 75 (25 Right Arm/ 25 Left Arm/25 Distance per Stroke) 15 sec. RBI PSS 3 x 400 (20 sec. RBI) KSS 2 x 25 (20 sec. RBI) CD 100 **Bike: 1:15 EM** 3 x 10 OU (3U, 20) (5 min. RBI)	Rest Day	**Bike: 45 min. EM** 3 x 8 min. SS (4min RBI) **Run: 15 min. ER** *Keep transition to less than 5 min.
WEEK 8	Rest Day	**Swim: 45 min. (1,750 m/yds.)** WU 300 Drill 4 x 75 (25 Right Arm/ 25 Left Arm/25 Distance per Stroke) 15 sec. RBI BIS 5 x 200 (20 sec. RBI) KSS 2 x 25 (20 sec. RBI) CD 100 **Run: 45 min. ER** 4 x 2 min. FI (2 min. RBI)	Rest Day	**Swim: 45 min.** **(1,600 m/yds.)** WU 400 Drill 6 x 50 Distance per Stroke (20 sec. RBI) VOS 6 x 100 (20 sec. RBI) KSS 4 x 50 (15 sec. RBI) CD 100 **Bike: 1:00 EM**

RBI = Rest between intervals | RBS = Rest between sets | WU = Warm-up | CD = Cooldown

FRIDAY	SATURDAY	SUNDAY	TOTALS
Rest Day	**Swim: 1:00 (2,000 m/yds.)** WU 300 Drill 6 x 50 Distance per Stroke (20 sec. RBI) VOS 12 x 100 (10 sec. RBI) CD 200 **Bike: 2:15 EM** 2 x [3 x 3 min. PI] 3 min. RBI/ 8 min. RBS	**Run: 1:15 ER** (hilly terrain)	SWIM: 1:45 BIKE: 3:30 RUN: 2:15 TOTAL: 7:30
Rest Day	**Run: 1:15 ER** (hilly terrain) **Swim: 1:00 (2,000 m/yds.)** WU 300 Drill 6 x 50 Distance per Stroke (20 sec. RBI) VOS 12 x 100 (10 sec. RBI) CD 200	**Bike: 2:30 EM** 3 x 10 OU (3U, 2O) (5 min. RBI) **Run: 15 min. SSR**	SWIM: 1:45 BIKE: 4:00 RUN: 2:15 TOTAL: 8:00
Rest Day	**Bike: 30 min. EM** 1 x 10 min. T 3 x 1 min. PI (1 min. RBI) **Run: 15 min. ER** 4 x 10 RS (60 sec. RBI)	**OLYMPIC- DISTANCE RACE**	SWIM: 1:30 BIKE: 2:30 RUN: 1:00 RACE TOTAL: 5:00 + RACE

TRAINING PLAN 5.4: Advanced Olympic Program

	MONDAY	TUESDAY	WEDNESDAY	THURSDAY
WEEK 1	Rest Day	**Bike: 1:00 EM** 3 x 8 min. SS (4 min. RBI) **Run: 15 min. ER** *Keep transition to less than 5 min.	**Swim: 45 min.** **(1,600 m/yds.)** WU 300 Drill 6 x 50 Catch-up (20 sec. RBI) BIS 4 x 200 (20 sec. RBI) KSS 2 x 25 (20 sec. RBI) CD 100	**Run:** **45 min. ER** 6 x 10 sec. RS (60 sec. RBI)
WEEK 2	Rest Day	**Bike: 1:15 EM** 3 x 8 min. SS (4 min. RBI) **Run: 15 min. ER** *Keep transition to less than 5 min.	**Swim: 45 min.** **(1,800 m/yds)** WU- 300 Drill 7 x 50 Closed Fists (20 sec. RBI) PSS 10 x 100 (15 sec. RBI) KSS 2 x 25 (15 sec. RBI) CD 100	**Run:** **45 min. ER** 4 x 6 min. SSR (4 min. RBI)
WEEK 3	Rest Day	**Bike: 1:00 EM** 3 x 10 min. SS (4 min. RBI) **Run: 15 min. ER** *Keep transition to less than 5 min.	**Swim: 45 min.** **(1,800 m/yds.)** WU 300 Drill 7 x 50 Fingertip Drag (20 sec. RBI) PSS 4 x 200 (15 sec. RBI) KSS 2 x 25 (15 sec. RBI) CD 100 **Bike: 1:00 EM** 4 x 8 min. SS (4 min. RBI)	**Run: 1:00 ER** 6 x 10 sec. RS (60 sec. RBI)
WEEK 4	Rest Day	**Swim: 45 min. (1,900 m/yds.)** WU 200 Drill 6 x 50 Distance per Stroke (20 sec. RBI) BIS 4 x 300 (20 sec. RBI) KSS 2 x 25 (20 sec. RBI) CD 150 **Bike: 1:00 EM** (hilly terrain)	**Run: 1:00 ER** 4 x 10 sec. RS (60 sec. RBI)	**Bike: 1:30 EM** 7 x 2 min. PI (2 min. RBI)

FRIDAY	SATURDAY	SUNDAY	TOTALS
Rest Day	Bike: 1:30 EM 3 x 8 min. SS (4 min. RBI) Run: 15 min. ER	Run: 45 min. ER Swim: 45 min. (1,600 m/yds.) WU 200 Drill 6 x 50 Catch-up (20 sec. RBI) BIS 3 x 300 (20 sec. RBI) CD 200	SWIM: 1:30 BIKE: 2:30 RUN: 2:00 TOTAL: 6:00
Rest Day	Bike: 1:30 EM 3 x 10 OU (3U, 2O) (5 min. RBI) Run: 15 min. SSR	Run: 60 min. ER 6 x 10 sec. RS (60 sec. RBI) Swim: 45 min. (1,800 m/yds.) WU 200 Drill 6 x 50 Closed Fists (20 sec. RBI) BIS 2 x 400 (20 sec. RBI) BIS 4 x 100 (15 sec. RBI) CD 100	SWIM: 1:45 BIKE: 2:45 RUN: 2:15 TOTAL: 6:45
Rest Day	Bike: 1:30 EM 3 x 10 OU (3U, 2O) (5 min. RBI) Run: 15 min. ER	Run: 1:00 ER 4 x 6 min. SSR (4 min. RBI) Swim: 1:00 (2,200 m/yds.) WU 300 Drill 6 x 50 Fingertip Drag (20 sec. RBI) PSS 2 x [300-200-100] (15 sec. RBI) KSS 5 x 50 (15 sec. RBI) CD 150	SWIM: 1:45 BIKE: 3:30 RUN: 2:30 TOTAL: 7:45
Rest Day	Run: 1:15 ER 5 x 3 min. FI (3 min. RBI) Swim: 45 min. (1,600 m/yds.) WU 400 Drill 6 x 50 Distance per Stroke (20 sec. RBI) VOS 6 x 100 (20 sec. RBI) KSS 4 x 50 (15 sec. RBI) CD 100	Bike: 1:30 EM 7 x 2 min. PI (2 min. RBI)	SWIM: 1:45 BIKE: 3:30 RUN: 2:30 TOTAL: 7:45

CONTINUES

CONTINUED

TRAINING PLAN 5.4: Advanced Olympic Program

	MONDAY	TUESDAY	WEDNESDAY	THURSDAY
WEEK 5	Rest Day	Swim: 1:00 (2,300 m/yds.) WU 200 Drill 6 x 75 (25 Right Arm/25 Left Arm/ 25 Distance per Stroke) 15 sec. RBI PSS 5 x 300 (20 sec. RBI) KSS 2 x 25 (20 sec. RBI) CD 100 Bike: 1:00 EM 2 x [3 x 3 min. PI] 3 min. RBI/8 min. RBS	Run: 1:15 ER 5 x 3 min. FI (3 min. RBI)	Bike: 1:00 EM (hilly terrain)
WEEK 6	Rest Day	Swim: 1:00 (2,500 m/yds.) WU 200 Drill 6 x 50 Distance per Stroke (20 sec. RBI) PSS 4 x 75 (15 sec. RBI) VOS 15 x 100 (10 sec. RBI) KSS 2 x 50 (10 sec. RBI) CD 100 Bike: 1:00 EM 2 x [3 x 3 min. PI] 3 min. RBI/8 min. RBS	Run: 1:15 ER 5 x 3 min. FI (3 min. RBI)	Bike: 1:00 EM (hilly terrain) Run: 15 min. ER
WEEK 7	Rest Day	Bike: 1:30 EM 3 x 12 OU (4U, 2O) (6 min. RBI)	Run: 1:00 ER 5 x 6 min. SSR (4 min. RBI) Swim: 1:00 (2,500 m/yds.) WU 300 Drill 6 x 75 (25 Right Arm/ 25 Left Arm/ 25 Distance per Stroke) 15 sec. RBI PSS 8 x 50 (15 sec. RBI) LTS 4 x 300 (15 sec. RBI) CD 150	Bike: 1:00 EM (hilly terrain) Run: 15 min. ER

	FRIDAY	SATURDAY	SUNDAY	TOTALS
	Rest Day	Run: 1:00 ER 4 x 10 sec. RS (60 sec. RBI) Swim: 1:00 (2,500 m/yds.) WU 400 Drill 6 x 50 Distance per Stroke (20 sec. RBI) PSS 6 x 50 (15 sec. RBI) VOS 6 x 200 (20 sec. RBI) KSS 4 x 50 (15 sec. RBI) CD 100	Bike: 1:45 EM 5 x 3 min. PI (3 min. RBI) Run: 15 min. ER	SWIM: 1:45 BIKE: 3:45 RUN: 2:30 TOTAL: 8:00
	Rest Day	Swim: 1:00 (2,600 m/yds.) WU 300 Drill 6 x 50 Distance per Stroke (20 sec. PSS 2 x [100- 200-300-200-100] (15 sec. RBI) CD 100 Bike: 2:00 EM 3 x 10 OU (3U, 2O) (5 min. RBI)	Run: 1:00 ER 5 x 6 min. SSR (4 min. RBI)	SWIM: 2:00 BIKE: 4:15 RUN: 2:30 TOTAL: 8:45
	Rest Day	Swim: 1:00 (2,800 m/yds.) WU 300 Drill 6 x 50 Distance per Stroke (20 sec. RBI) PSS 2 x 300 (20 sec. RBI) PSS 3 x 200 (15 sec. RBI) PSS 6 x 100 (10 sec. RBI) KSS 4 x 50 (15 sec. RBI) CD 200 Bike: 1:30 EM 3 x 12 OU (4U, 2O, 4U, 2O, 4U, 2O) (6 min. RBI)	Run: 1:00 ER 4 x 10 sec. RS (60 sec. RBI)	SWIM: 2:00 BIKE: 4:30 RUN: 2:15 TOTAL: 8:45

CONTINUES

CONTINUED

TRAINING PLAN 5.4: Advanced Olympic Program

	MONDAY	TUESDAY	WEDNESDAY	THURSDAY
WEEK 8	Rest Day	Swim: 1:00 (2,800 m/yds.) WU 300 Drill 6 x 75 (25 Right Arm/25 Left Arm/ 25 Distance per Stroke) 15 sec. RBI PSS 6 x 50 (15 sec. RBI) BIS 7 x 200 (20 sec. RBI) KSS 4 x 50 (15 sec. RBI) CD 150 **Bike: 1:00 EM** 3 x 10 OU (3U, 2O) (5 min. RBI)	**Run: 45 min. ER** 4 x 2 min. FI (2 min. RBI)	Swim: 45 min. (1,600 m/yds.) WU 400 Drill 6 x 50 Distance per Stroke (20 sec. RBI) VOS 6 x 100 (20 sec. RBI) KSS 4 x 50 (15 sec. RBI) CD 100 **Bike: 45 min.** easy spinning

RBI = Rest between intervals | RBS = Rest between sets | WU = Warm-up | CD = Cooldown

FRIDAY	SATURDAY	SUNDAY	TOTALS
Rest Day	**Bike: 30 min. EM** 1 x 10 min. T 3 x 1 min. PI (1 min. RBI) **Run: 15 min. ER** 4 x 10 RS (60 sec. RBI)	**OLYMPIC-DISTANCE RACE**	SWIM: 1:45 BIKE: 2:15 RUN: 1:00 RACE TOTAL: 5:00 + RACE

TRAINING PLAN 5.5: Transition Program

	MONDAY	TUESDAY	WEDNESDAY	THURSDAY
WEEK 1	Rest Day	Bike: 1:00 EM	Run: 30 min. ER 4 x 10 sec. RS (60 sec. RBI)	Rest Day
WEEK 2	Run: 30 min. ER 4 x 10 sec. RS (60 sec. RBI)	Bike: 1:00 EM 2 x 10 min. T (5 min. RBI)	Rest Day	Run: 30 min. ER 4 x 10 sec. RS (60 sec. RBI)
WEEK 3	Bike: 1:00 EM 2 x 10 min. T (5 min. RBI)	Run: 30 min. ER 4 x 10 sec. RS (60 sec. RBI)	Swim: 30 min. (1,300 m/yds.) WU 150 Drill 6 x 50 Fingertip Drag (20 sec. RBI) PSS 4 x 200 (15 sec. RBI) KSS 2 x 25 (15 sec. RBI) CD 100	Rest Day
WEEK 4	Rest Day	Run: 30 min. ER 4 x 10 sec. RS (60 sec. RBI)	Swim: 30 min. (1,400 m/yds.) WU 150 Drill 4 x 75 (25 Right Arm/ 25 Left Arm/ 25 Distance per Stroke) 15 sec. RBI BIS 4 x 200 (20 sec. RBI) KSS 2 x 25 (20 sec. RBI) CD 100	Bike: 1:15 EM 2 x 15 min. T (5 min. RBI)

RBI = Rest between intervals | WU = Warm-up | CD = Cooldown

	FRIDAY	SATURDAY	SUNDAY	TOTALS
	Swim: 30 min. (1,200 m/yd.) WU 200 Drill 8 x 50 (alternate 50s, 1 x Right Arm/ 1 x Left Arm) 15 RBI SPS 3 x 100 (10 sec. RBI) KSS 4 x 50 (15 sec. RBI) CD 100	Bike: 1:30 EM	Rest Day	SWIM: 0:30 BIKE: 2:30 RUN: 0:30 TOTAL: 3:30
	Swim: 30 min. (1,400 m/yd.) WU 100 Drill 4 x 75 (25 Catch-up/ 25 Fingertip Drag/ 25 free swim) (15 sec. RBI) BIS 100-200-300-200-100 (15 sec. RBI) CD 100	Bike: 1:30 EM	Rest Day	SWIM: 0:30 BIKE: 2:30 RUN: 1:00 TOTAL: 4:00
	Rest Day	Bike: 1:30 EM (or group ride)	Swim: 30 min. (1,300 m/yds.) WU 150 Drill 6 x 50 Closed Fists (20 sec. RBI) PSS 5 x 100 (15 sec. RBI) VOS 4 x 50 (15 sec. RBI) KSS 2 x 25 (15 sec. RBI) CD 100	SWIM: 1:00 BIKE: 2:30 RUN: 1:00 TOTAL: 4:30
	Rest Day	Bike: 1:30 EM (or group ride) Run: 15 min. ER	Run: 30 min. ER 4 x 10 sec. RS (60 sec. RBI)	SWIM: 1:00 BIKE: 2:45 RUN: 1:15 TOTAL: 5:00

6

RACING TO YOUR STRENGTHS

In endurance sports, we sometimes talk about an athlete's preparedness in terms of "matches." Everyone starts a competition with a finite number of matches, and every time you dig deep or put forth a big effort, you've burned a match. When they're all gone, so is your ability to surge, accelerate, or perhaps even stay on your goal pace. As a time-crunched athlete, it's easy to assume that you're at a disadvantage when you step up to the start line with athletes who train twice as much as you do. But what we've found through years of training time-crunched athletes is that even though you start competitions with fewer matches than athletes who have a deeper aerobic base, the matches you do have burn just as hot as everyone else's. In other words, you must be careful about how you use your big efforts because you can't afford to waste them, but when you do decide to unleash a big move, there's no reason to hesitate or hold back. You have what it takes to be competitive, with yourself and with your competition. The sprint and Olympic programs in this book aren't designed merely to get you through your events; they are designed to provide the strength, power, and endurance to enable you to *race* your next triathlon.

In order to be competitive in your next event, and to beat athletes who will be starting with more matches, you will need to race intelligently. As with other areas in this book, I'm not going to cover the absolute basics of triathlon strategy. I'm assuming you know what to bring to the race and how to organize your transition area, and that you're familiar with the rules of triathlon. And race-day nutrition is covered in Chapter 4. Since this book is not a beginner text, I'd rather spend this chapter talking about tips and strategies for making your race faster, not rehashing basic information you already know.

The tips and strategies in this chapter can be beneficial to all triathletes, and are of special importance for time-crunched triathletes because on race day your attention to detail can significantly elevate your performance. Athletes who use high-volume, high-frequency training programs can afford to be sloppy. They can waste energy without paying a heavy price because they have such a deep aerobic base to pull from. You're going to be operating at a higher proportion of your capacity and you have less room for error, so it's important to optimize as many elements of your race strategy as possible.

Your Race-Day Warm-up

A structured and comprehensive warm-up prior to competition is essential for achieving optimal performance. The morning of your race, your body has all the necessary tools for you to have a great race, but you need to get your energy systems, muscles, and joints moving and primed for action. The first few minutes of an open-water swim are hectic, and that's not the time to expect your body to go from rest to race pace at the sound of a starting pistol.

A good warm-up is long enough to activate all the energy systems necessary for endurance performance (aerobic, glycolytic, and VO_2max), but not so long that it leads to a significant increase in core temperature, costs you enough fluids to become dehydrated, or expends so much energy that you're burning matches before the race even starts. It's that last point, energy expenditure, that prevents athletes from accomplishing a truly effective warm-up—though perhaps not in the way you expect. The *fear* of expending too much energy during a warm-up often keeps athletes from pushing themselves hard enough to activate the VO_2max system. In fact, though, the extra energy you expend during the warm-up increases the workload you're able to maintain throughout the race. Without a good warm-up, your subsequent efforts in the race will not access or utilize your full capacity. In essence, the energy you burn during the warm-up is not as costly as the amount of performance capacity you lose by not warming up.

Race-Day Warm-up, 25 Minutes

10 minutes bike:

    4 minutes easy spinning

    3 minutes at SteadyState intensity

    Move directly into 2 × 1-minute PowerIntervals separated by 1 minute of easy spinning

15 minutes swim:

    5 minutes easy

    2 × 2 minutes at race effort (1 minute RBI), 2 minutes easy, and then 4 × 30-second accelerations that build from moderate pace to max effort (30 seconds RBI)

Then get to the start!

The swim warm-up is the more important piece. A bike warm-up can be cursory, in that it's only really meant to check your gear to make sure that everything is working smoothly. On the other hand, if you do have the opportunity to spend 10 more minutes warming up, then a short ride or run for about 10 minutes prior to your swim warm-up is a great idea; it'll get your systems humming without tiring your swimming muscles.

If you can't get your bike out of transition at that time, a short easy run with about 4 RunningStrides would be a good substitute for the bike.

Additional Pre-Race Tips

Get to the race early, with ample time to check in, set up your spot in transition, warm up, and get to the swim start on time. This usually will mean arriving at the race site two hours before the race begins. Often race directors will kick you out of transition even if your swim wave doesn't start for 20 to 30 minutes. Check the posted information beforehand so you know your particular start time, how far ahead you'll need to be on the beach or pier, and how far the start is from the transition area.

In many lower-key local events, you can rack your bike, get into your wetsuit, and report to the beach within minutes of your wave start. As events become larger, or when events are part of a structured series (like Ironman or Xterra), it's more likely that you will have to rack your bike and report to the beach a lot earlier. It's important to plan ahead for this delay, because it can be anywhere from 10 minutes to an hour or more. At the Ironman 70.3 in New Orleans in 2010, the transition area closed 30 minutes before the first athletes started. Because athletes needed to pass through transition to get to the beach, all 2,000 competitors had to report to the beach at the same time as the folks in the first wave. CTS Coach Patrick Valentine was in the twelfth wave, so he waited 44 minutes to start. The athletes in the twenty-second wave had to wait 88 minutes between the time they reported to the beach and when they started.

At the Memphis in May Olympic-distance triathlon, competitors don't start in waves at all. Because of the nature of the swim course, athletes start one at a time every three seconds. Some triathlons start from a beach; in this case, you'll be able to get into the water ahead of time to do a little swimming. Other races start with a leap off a pier, and you're rarely able to get in the water ahead of time at these events. The point is, the starting environment and procedures vary from race to race, and your choices in this crucial period can enhance or undermine your performance.

MANAGE CORE TEMPERATURE

Your warm-up is designed to increase circulation and activate energy systems, and core temperature will increase as a result. A small rise in core temperature is expected and normal, and you want to start the race sweating lightly. The delay period between the end of your warm-up and the start of the swim can significantly impact your core temperature. If it's hot out and you're going to be sitting in the sun on the beach for 30 minutes, keep your wetsuit off your upper body and make sure you take some fluids with you—even if it means you're going to leave a water bottle behind. If there's a greater chance that you're going to cool down significantly while you wait to start the race (getting sweaty and then sitting around in a slight breeze can really bring your core temperature down), take a sweatshirt, jacket, towel, or blanket with you to the starting area. Ideally, you'll be able to hand this garment to a friend or relative before the start, but if you're going to the race alone, take an old sweatshirt you don't mind losing.

Staying warm before starting your swim is very important, especially if the water is cold. When you're cold, you're slow. Your body starts directing blood to your organs and core rather than your extremities, but that's where your muscles are, and as the starting gun goes off, that's where you want plenty of oxygenated blood to be! When you start cold, you must dig deeper to deliver the energy necessary to surge through the first few minutes of the swim. That means burning more matches than necessary, and you'll pay for that effort later.

Similarly, if it's hot and you're going to be waiting for a while, you don't want your core temperature to rise out of control. When you're too hot, you're also slow. There's plenty of blood circulating to the muscles and skin, but a high core temperature leads to lethargy and diminished motivation. When you're really hot, it's more difficult to push yourself to go harder, partly because you know it's just going to make you even hotter.

Either of these conditions—too hot or too cold—can hurt your race performance, no matter how great your fitness and preparations are. Being too cold is typically more of a problem, because when you're too hot, getting in the water to start the race will typically alleviate the elevated core temperature problem (at least for a few minutes before your effort level brings core temp back up). But being cold and then getting into cold water—even when wearing a wetsuit—can sap your energy and motivation. Not only will that slow your swim, but it can take a long time after that to finally get rid of the chill.

MANAGE NUTRITION AND HYDRATION

If you're going to be on the beach for more than 20 minutes before your start, you're going to want to bring some fluids. Take a sports drink or water, based on your preferences, and take a full bottle (anticipating you could be there for up to an hour). From the standpoint of being prepared for the unexpected, I recommend that athletes take at least one GU Gel or a package of GU Chomps to the starting area, along with a bottle. For local events, where you know you're going to walk onto the beach and start within a few minutes, you may not need any food or fluids (and you may not need to worry about considerations mentioned in the previous section, either), but in larger events it's good to plan ahead. You may not eat the food or drink the fluid, depending on the conditions, but if you need it and don't have it, your performance will start diminishing with every additional minute you're stuck on that beach. As I see it, it's worth having the food and fluids that could save your race, even if it means potentially donating a gel and a water bottle to the race staff or spectators.

The Race

THE SWIM

Lining up for the swim start is a strategic component of your race. Instead of starting a few rows behind the leaders and directly in line with the first buoy, line up in the front a bit to the side of the group. Think about your positioning as the hypotenuse of a triangle. It is easier to swim directly to the buoy than to swim over and around slower swimmers who are lined up directly in line with the buoy. Sure, you'll be swimming a very slightly greater distance, but you will also be swimming faster. In the water, there's a significant draft directly behind a swimmer, and there's also a good draft when you swim on someone's hip. As the straight line of athletes becomes an arrow pointing toward the first buoy, you can ride this draft and start moving diagonally forward and toward the center of the pack. Draft on the hip of the person in front of you instead of on their feet to cut down the distance from you to the first turn buoy. You will still reap the rewards of drafting, and you'll largely avoid the clustered masses in the center.

When the gun goes off, it's time to haul ass. Go out hard and fast and hang on. There is merit to going out very hard at the start of the swim: You can get into a pack that is going slightly faster than you could sustain on your own. Remember, you've done plenty of threshold and VO_2max work in training, and this is the time when you want to burn a match and tap into that fitness. Starting hard can help you get out of the chaos of the start sooner, and can put you in a fast group. And if it turns out you get dropped out of that group, your fast start means there are still reasonably fast people behind you, and you can settle into a more sustainable pace and still draft off of those people. Once you are in position with a pack, draft by maintaining a position where your outstretched arm is only a few inches from the feet of the person ahead of you. Drafting is something you can practice during workouts; find someone who swims at a 100 meter pace 5 seconds faster than you (perhaps someone who is in one lane ahead of you in a masters class) and swim on that person's toes. They will pull you to a faster swim and you will conserve energy! You know you are in the right spot if you come out of the draft to try to pass the swimmer in front of you and find that you are losing the group. Tuck back in on their toes and hold on.

If you're feeling like you want to get around someone during the swim, give it some thought before you act. What are you going to gain? If there's a gap opening in front of the swimmer ahead of you and getting in front of him or her will keep you with a good group or within a line of swimmers, then it may be a good idea. But you also have to consider whether you have the speed to accelerate around this swimmer, get across the gap, and settle back into a sustainable pace before you fatigue and start floundering. One of the worst scenarios is to accelerate all the way past a swimmer and then tire to the point where that athlete comes by you again, but this time you're too tired to even hold on to his or her draft. The effort to go forward can send you backward. Of course, if you're behind someone who started way too fast and he or she is struggling and going backward, then you need to figure that out quickly and get around that person before the gap to the next person becomes too large. But if there's little to be gained by passing someone, it's sometimes better to stay in the draft and conserve energy. Think of it this way: You could expend a ton of energy in the water to hit the beach 1 minute sooner, or save that energy and use it to go 3 minutes faster on the run.

When you get to about 150 meters from the beach, start picking up your speed to surge into the exit from the water. If you haven't been focusing on your kick, now's the time to start. Bring your kick up to a 3- or 5-beat kick per stroke. This helps to engage more muscles in the lower body, which will be useful when you go from prone to standing, and unweighted to weight-bearing. And if you're going to be kicking faster and more forcefully (originating from your core and hips, not your knees), you might as well pull more water with your arms too. Instead of churning your arms faster, focus on extending your stroke. Get your elbow out of the water on the recovery and reach forward farther to catch more water during your stroke. As the swim progresses, athletes tend to shorten their stroke; this is a good time to proactively extend it again. This is the same technique you should use when accelerating around another swimmer; increase the rate and force of your kick, and catch more water by extending your stroke.

As soon as you can touch the bottom with your hands, stand up and start running out of the water as you remove your cap and goggles. As soon as you exit the water, you should start removing your wetsuit. To facilitate this, apply a lubricant to the neck, arms, and legs of the wetsuit before competition. As you are running toward T1, undo the Velcro at the neck, grab the cord attached to the zipper, and unzip your wetsuit fully. Continue running and pull your wetsuit off your upper arms, then off each individual lower arm (this should be easy with the lubricant on them). Run with your wetsuit hanging down at your waist until you get to your transition spot. After dumping your cap and goggles, you should pull the wetsuit down from your thighs, and then step out of each leg (once again, lubricant helps a lot).

T1

If, in the weeks leading up to your race, you've practiced your transitions, you should now be reasonably quick and fluid as you get your helmet and glasses on, get any additional gear together, and start walking/running toward the mount line. I recommend lining the opening of your cycling shoes with Aquaphor to make it easier to get your damp foot into a dry shoe; the Aquaphor will also help prevent chafing and blistering from the shoe rubbing against your skin. Next, as much as you want to get into and out of transition as fast as possible, it's a good idea to take a moment to check yourself. If you're frantic, take a few deep breaths and slow down. It will feel like you're wasting valuable time, but when you're frantic everything seems like it's in fast-forward. Proactively calming yourself brings you back to a fast and controlled pace, and you're more likely to get everything right the first time (instead of putting your helmet on backward and sticking your glasses in your eye). An engaged but calm mind makes quicker and more accurate decisions.

THE BIKE

Once you're clipped in and rolling away from transition, don't immediately peg your maximum power output. Even if you're a cyclist-turned-triathlete and you're looking forward to using your experience and accumulated cycling strength to crush the bike leg, remember that everything you do in the first two legs of a triathlon impacts your run performance—and a great run can do you more good than an exceptional ride. Spend the first 2 to 3 minutes of the bike leg gradually bringing your pace and effort level up to race intensity. Accelerate by spinning faster and then shifting into a harder gear, not shifting into a harder gear and then pushing to accelerate against that larger resistance. Many times, the environment of the first mile of the bike leg makes it tempting to spike big power outputs, but you should take pains to avoid doing so.

Getting out of the transition area often means going through a series of corners, short straightaways, and even chicanes. This terrain tempts some racers to sprint out of every turn, brake into the next, and accelerate again. Instead, keep your gearing lower so your cadence is higher, and use this time to get your cycling legs under you without building up a lot of lactate. Soon enough you'll be out on more open terrain and you'll be ready to open the throttle.

Once out on the open area of the course, you want to settle into your pace. The appropriate pace for the bike leg depends on several factors, but generally it will be closer to lactate threshold, or maximum sustainable power, for shorter triathlons (sprint distance) and get progressively slower as the distance gets longer. You should be under threshold for an Olympic-distance bike leg, but not by that much. You can ride in your SteadyState range or the high end of your Tempo range and still have the legs for a great run. For a 70.3 race, you're going to want to stay in your Tempo range when you can and go into your SteadyState range on climbs and through headwinds.

When you come to a hill, keep your cadence up around 85 to 90 and spin up the grade. Resist the urge to stomp your way up the hill with a low cadence, unless the hill will only take 15 to 20 seconds to complete. Instead, shift down so you can keep your cadence up until you summit the hill. Once your speed falls below about 16 mph, you're not getting much of an advantage by staying in your aerodynamic position. At this point on a hill, you're better off putting your hands on the outside of your bars and bringing your head and shoulders up. This will open your chest for easier breathing and open your hip angle for greater climbing power. When your speed really falls on particularly steep sections of climbs, it's OK to stand up in order to keep your speed up. If you can, try to shift into one harder gear before you get out of the saddle. Once you stand, your cadence will fall, but you also have your body weight to help push the pedals. You can maintain your momentum and speed by pushing a bigger gear when out of the saddle. Just remember to shift back into an easier gear once you sit back down. Standing on a climb and pushing a bigger gear can help you stretch out a bit, but be careful not to go too hard or too long out of the saddle. Really hard efforts out of the saddle generate a lot of lactate, and the effort can come back to haunt you on the run.

The nature of the course dictates how and when you use an aero position, and so does the wind. In a headwind, you want to stay in your most streamlined aero position because your speed and the opposing wind create additive resistance. When you're in a tailwind, you're going faster, and air resistance increases as the cube of your speed. That's why it's so much harder to accelerate from 27 mph than to accelerate from 22 mph. So even though the wind is at your back, you want to stay in a streamlined aerodynamic tuck because you're going fast and you have the opportunity to take advantage of aerodynamics for going even faster. The same goes for descents or any other time when your speed is very high. When the wind is all over the place, or you're going through a series of technical turns, there's no benefit to rising up out of your streamlined aero position, but there's no heightened need to stay as streamlined as possible either. In other words, aerodynamic positioning on the bike is a behavior, not a static thing.

Optimizing aerodynamic position on the bike is a matter of balancing three components: drag, power, and comfort. The more you optimize one component, the more you take from the other two. You want the position that allows you to produce the most power with the lowest amount of drag, and that you can sustain for the duration of your ride. That almost always means that your race position is not the most aerodynamic position you can achieve; rather, it's the best you can hold while riding at a high power output. But if you treat aerodynamic positioning as a behavior, you realize that for short periods of time you can adjust your aerodynamic position on the bike to maximize a particular component. When you're ripping downhill with a tailwind, get into the fastest aero position you can. When you start to go up a hill and your speed comes down, focus on power generation by opening up your hip angle a bit, even if it means raising your head and shoulders a bit to a slightly less aerodynamic position. And when you're doing a 70.3 or Ironman triathlon, remember that you have either 56 or 112 miles to ride. A longer bike leg tips the priority to the comfort component of bike position, so you need a less aggressive aero position than when you're racing a sprint- or Olympic-distance event. One more thing about aerodynamic positions: It takes time and distance to accumulate a meaningful benefit from aerodynamics. During a race, it might take 10 minutes of careful attention to your position to gain 15 seconds' advantage, and you can give up all of that by sitting up in a headwind to take a drink. You need to practice as much as possible staying in your aerodynamic position while eating, drinking, and cornering so you minimize how much of your advantage you inadvertently give back.

In terms of aero equipment, I'll cover that on page 236, but for now I need to include this: An aero helmet can be very advantageous compared to a traditional helmet, as long as you are holding your head in proper position. When the tail of the helmet comes up (when you look down instead of forward), it can create more drag instead of reducing it.

If you're having a good race, you're most likely going to be passing people on the bike. Since you're most likely not entering draft-legal International Triathlon Union (ITU) events, you will have to remember your USA Triathlon rules in order to avoid drafting and blocking penalties. As with passing competitors during the swim, you have to evaluate whether it's worth the effort to pass the person ahead of you, and you have to choose the right time to do it. You want to get the pass over and done with quickly and at the lowest energy cost to you. If passing means you have to accelerate and then return to a sustainable pace once you're past the person, then uphills and areas where speeds are low to moderate are good times. Passing when you're going downhill with a tailwind is difficult because it takes a lot of additional power to go even faster (remember the speed cubed aspect of air resistance).

Remember that once your front wheel gets ahead of the front wheel of the rider you're passing, it is incumbent upon the passed rider to drop back. This is typically not an issue when you're rolling up on slower riders and blowing right by them. But when you're in a line of pretty equally matched athletes, you don't have to kill yourself for the entire pass; get in front and hold your pace and the athlete you're passing will have to adjust or risk the drafting penalty.

The situation where you're in a line of pretty equally matched athletes is when you really need to evaluate the value of expending energy to pass. It's kind of like driving in slow traffic (even if you're all racing pretty fast). There's always that impatient driver trying to weave through traffic, and an hour later you and he turn off at the same exit ramp and he gets there all of 10 seconds sooner. It doesn't cost much extra energy when you're just tapping the accelerator, but when your aerobic and glycolytic systems are the engine, you have to decide if being patient is better policy.

Having said that, moving up through turns in a well-matched group can be most advantageous. You make the pass and get back up to speed and everyone stays in line, just in a different order.

Similarly, in long events like a 70.3 race, being patient in the first half of the ride can give you the ability to maintain a higher effort level and higher speed in the second half of the bike leg. If you do this successfully, you may pass very few riders in the beginning of the ride but start streaming by them in the final 15 miles leading to T2.

In the final few miles of the ride, try to keep your cadence up, grab the last of your food and drink about 10 to 15 minutes before T2 (see Chapter 4 for more information on race-day nutrition), and start to envision your T2 procedure. Your power on the bike in the last few miles shouldn't change. You don't need to increase or decrease it, just watch that cadence and keep it around 90. As with the start of the bike leg, you may find that the environment changes significantly as you near T2, going from open roads to tighter turns, and threading through narrow passages between barriers or cones. Although you want to keep your speed up, remember that everyone has to negotiate the same environment and everyone will lose a bit of speed there. Take the opportunity to keep your legs spinning with less tension as you twist and turn your way to T2 and mentally rehearse your dismount and transition to the run, so all you have to do is execute it when you arrive. The more mentally prepared you are, the faster you will be through T2. And remember, quickness in transition is "free" time. Be prepared and be calm, and you'll be quick.

T2

When approaching the dismount line, you will need to undo the straps on your shoes and put your feet on top of them. Ride with your feet on top of the shoes until you are within 10 meters of the dismount line, then stand up and swing one leg over your saddle, bringing your foot to rest behind your other foot (which is still on top of the shoe). Coast in this position until you reach the dismount line, where you will step down and start running with your bike toward your transition spot. Hook your handlebars over the bar, put your running shoes on, and then take your helmet off. As with your cycling shoes, I recommend putting Aquaphor around the opening of your running shoes, as well as in the toe box, as both a lubricant and skin protectant.

THE RUN

Now it's time to race the run! First, though, you need to get out of transition and up to speed. If everything is going right, your nutrition strategy has enabled you to start the run feeling light, as opposed to running with a boulder in your gut. And if you're pacing and cadence strategies on the bike were good, your legs should feel like you've already completed a swim and a bike leg, but not like two chicken legs. Resist the urge to sprint out of T2. Instead, start at a pace that's slightly below your target race pace and spend 3 to 4 minutes getting up to your goal race pace. Patience is a virtue here, because trying to get to race pace too quickly can be very costly in terms of energy. Instead of working too hard to go a little faster early in the run, make that energy available at the end of the run so you can maintain a higher pace for longer. Almost everyone slows down toward the end of the run; the athletes who slow down the least often end up doing the best.

Too many triathletes go out too hard and are left walking at the end of the race. The race is still going on as long as you haven't crossed the finish line. Remember this when you are crushing the hill on the bike and sprinting in the first mile of your run leg. Save enough of your time-crunched fitness to run hard and strong all the way through the finishing chute.

As an experienced triathlete, you probably already have a good idea of your target paces for triathlons of various lengths. But if you're not sure about yours, here's a basic set of run leg pacing strategies you can use as a starting point:

- Sprint triathlon: TempoRun/5K race pace, plus 10 to 15 seconds/mile
- Olympic-distance triathlon: Upper end of SSR/10K pace, plus 15 to 20 seconds/mile
- Ironman 70.3 triathlon: Lower end of SSR/upper end EnduranceRun/ half-marathon pace, plus 30 seconds/mile

If you're running with a heart rate monitor, remember the discussion earlier in the book regarding cardiac drift. By the middle of the run in a triathlon, you'll be at least 45 minutes into your race, if not a few hours, and there's a good chance that the numbers on your monitor are reflecting some amount of cardiac drift. This is likely to be more pronounced during longer races in hotter conditions, and may be less pronounced in cooler conditions and for athletes who are very diligent about hydration. The point is, during the run in a triathlon, your pace and RPE take priority over heart rate in terms of adjusting your effort level. If your heart rate seems a bit high, but your RPE is telling you that you're maintaining race pace at about the right effort level, then keep going. In that scenario, though, it's a good idea to try to consume more fluids if you can tolerate them.

If the effort necessary to maintain your goal pace rises to the point that you know you're not going to be able to sustain that pace all the way to the line, you have to make a decision: Either you slow down now, or you run as far as you can at this pace and just wait to see what happens when you hit the wall. The latter is analogous to people who drive as fast or faster when the gas warning light comes on in the car, figuring they need to cover as much ground as possible before running out of fuel. The difference is that as an athlete you have a chance to add fuel without stopping, so slowing down slightly now is the better decision. Slowing down by 10 seconds per mile can be an entirely different effort level, one that is sustainable for much longer. And if slowing by 10 seconds per mile for a mile allows you to get some fluid and simple sugar on board and into your system, then you might actually be able to get back up to your goal pace before long. The other strategy of maintaining your race pace until the lights go out might make you feel tough initially, but you're more likely to be shuffling your way to the finish line in the end.

CHOOSING A BIKE FOR YOUR NEXT TRIATHLON

ONE OF THE MOST FREQUENT DISCUSSIONS MY COACHES AND I HAVE WITH TRIATH-letes revolves around their choices for cycling equipment. Do you need a triathlon-specific bike? Should you always train on your tri bike? What pieces of equipment are most worthwhile to spend money on? CTS Pro Coach Kirk Nordgren runs the 3D Dynamic Bike Fit Lab in our Colorado Springs training facility, and he's used his experience as a coach and biomechanics expert to develop some answers.

Whether you've just completed your first sprint triathlon or your tenth Ironman, you've just spent about half of your total race time on the bike leg. We know cycling fitness is the most important factor in improving your results on the bike, but there's no doubt that the bike you're riding has a big impact on your performance as well. Besides looking good (and don't underestimate the lengths some triathletes will go to look "right," even in the face of data that say they're actually slower than before), the aerodynamics, comfort, and handling characteristics of a bike can play a significant role in your bike split. But before you run out to drop a few grand on a tri bike, let's go through some of your options.

IF YOU ARE RELATIVELY NEW TO TRIATHLON AND HAVE BEEN RACING PRIMARILY SPRINTS

Unless you literally didn't own a bicycle prior to becoming a triathlete, chances are you have a standard road bike. Obviously this is not true for everyone, but a triathlon-specific bike is most often a second or third addition to an athlete's stable of bikes. So the question often becomes, do you need a triathlon-specific bike for sprint-distance events?

An aerodynamic position on a tri-specific bike can certainly help you in a 20K bike leg, so there's no downside to a sprint triathlete owning or using a tri bike. However, the impact of the dedicated bike won't be as great as it would be in longer events. It's wise to consider your overall lifestyle in your decision. If you want to do some single-sport bike racing, participate in local group rides, or like riding in the mountains, then you would benefit from having a standard road bike in addition to, or instead of, a triathlon-specific bike. You can still gain significant aerodynamic advantages with an aero helmet and clip-on bars, and your position on the road bike can be a hybrid of aero and road positioning (higher and more forward saddle position than a single-sport road rider, but not as far forward as on a tri-specific bike).

You don't want to put yourself in an extreme triathlon-specific position on a standard road bike, however. A road bike works well for climbing, descending, and flat terrain; provides multiple hand positions for variety; and handles well in technical situations. But it's designed to do all that with the assumption that your weight and center of gravity will be in a relatively small range of positions. When you confound the geometry of the bike by trying to achieve a position equal to one you can achieve on a

CONTINUES

CONTINUED

triathlon-specific bike, the handling characteristics and stability can be seriously compromised. After all, tri bikes are designed to accommodate more aggressive and sport-specific aerodynamic positions with comfort and stability.

IF YOU ARE DOING OLYMPIC-DISTANCE RACES AND CONSIDERING GOING LONGER IN THE FUTURE

You have options. You don't necessarily need to change your bike selection right now. You can still perform well in an Olympic-distance triathlon with clip-on aerobars and some adjustments to your saddle position. Because of the longer bike leg, however, it's worthwhile to have your aero position evaluated and optimized with a triathlon-specific bike fit. You want to make sure the reach to your clip-ons is not so long that it sacrifices long-term comfort or makes you vulnerable to back injuries.

Once an athlete has completed about a half-dozen Olympic-distance races and has committed to sticking with triathlon for a long while, it's not uncommon to make the jump to a tri-specific bike. With a 40K bike leg, the impact of aerodynamic equipment—including wheels, helmet, and bike frame design—can be quite pronounced. Of course, so can the cost. When you make the investment in a tri bike, it's a good idea to invest also in a triathlon-specific bike fit. Or, if you want to go all the way, book a session in the wind tunnel with an experienced coach trained in wind-tunnel bike fits. Great equipment can make you faster, but the optimal position on top of great equipment allows you to get the full value out of your purchase.

Note that ITU racers and professional Olympic-distance triathletes who race in draft-legal races do use "shortie" aerobars on an International Cycling Union (UCI)–approved road bike per race regulations.

IF YOU ARE RACING HALF-IRONMAN TO FULL-IRONMAN-DISTANCE RACES

Invest in a triathlon bike. The idea behind tri bikes is to modify the traditional geometry of a road bike to allow for a more aerodynamic position that is sustainable for the duration of the bike leg. When comparing the 73-degree seat-tube angle in a typical road bike with the 79-degree seat-tube angle in an average tri bike, the saddle position is 10 cm farther forward on the tri bike. This forward position allows a rider's torso to be lowered (aerobars of the bike are lower) without the torso restricting the range of motion of the thigh at the top of the pedal stroke. The rider's upper-body weight is supported more directly by the skeletal system (shoulder angle and elbow angle near 90 degrees). There is sometimes a sacrifice of maximum sustainable power in this forward position, but since the fastest bike leg doesn't necessarily win a triathlon, the loss in power is usually an acceptable trade-off for the increased aerodynamic benefits.

The aerodynamic gains made on a tri bike sound appealing, but it's important to acknowledge that there are a few drawbacks. First off, the aero position, even on a tri bike, is not the most comfortable or natural position for the body. Tri bikes are made for speed; they are not a great choice for taking a spin down to the coffee shop. If you're going to race on a tri bike, but also enjoy group rides or just spending lots of time on your bike, you'll want a road bike as well. But keep in mind that optimum performance on a bike is position-specific. Riding fast on your tri bike means spending time training in that aero position. Handling on a tri bike is also different than on a road bike, with the added body weight over the front wheel, and is further complicated when steering the bike from the aerobars. In addition, many racers find they can't produce adequate power on the aerobars in the later portion of the bike leg or can't maintain their aero position due to comfort issues. They end up riding half the race with hands on the bullhorns, resulting in a less aerodynamic and useful position.

To get the most out of your tri bike on race day, the majority of your triathlon-specific workouts should be completed in your aero position on your race bike (or at least in your race position, if you have a training bike). You don't need to train on race wheels all the time, however, unless you're willing to accept the additional wear and tear on the wheels and tires.

CONTINUES

CONTINUED

Whether it's optimizing your road bike setup for maximal power production, dialing in the aerodynamic position on your tri bike, or using a hybrid combination as a solution, a good fit on the right bike will place you in the position that safely and effectively suits your goals. In summary:

- Identify where you fit on the spectrum as a triathlete.
- Decide which bike option works best for you and your goals.
- Get a bike fit.
- Train in your race position as much as possible.

7

STEPPING UP
TO 70.3

In 2006, USA Triathlon (USAT) commissioned a survey to investigate the demographics, training habits, and ambitions of its members. Among many interesting insights, the survey results indicated that within five years of an athlete's first triathlon, more than half (52 percent) had completed a half-Ironman-distance race. By far, the most popular events remained sprint and Olympic-distance events, partly because the biggest factors influencing choice of races are proximity and time of year. Seventy-eight percent of respondents had participated in a sprint-distance event in the past 12 months, 58 percent had competed in an Olympic-distance event, 39 percent in a half-Iron event, and 17 percent in an Ironman-distance race.

A more recent review of our CTS athletes competing in triathlons reveals a similar trend. Sprint and Olympic-distance events make up the bulk of the races our athletes compete in, both because they are used as training races in preparation for longer events and because they are easier for a time-crunched athlete to fit into his or her busy schedule when holding down a full-time career and supporting a family. However, we also see the same trend that USAT's survey found in terms of experience and longer events. Within a handful of years, many triathletes are drawn to the half- and full-Ironman events.

I've included this chapter and this 70.3 training program because I know there are athletes who have the experience and the desire to train for a half-Ironman race on limited time. My coaches and I have successfully used this program to prepare time-crunched triathletes for 70.3 races. It stretches the limits of time-crunched training, but the whole point of creating these programs was to give motivated but time-limited athletes the opportunities to participate and compete in the sports they love. Some events are outside the scope of what you can realistically expect to be prepared for; I hope I have been quite clear that the Time-Crunched Triathlete Programs are not designed to prepare you for an Ironman event. But a half-Ironman race is well within your grasp.

Ironman Experience Is Beneficial, but Not Required

When it comes to time-crunched triathletes and half-Ironman races, athletes tend to fall into two categories: the Haves and the Have-Nots. The Haves have completed at least one Ironman race, and sometimes several Ironman races, perhaps even the world championships in Kona, Hawaii. The Have-Nots have not yet attempted an Ironman-distance race. Whether you are a Have or a Have-Not, you can race a successful 70.3 triathlon. How you get there, though, may vary, as you'll see here.

THE HAVES

John is a Have. He has been a triathlete for seven years, after being drawn into the sport by a coworker who thought it might help the account executive lose weight and regain the energy that had waned over the years. In the first year, he entered three sprint triathlons, none more than an hour from his home in Philadelphia. The following year, he entered a few more races, including one Olympic-distance race. In his fourth year as a triathlete he raced his first half-Ironman event (he raced two that year), having already decided that he wanted to compete in an Ironman race the following year. The half-Ironman races required some travel, and his wife and two children, four and seven years old, went along to cheer him on. John's preparation for his first Ironman consumed a great deal of time; he was training 12 to 16 times each week, including masters swim sessions in the morning, rides and runs at lunch, sometimes longer rides or runs after work. And his weekends were packed, between attending soccer and baseball games with his seven-year-old, trips to the zoo and the playground, birthday parties, and of course training.

John's commitment paid off and he performed well in his first Ironman. It was the hardest physical challenge of his life, he said, but he swam, rode, ran, and finished within 10 minutes of his goal time. Not bad for a first-timer with only two half-Iron-distance races under his belt. But his commitment to training had come at a cost. Although he was very good at making time for his family and keeping up with his responsibilities at work, he constantly felt as if he was stretched very thin. Soon after completing his Ironman race, he and his wife went out for a nice dinner (something they hadn't done together in quite a while) and talked about the future of his racing career. It wasn't his wife who suggested that he back off on his training time; it was he who felt it was time to focus more on spending time with his family. Career opportunities also impacted his decision; there was a senior-level management position opening up at his office, and in order to increase his chances of getting the promotion, he decided he needed to focus more of his energy on excelling in his career.

John's wife encouraged him to continue training and competing, if not in Ironman events, then in shorter races. She realized how much he enjoyed training and competing, how being an athlete had improved his demeanor, his health, and even his self-image. The next conversation he had was with his coach, who realized he was a great candidate for the Time-Crunched Triathlete Program. They sketched out a plan that focused on Olympic-distance races, using sprint races and local 10K running races as training events. In the season following his Ironman race, John concentrated on building the speed necessary to be competitive in local and regional sprint and Olympic-distance triathlons, and did so on a five-workouts-per-week training program. It worked very well, and he enjoyed improved performances in all aspects of his life: He was more present in his children's lives, got the promotion he was seeking at work, and went out on more dates with his wife. And he had a blast racing.

But the itch to return to longer triathlons resurfaced, as it does with many triathletes, and he started talking with his coach about getting back into condition for a half- or full-Iron-distance race. John and his coach had long conversations about what he was looking to get out of being a triathlete, what he was willing to sacrifice for his athletic ambitions, and what he was hoping to achieve, both in and out of triathlon. As much as he loved the sense of accomplishment he felt when he crossed the finish line of his first Ironman, he decided that the time and effort required to race another one was more than he was ready to commit to, at least that year. But he wanted to push beyond the local and regional sprint and Olympic-distance triathlons as well; he was looking to train for an event more substantial than a 2-hour triathlon. He decided that a half-Ironman race was a challenge great enough to keep him excited. As I will cover in the coming pages, his coach was frank with him about the realities of using the Time-Crunched Training Program to prepare for a half-Ironman event. John accepted the fact that he may not have the endurance and speed to set a new personal record (PR) for the 70.3 distance (per the terms and conditions outlined in Chapter 2), but reveled in the challenge presented by the workouts and the race itself.

As they had for his previous 70.3 events and his Ironman race, John's family traveled with him to his half-Iron race. They actually used the event as the kickoff to a family vacation; the race was on a Sunday and the family spent the following week at the beach (John rode his bike once, went for two runs, and swam in the ocean with his kids). He performed well, finishing in 5:37:32, and even though he wasn't as fast as he'd been when he trained with twice as many weekly workouts, he paced himself well and finished strong. It was exactly the experience he had hoped it would be: challenging, substantial, valuable, and enjoyable.

There are a lot of athletes out there like John, men and women who have completed at least one Ironman and now have other priorities that have put the training time and commitment necessary for Ironman triathlons out of reach. There is no shame in refocusing your attention on shorter races, and doing so is not tantamount to taking a step backward. Changing the focus of your training to races that are more appropriate for the overall demands on your time is a smart choice; it allows you to continue challenging yourself and keep competing, and perhaps even more important, keeps you engaged in the positive and supportive triathlon community.

THE HAVE-NOTS

On the other end of the spectrum are the Have-Nots, and there are far more Have-Nots than Haves. According to USAT's 2006 survey, only one in six triathletes had competed in an Ironman-distance race within the previous 12 months, but the data also showed a constant stream of athletes stepping up to complete their first Ironman event. Along the way, as we have found, 70.3 events are almost always included in an athlete's preparation for the big one, and for many triathletes it's their first foray into a competition that can last anywhere from four to seven hours.

Ashley started racing triathlons only three years ago, and like John she started with a few sprint events near her home in Austin. It didn't take long for her to fall in love with the sport, which welcomed her eagerly. Ashley's enthusiasm for the sport, though, wasn't fueled so much by her competitive drive as by the camaraderie she experienced as a member of her local triathlon club. By day she worked at a downtown software company, and although her coworkers were nice people, she quickly discovered that her active lifestyle was an anomaly among her colleagues. As so many endurance athletes experience, her accounts of weekend runs and long rides drew surprise and astonishment from those around her; some even seemed to think it was bizarre that she would voluntarily run 10 miles at a time. In triathlon she found a community of like-minded individuals, people who reveled in the challenge of strenuous exercise.

In her first two years as a triathlete, the concept of attempting a half-Ironman or an Ironman triathlon never crossed Ashley's mind. Sprint events and the occasional Olympic-distance triathlon were fun, and she looked forward to swapping stories after the race as much as actually crossing the finish line. But as her fitness improved across all disciplines, and especially as she gained more confidence in the water (I've definitely found that apprehension about the 1.2-mile swim leg of a 70.3 event has more impact in keeping athletes from attempting their first half-Ironman than any perceived weakness as a cyclist or runner), the challenge of a 70.3 race began to gain appeal.

Ashley's schedule, however, was pretty packed. Her boyfriend, though supportive of her training goals, was not an athlete. Beyond that, Ashley was not going to make more time for training by taking it away from the volunteer work she did with children. And then there was her job, which frequently, yet unpredictably, called for working well into the night or on weekends. As with many triathletes, it wasn't so much the training hours that were the problem, but rather the frequency of the workouts.

Ashley started working with a CTS coach in her second year as a triathlete, and in the fall of that year started talking with her coach about attempting her first 70.3 race the following season. During the winter, life got a little bit more complicated with the addition of a new dog to the household and an illness in the family that required several trips back home and a lot of missed training. In the early spring, her coach put her on a program quite similar to the one in this chapter as she prepared for her first event longer than an Olympic-distance triathlon.

Going into the race, Ashley was excited and a little bit nervous. From the shoreline, the 1.2 mile open-water swim still looked somewhat intimidating, but as soon as the gun went off and she made it through the initial flurry of the swim start, she settled into a great rhythm and swam a pace she knew she could maintain. She later recalled that the swim went by much faster than she thought it would, partly because she was swimming with a pack of athletes. Coming out of T1, she felt remarkably fresh, and noticing that the athletes around her were struggling more with the shift from swimming to cycling, she was thankful for all the swim-bike brick work she had completed during her training.

Although Ashley was a strong cyclist, she used her power meter to pace herself conservatively during the 56 mile cycling leg. She resisted the urge to increase her pace to stay with the people who rode by, but even so, she passed far more athletes than passed her. As the end of the ride approached, she was careful to follow the nutrition advice her coach had given her (which was right in line with the race-day nutrition strategy discussed in Chapter 4). Through T2 she again noticed that she seemed to have more spring in her stride than the competitors around her, and after the first mile decided it was time to let it rip. As expected, her running pace wasn't as fast as it had been in her previous Olympic-distance races, but she stayed steady. In fact, her pace in the final 2 miles was only 10 seconds per mile slower than she ran that second mile.

More important than her finishing time (which was 4 minutes faster than her goal time), Ashley crossed the line with a huge smile on her face. The race was a resounding success; she had accomplished the training without sacrificing the other important areas of her life, felt in control and confident from start to finish, and was able to push herself right to the end instead of merely reaching the finish line. After the race she told her coach she would absolutely enter another 70.3 triathlon, and she has, but thus far she has not been enticed by the allure of a full Ironman. Maybe someday, but for right now, the challenge and exhilaration of the half-Ironman are fulfillment enough.

Ashley's path to 70.3 is more common than John's, partly because almost every athlete who ends up competing in an Ironman came up through the shorter events, and at some point faced the jump from Olympic- to 70.3-distance races. For those triathletes who have not completed their first half-Ironman race, the Time-Crunched Triathlete Program in this chapter will get you to the starting line prepared to complete the race and feel strong, confident, and steady throughout. You're not likely to be contending for victory because the training necessary to achieve that level of fitness requires a higher weekly training load than is presented here, but getting your first 70.3 race under your belt is a necessary step toward either winning at this distance or using 70.3 races as a stepping-stone to future Ironman events.

Is This the 70.3 Training Plan for You?

If your goal is to complete a half-Ironman triathlon, this program can get you to the starting line prepared to have a great day, but there are some caveats you need to be aware of.

BASE FITNESS

The program at the end of this chapter is not meant to take you from zero fitness to a half-Ironman in eight weeks. Rather it assumes that you are already an active triathlete and that you are in reasonable shape. That means you would be able to enter and complete an Olympic-distance triathlon tomorrow. I'm not saying you would be optimally prepared for a race-winning or personal-best performance tomorrow, but if you had to complete one, you could. If you don't have the conditioning to at least complete the distance of an Olympic event right now, you're not ready to move up to the 70.3 distance in eight weeks. Start with the Olympic-distance training program in Chapter 5, and after you complete your event, take two weeks of active recovery before starting on this half-Ironman program. If the race calendar in your area isn't conducive to that schedule, at least get into the condition necessary to complete an Olympic-distance event before starting this program.

EXPECTATIONS

You're going to have the fitness to complete a 70.3 triathlon, but it's not likely to be the fastest performance you're capable of at this distance. You're making a trade-off between training time and race-day performance, and this program stretches the limits of what's possible with so little training time. The program has worked for many athletes, and I wouldn't bother putting it in a training book if I wasn't 100 percent confident that it is sound and effective. All the same, it is crucial that you accept and internalize the reality of what you're preparing for. With rare exceptions, the people who have been dissatisfied with the results they achieved on this program were people who went through the training and into the event with the notion that they were preparing for a PR or race-winning performance. This plan will prepare you to have a good, strong performance, one you can be proud of and enjoy. If you're looking to win an Ironman 70.3 race, or if you've done the distance before and you're looking to set a new PR, you're going to need a more comprehensive and time-consuming training program than presented here.

On the other hand, if you're a time-crunched Have or Have-Not who's reasonably fit and ready to step up to the Ironman 70.3 distance to give it a whirl, then let's get going!

The Time-Crunched Triathlete Half-Ironman Training Plan

Like the sprint and Olympic-distance training plans in this book, the half-Ironman plan is 8 weeks long. There are two complete rest days each week, making this a 5-days-a-week training schedule, and the majority of the workouts are either swim-bike or bike-run bricks. However, with the increased race distance you're preparing for, it's necessary to increase the duration of the individual training sessions. This is where the half-Ironman program can get tricky, because in some cases it calls for weekday workouts that last a bit more than 2 hours. Depending on your personal and professional schedule, carving out a 2-hour block of time on a weekday might be easier than scheduling two shorter workouts on the same day (the more typical scenario for triathlon programs). On the other hand, a 2-hour block of time for training could be difficult for some busy professionals. See page 213 in Chapter 5 for tips on fitting your workouts into your lifestyle. On the weekends, the workouts reach the 3-hour mark once only. For information and instructions on individual workouts, see Chapter 5.

TRAINING PLAN 7.1: Half-Ironman Program

	MONDAY	TUESDAY	WEDNESDAY	THURSDAY
WEEK 1	Rest Day	**Swim: 45 min. (1,800 m/yds.)** WU 300 Drill 8 x 50 (15 RBI) 2 x [25 Catch-up/25 free, 25 Fingertip Drag/25 free, 25 Closed Fists/25 free, 50 free] SPS 2 x 400 (30 sec. RBI) CD 300 **Run: 30 min. ER** 4 x 10 sec. RS (60 sec. RBI)	**Bike: 1:15 EM** 4 x 8 min. SS (5 min. RBI)	**Run: 45 min. ER** 4 x 10 sec. RS (60 sec. RBI)
WEEK 2	Rest Day	**Swim: 45 min. (2,000 m/yds.)** WU 300 Drill 6 x 50 (15 RBI) 2 x [25 Catch-up/25 free, 25 Fingertip Drag/25 free, 25 Closed Fists/25 free] BIS 5 x 200 (15 sec. RBI) KSS 4 x 75 (15 sec. RBI) CD 100 **Run: 30 min. ER**	**Bike: 1:15 EM** 4 x 8 min. SS (5 min. RBI)	**Run: 45 min. ER** 4 x 10 sec. RS (60 sec. RBI)
WEEK 3	Rest Day	**Swim: 1:00 (2,400 m/yds.)** WU 400 (100 swim, 200 KSS, 200 SPS) Drill 4 x 75 (25 Right Arm/25 Left Arm/ 25 free) (15 sec. RBI) PSS 2 x 600 (30 sec. RBI) SPS 4 x 75 (15 sec. RBI) KSS 2 x 50 (15 sec. RBI) CD 100 **Bike: 1:00 EM**	**Bike: 1:00 EM** 3 x 8 OU (2U, 2O) (5 min. RBI) **Run: 15 min. EM** *Keep transition to less than 5 min.	**Run: 1:00 ER** 5 x 5 min. TR (5 min. RBI)
WEEK 4	Rest Day	**Swim: 1:00 (2,300 m/yds.)** WU 300 Drill 6 x 50 2 x [25 Catch-up/25 free, 25 Fingertip Drag/25 free, 25 Closed Fists/25 free] (15 RBI) PSS 3 x 500 (20 sec. RBI) KSS 100 CD 100 **Bike: 1:00 EM** 3 x 9 OU (2U, 1O) (5 min. RBI)	**Bike: 1:00 EM** **Run: 15 min. ER** *Keep transition to less than 5 min.	**Run: 1:00 ER** 3 x 10 min. SSR (5 min. RBI)

FRIDAY	SATURDAY	SUNDAY	TOTALS
Rest Day	**Swim: 45 min. (1,800 m/yds.)** WU 400 (200 swim, 200 KSS, 200 SPS, 200 swim) Drill 8 x 50 (15 RBI) 2 x [25 Catch-up/25 free, 25 Fingertip Drag/ 25 free, 25 Closed Fists/ 25 free, 50 free] BIS 5 x 100 (15 sec. RBI) SPS 4 x 75 (15 sec. RBI) KSS 2 x 50 (15 sec. RBI) CD 100 **Bike: 1:30 EM** 4 x 8 min. SS (5 min. RBI)	**Run: 45 min. ER** 4 x 5 min. TR (5 min. RBI)	SWIM: 1:30 BIKE: 2:45 RUN: 2:00 TOTAL: 6:15
Rest Day	**Swim: 1:00 (2,200 m/yds.)** WU 200 Drill 4 x 75 (25 Right Arm/25 Left Arm/ 25 free) (15 sec. RBI) PSS 8 x 100 (15 sec. RBI) BIS 2 x 200 (15 sec. RBI) SPS 4 x 75 (15 sec. RBI) KSS 2 x 50 (15 sec. RBI) CD 100 **Bike: 1:45 EM**	**Run: 1:00 ER** 5 x 5 min. TR (5 min. RBI)	SWIM: 1:45 BIKE: 3:00 RUN: 2:15 TOTAL: 7:00
Rest Day	**Swim: 1:15 (2,800 m/yds.)** WU 300 Drill 4 x 75 (25 Right Arm/25 Left Arm/ 25 free) (15 sec. RBI) PSS 6 x 300 (15 sec. RBI) KSS 3 x 100 (10 sec. RBI) CD 100 **Bike: 1:45 EM** 3 x 9 OU (2U, 1O) (5 min. RBI)	**Run: 1:15 ER** 4 x 10 sec. RS (60 sec. RBI)	SWIM: 2:15 BIKE: 3:45 RUN: 2:30 TOTAL: 8:30
Rest Day	**Swim: 1:15 (2,800 m/yds.)** WU 500 (100 swim, 200 KSS, 200 SPS) Drill 6 x 50 (15 RBI) 2 x [25 Catch-up/ 25 free, 25 Fingertip Drag/25 free, 25 Closed Fists/25 free] PSS 3 x 200 (15 sec. RBI) VOS 3 x 100 (15 sec. RBI) PSS 3 x 200 (15 sec. RBI) VOS 3 x 100 (15 sec. RBI) CD 100 **Run: 1:15 ER** NSR (out and back). Run out in 39 min./ back in 36 min.	**Bike: 2:30 EM** 2 x [3 x 3 min. PI] 3 min. RBI/ 8 min. RBS	SWIM: 2:15 BIKE: 4:30 RUN: 2:30 TOTAL: 9:15

CONTINUES

TRAINING PLAN 7.1: Half-Ironman Program

	MONDAY	TUESDAY	WEDNESDAY	THURSDAY
WEEK 5	Rest Day	Swim: 1:00 (2,800 m/yds.) WU 300 Drill 6 x 50 Fingertip Drag (20 sec. RBI) PSS 3 x [300-200-100] (15 sec. RBI) KSS 5 x 50 (15 sec. RBI) CD 150 **Bike 1:00 EM**	**Bike: 1:30 EM** 7 x 2 min. PI (2 min. RBI) **Run: 20 min. ER** *Keep transition to less than 5 min.	**Run: 1:00 ER** 3 x 10 min. SSR (5 min. RBI)
WEEK 6	Rest Day	Swim: 1:00 (2,800 m/yds.) WU 400 Drill 6 x 50 Distance per Stroke (20 sec. RBI) PSS 8 x 50 (15 sec. RBI) VOS 7 x 200 (20 sec. RBI) KSS 4 x 50 (15 sec. RBI) CD 100 **Run 1:00 ER** 5 x 3 min. FI (3 min. RBI)	**Bike: 1:30 EM** **Run: 15 min. ER** *Keep transition to less than 5 min.	**Bike: 1:30 EM**
WEEK 7	Rest Day	Swim: 1:00 (2,800 m/yds.) WU 300 Drill 6 x 50 Distance per Stroke (20 sec. RBI) PSS 6 x 75 (15 sec. RBI) VOS 15 x 100 (10 sec. RBI) CD 150 **Run 1:00 ER** 5 x 3 min. FI (3 min. RBI)	**Bike: 1:30 EM** 1 x 30 T (5 min. RBI)	**Bike: 1:30 EM** **Run: 15 min. ER** *Keep transition to less than 5 min.
WEEK 8	Rest Day	Swim: 1:00 (2,800 m/yds.) WU 300 Drill 6 x 75 (25 Right Arm/ 25 Left Arm/ 25 Distance per Stroke) 15 sec. RBI PSS 3 x 100 (15 sec. RBI) BIS 7 x 200 (20 sec. RBI) KSS 4 x 50 (15 sec. RBI) CD 150 **Bike: 1:00 EM**	**Run: 45 min. ER** 4 x 2 min. FI with 2 min. RBI	**Swim: 45 min.** **(2,000 m/yds.)** WU 400 Drill 6 x 50 Distance per Stroke (20 sec. RBI) VOS 4 x 100 (20 sec. RBI) BIS 3 x 200 (15 sec. RBI) KSS 4 x 50 (15 sec. RBI) CD 100 **Bike:** 45 min. EM

RBI = Rest between intervals | RBS = Rest between sets | WU = Warm-up | CD = Cooldown

FRIDAY	SATURDAY	SUNDAY	TOTALS
Rest Day	**Swim: 1:30 (3,200 m/yds.)** WU 800 (200 swim, 200 KSS, 200 SPS, 200 swim) Drill 8 x 50 (15 RBI) 2 x [25 Catch-up/ 25 free, 25 Fingertip Drag/25 free, 25 Closed Fists/25 free, 50 free] BIS 12 x 100 (15 sec. RBI) SPS 8 x 75 (15 sec. RBI) CD 200 **Run: 1:20 ER** 5 x 3 min. FI (3 min. RBI)	**Bike: 2:45 EM** 2 x [3 x 3 min. PI] 3 min. RBI/ 8 min. RBS	SWIM: 2:15 BIKE: 5:15 RUN: 2:40 TOTAL: 10:10
Rest Day	**Swim: 1:30 (3,500 m/yds.)** WU 600 (200 swim, 200 KSS, 200 SPS) Drill 3 x 100 (15 sec. RBI) [25 Right Arm/ 25 Left Arm/50 free] BIS 4 x 200 (15 sec. RBI) PSS 4 x 200 (10 sec. RBI) SPS 4 x 200 (15 sec. RBI) CD 200 **Run: 1:30 ER** 4 x 10 sec. RS (60 sec. RBI)	**Bike: 2:45 EM** 3 x 15 T (5 min. RBI) **Run:** **15 min. SSR** *Keep transition to less than 5 min.	SWIM: 2:30 BIKE: 5:45 RUN: 3:00 TOTAL: 11:15
Rest Day	**Swim: 1:30 (3,200 m/yds.)** WU 400 Drill 6 x 50 (15 RBI) 2 x [25 Catch-up/ 25 free, 25 Fingertip Drag/25 free, 25 Closed Fists/25 free] BIS 5 x 400 (20 sec. RBI) KSS 4 x 75 (15 sec. RBI) CD 200 choice **Run: 1:00 ER** NSR (out and back). Run out in 39 min./ back in 36 min.	**Bike: 2:00 EM** 1 x 30 T (5 min. RBI)	SWIM: 2:30 BIKE: 5:00 RUN: 2:15 TOTAL: 9:45
Rest Day	**Bike: 30 min. EM** 8 min. EM 5 min. T (3 min. RBI) 6 min. SS (4 min. RBI) 2 x 1 min. PI (1 min. RBI) 6 min. EM **Run (off the Bike): 0:15 EM** 4 x 10 sec. RS (60 sec. RBI) **Swim: 20 min. (1,000 m/yds.)** WU 200 Drill 6 x 50 Distance per Stroke (20 sec. RBI) VOS 6 x 50 (10 sec. RBI) CD 200	**HALF-IRONMAN RACE**	SWIM: 2:05 BIKE: 2:15 RUN: 1:00 TOTAL: 5:20 + Race

8

STRENGTH TRAINING
ON LIMITED TIME

I've been an endurance athlete for more than 40 years, and almost exclusively a cyclist for that time, but all things being equal, I'd probably be in better overall condition at 50 years old if I had been a triathlete as long as I've been a cyclist. The advantage you have over me is that your athletic training involves a wider range of activities and develops muscle strength, endurance, and power throughout the body. In contrast, single-sport cycling is a pretty one-dimensional activity; it's not weight-bearing, it's not significantly impacted by upper-body strength, and the lower body operates in one well-defined and highly repetitive movement. As a triathlete you use your lower body to kick in the water, pedal on the bike, and stride during the run, and each of these activities has a different neuromuscular and muscle-recruitment pattern. During the swim and again on the run, upper-body strength and endurance come into play, and throughout all multisport activities, you depend on core muscles for stability, maintenance of proper body position, and power transfer. As a result, strength training has a much bigger role in triathlon training than it does in single-sport cycling.

However, although strength training can be beneficial to a triathlete, there is the ever-present issue of time. Given the time constraints that make the Time-Crunched Triathlete Program appealing to busy career professionals and working parents, you have to consider whether you have the time to incorporate strength training into your schedule. Again, this becomes a question of specificity. Strength training may improve your performance as a triathlete, but not as much as spending your available time in the water, on the bike, and on your feet performing triathlon-specific workouts. When you divide your limited training time into too many subsets, by running, swimming, cycling, strength training, yoga, Pilates, and so on, you end up doing a great deal of total work. But you fail to accumulate enough focused work in any one area. Dividing your limited time among too many modes of exercise often results in work-loads that are insufficient to lead to significant progress in any of them. This is why I have not written strength training workouts directly into the training programs in Chapters 5 and 7. They are included here as an op-tional supplement for those athletes who have enough time to use them.

But, you might ask, why bother including strength training in this book at all if it's unlikely that you are going to have the time to perform enough strength training to make a positive impact on your performance? Because, as mentioned in Chapter 2, the Time-Crunched Periodization Plan calls for a relatively significant period of less-intense training once you're done with the program. I believe that it is during this recupera-tion/maintenance phase that strength training will enhance your overall health and performance in life.

I've also designed the strength training workouts in this book to be short and simple enough to perform at home without the need for much exercise equipment. So if you can find the time to append a 20-minute strength workout to the end of two training sessions each week, then these strength training workouts can enhance your overall progress as a triathlete.

Strength Training for Performance

Beyond having the necessary time to devote to strength training, it's also important to look at your current strengths and weaknesses to determine whether strength training is actually going to enhance your performance. The athletes who benefit most from the program in this chapter are those who have deficiencies in strength, flexibility, and joint mobility. More than attempting to build additional muscle mass, the exercises in this chapter are designed to enable you to use your muscles effectively through a greater range of motion. That's why you'll notice that most exercises require you to apply force while muscles are in a lengthened position (Medicine Ball Pull-over and Reach-out, Single-Arm/Single-Leg, etc.). Other exercises, like Mountain Climber, work to increase joint mobility by requiring you to perform a movement that is essentially an exaggerated version of the motion a particular joint—in this case the hip—performs during triathlon-specific activities (running and cycling).

In addition to improving the effectiveness of muscles over a larger range of motion, the strength exercises in this program are designed to enhance stability and coordination throughout the body. There is a specific set of exercises that targets the muscles of your torso, but core muscles are activated during almost all of the other movements as well. By using exercises that challenge your upper body, lower body, and torso simultaneously, you're enhancing your ability to smoothly coordinate complex movements. Improved muscular coordination helps to enhance economy of motion, meaning you end up using less energy to travel the same speed and distance.

Another reason that so many of the exercises in this program either target the core specifically or at least use core muscles in the course of the movement is that in triathlon, your torso is the linchpin of your race-day performance. In the water, core muscles are crucial for maintaining a streamlined position in the water and executing an effective and powerful stroke. On the bike they resist twisting to provide a stable platform against which the legs can push. And on the run they are essential for maintaining proper posture and form for maximum speed. With a weak core, you're a less effective swimmer, your hips rock and roll on the bike, and your running stride turns to a shuffle.

The key to enhancing core strength is not more sit-ups, but rather to engage the muscles of the torso in a wide variety of movements and from every conceivable direction. The exercises in this program involve twisting, resisting twisting, flexion, and extension. You'll be engaging your core muscles while standing on one foot and both feet, while lying on your back and your front, while crouching and holding weights over your head. By hitting these muscles in a variety of ways, they will be prepared to support you from one end of your triathlon to the other—and that's crucial because core muscle fatigue often has the greatest impact on a triathlete's running performance. Even if you have the aerobic fitness and energy reserves to crank out a great run, a fatigued core can wreck your day. Your running form deteriorates, your stride shortens to more of a shuffle, your back starts to hurt, and you slow down. In order to race the run, you need to have the core stability to support a strong running stride.

Strength Training for Life

To be perfectly honest with you, I think the best reasons for athletes to incorporate strength training into their lives have little or nothing to do with sport-specific performance. Even if strength training did absolutely nothing to make you a better triathlete, there are still compelling reasons why you should do it. The strength training program described in this chapter promotes full-body strength so you can live an active and healthy life for years to come.

There is a lot of talk these days about metabolism (the energy your body burns on a daily basis through a combination of normal bodily functions, the thermal effect of digesting food, and your activity level and exercise), particularly the notion that metabolism inevitably declines as we get older. This idea has fueled countless late-night infomercials that blame

middle-age weight gain on declining metabolism and tout pills and po-
tions that claim to reverse the effects of aging by boosting said metabolism.
The truth is, the primary reason metabolism declines as we age is that we
tend to be less active as we grow older. When we were younger, we were
more active, so we needed, and therefore carried, more lean muscle mass
on our bodies. That muscle burned calories, not only to maintain itself
but also to power our activities, and as we grew less active we lost some
of this calorie-burning muscle. At the same time, we either maintained
or increased our caloric intake, and hence gained weight.

Triathletes and other adult endurance athletes don't always fit this
model for declining metabolism. In many cases, triathletes between the
ages of 30 and 50 have become *more* active since becoming triathletes
than they were in their teens and twenties. But endurance athletes, especially those who have been involved in their sports for several years or
more, tend to lose muscle mass. It's not that you've become weaker; in
fact, it's because you've grown stronger. Over time, your body has burned
up excess muscle mass and only retained and strengthened the muscle
mass you need to perform at your best. This is part of the reason that you
see older, more experienced endurance athletes who appear somewhat
spindly but are extremely fit and successful. The fact that triathlon training engages and develops muscles throughout the body helps triathletes
maintain a good base of muscle mass (relative to overall weight), especially compared to single-sport endurance athletes like cyclists.

However, for time-crunched athletes who face a reduction in their
training workload, either year-round or in periods between preparing
for races, strength training can be a good way of retaining muscle mass.
The strength training program in this chapter probably won't build a significant amount of muscle on your upper body (endurance athletes are
generally averse to increased upper-body bulk, anyway, as it detracts from
power-to-weight ratio, or PWR), but it provides a balanced approach that
will help you build a good base of strength and keep the lean muscle you
have now.

I believe the benefits of generalized strength training go beyond maintaining or boosting a person's metabolism. I turned 50 years old in 2010, and I have three kids. Anna is in high school, Connor is in elementary school, and Vivian is almost four years old. For me, strength training is an essential part of being the kind of father I want to be for my kids. At least for right now, Anna is an avid equestrian, Connor is into BMX racing and snowboarding, and little Vivian doesn't stand still for more than a few seconds. I don't want to sit in a chair and watch them; I want to be a part of their activities, and that requires not only a lot of energy but also the ability to jump, twist, lift, push, and pull. I'm a devoted cyclist because cycling is the sport I fell in love with as a kid, but I'm a well-rounded athlete because my overall fitness and strength give me the opportunity to be a fully engaged father and still keep up with the demands of my travel and business schedule.

Making Strength Training Work for You

I hate having to travel somewhere just so I can start training. As a cyclist I put on my clothes, grab my bike from the garage or the rack in the office, and I'm training as soon as I roll out the door. There was a time during the early years of CTS when I had pretty much given up on being an athlete at all. One particular winter, I think it was 2001 to 2002, I barely touched my bike for about four months. During that time, I decided I'd follow the "normal" path to fitness for a middle-aged guy: I joined a gym. I quickly realized that the most frustrating part of my entire day was the drive to and from the gym. The whole point of going to the gym was to work out, but between getting there and getting back, I was in the car nearly as long as I worked out. Clearly this was not a good use of limited time, so I got back on my bike and started doing my strength training at home (these days I can do it in the workout space we have at CTS headquarters in Colorado Springs).

To make strength training work for you, it has to address certain principles.

CONVENIENCE AND COST

First off, strength training has to fit into your personal and professional schedule. That's why I believe in at-home strength training as opposed to going to the gym. At the same time, it has to be cost-effective. I don't expect you to spend thousands of dollars on a home gym setup and a menagerie of equipment just so you can work out effectively in your house. With a small investment in a limited amount of equipment (and some creativity), you can achieve all the benefits you're looking for. The only pieces of equipment you need to complete the workouts in this chapter are a medicine ball (although I suggest purchasing a set that includes weights from 6 to 12 pounds) and a dumbbell or kettlebell. These things don't take up much room, and they can be used for a wide range of exercises. Dumbbells and kettlebells (you can buy sets of these as well) are great for chest and shoulder presses; can be used for some pulling exercises like a bent-over row; and can even be used to add resistance to step-ups, lunges, and squats. Medicine balls can be used alone or with a partner for a wide range of dynamic, and even ballistic, exercises.

NOTHING WRONG WITH THE BASICS

Some of the best strength training exercises are the simplest, and there's nothing wrong with continuing to perform some of the basic movements you learned in middle school. Push-ups and pull-ups, for instance, are solid exercises for upper-body strength. A body-weight squat and lunges are good exercises for lower-body strength. You can make these exercises more challenging by adding weight to a squat or lunge, or by putting your feet up on a bench or chair for push-ups. Or you can simply add more repetitions or incorporate more speed into the movement to develop power as well as strength.

BALANCE MATTERS

Because I consider maintaining a healthy and active lifestyle the primary reason for including strength training in your exercise program, I believe a balance component is essential. When you perform movements that challenge your balance, you engage muscles throughout your body. For instance, when you start doing lunges, you may notice you have a hard time keeping your upper body balanced over your legs. As you practice the movement, you will engage muscles in your core and hips and learn to better balance your body in this position. The same is true of overhead lifts. As you press or hold a weight over your head, you will engage muscles from your feet to your fingers to control the weight in space. This whole-body integration is as important as the weight you're able to move, because when you train your body to act as one coordinated unit, you are better able to maintain your balance in increasingly unstable conditions.

Outside the realm of athletics, researchers have examined the impact of strength training on mobility and longevity in elderly populations. Engaging in resistance training consistently throughout our adult years can help us maintain greater bone density as we get older, as well as preserve more lean muscle mass. From a balance perspective, older people who exercise regularly are less likely to fall, are more able to catch themselves when they trip or slip, and suffer fewer or less severe injuries when they do fall down. Breaking a hip, a common injury among elderly men and women, reduces a person's lifespan. Not only does it involve a significant period of recovery, but also people often lose confidence in their stability and further reduce their activity levels. You may be many years away from having to worry about slipping in the kitchen and breaking your hip, but the point is that the positive effects of training—and the negative ramifications of not training—have wide-ranging impacts on the quality of your life, now and in the future.

MOVEMENTS MATTER

When we get to the actual exercises in the strength training program, you'll notice that there are no isolated movements to target your triceps, biceps, or hamstrings. Instead you'll find multijoint exercises that engage large muscle groups, because these are the exercises that prepare you for real-world demands. An exercise like a push-up or an up/down, for example, engages your triceps, but also works muscles in your chest and shoulders at the same time. All of these muscles must work together to complete the movement, just as you rarely use your triceps in isolation. Similarly, you'll be using exercises like step-ups and lunges to work your hamstrings, but these movements also engage muscles throughout your legs, hips, and torso.

You'll also notice that some of the exercises take you out of that standard "feet shoulder-width apart" stance that's so common in strength training movements. I'm not really concerned about what you're capable of lifting or doing while you have both feet planted firmly on the ground, shoulder-width apart. Think about the last time you needed strength or power in an unexpected moment (something or someone was falling and you needed to catch and hold the weight, perhaps). Were you perfectly balanced? My family moved into a new house a few years ago, and we did a lot of the furniture moving ourselves. The old house had a stairwell with a landing in the middle and a 180-degree turn to get down the rest of the stairs. My wife and I were in the process of carrying a dresser down the stairs, and like many before us who have tempted fate by leaving the drawers in while trying to move a dresser, we suddenly found ourselves with a much more ungainly piece of furniture in a tight space. My wife, who was on the upstairs end of the dresser, tried to reach out and close one of the drawers before it marred the wall, but letting go with one hand caused the dresser to shift. That meant it was my turn to get a hand free and try to support more of the dresser's weight before it crashed into the wall. Honestly, at that point I cared more about the walls than the dresser, because the house was sold and I didn't want to have to fix the wall! Together we managed to get the dresser out of the stairwell without damaging it or the walls, and my point in all of this is that it required strength and balance to protect the wall and keep the dresser from crashing down the stairs. We weren't in textbook, stable positions with our feet firmly planted and our knees bent just so. We were both slightly off balance, grappling with a piece of furniture as it was tilting to the side. But because we were both in decent shape from exercises like those in this chapter, we had the strength we needed to get the job done—even when it appeared to be going all wrong—and we didn't injure ourselves in the process.

The movements included in the strength training program in this chapter are the most applicable to real-life situations. You're going to develop strength with flexibility, power when you're extended or reaching, instead of just when your feet are firmly planted and your arms are close to your chest. And as an added benefit to your performance as a triathlete, these exercises are highly effective for improving your range of motion, joint mobility, and stability.

How to Use the Time-Crunched Strength Training Program

Three workouts make up the Time-Crunched Triathlete Strength Training Program. The first is a simple core strength workout, and then there are two full-body routines. If you have the time to complete the core strength workout and one full-body routine together (which takes about 30 minutes) twice a week, I'd recommend integrating this program into the Time-Crunched Triathlete Program as you're preparing for an event or series of events. If you don't have time to fit it in completely with your triathlon-specific workouts, I recommend at least trying to incorporate the core strength portion of this program twice a week. In the periods between preparing for triathlon events, while you're exercising in a less structured or less intense manner, I suggest incorporating the full strength routines two or three times per week.

Variety is an important component of an effective strength training program, because different exercises present specific challenges, even when they target similar muscle groups. For instance, squats and step-ups are both good exercises for developing lower-body strength and power, but squats work both legs at the same time, and step-ups incorporate a balance component because you're lifting your body weight with one leg at a time. Because I want to keep the strength workouts short, and there's little reason to target the same area of the body more than once during each workout, I have created two routines so you can complete a wide variety of exercises each week. You should aim to complete two strength workouts a week while following the structured Time-Crunched Triathlete Program, leaving a full day between them, and I recommend alternating the two full-body routines. That could mean doing Routine 1 on Monday, Routine 2 on Wednesday. Whatever days of the week you choose, the point is to add the strength training onto the end of your workout instead of scheduling strength training on the days you're supposed to be recovering.

Whichever strength routine you're doing, core strength is such a vital aspect of sports performance and an active lifestyle that you should always perform the core routine. As I mentioned before, the core routine and one of the strength routines should take only about 30 minutes to complete.

In terms of how much resistance you should use, the final few repetitions of each exercise should be challenging, but maintaining good form is more important than working to failure. This is especially true when working with medicine balls, dumbbells, and dynamic movements, because failure typically means losing control of the weight or compromising your balance. As you get stronger and need to increase your workload, do so by increasing the resistance (heavier ball or dumbbell, or holding weights during some of the dynamic movements) rather than increasing the number of repetitions or sets you complete.

Just as there is debate about endurance training methods, there are different approaches to strength training. In terms of repetitions and sets, you can move more weight or against more resistance if you reduce the number of repetitions in a set. In other words, I may be able to press 50-pound dumbbells over my head 6 times, but could complete the same movement 12 times if I used 30-pound dumbbells. As you manipulate these two variables (resistance and repetitions), you start to change the impact the exercise will have on your muscles. If you're going for sheer strength gains, doing fewer reps (1 to 6) with very high resistance is generally the way to go. If you're going for muscular endurance and little or no increase in muscle mass, then 15 to 20 reps with relatively light resistance will do the trick. In the middle you get a significant increase in strength and a moderate increase in muscle mass, which is exactly what we're looking for. As a result, you'll be doing sets of 12 repetitions per exercise in the strength routines and 20 repetitions per exercise in the core routine (see Table 8.1).

TABLE 8.1: Time-Crunched Strength Training Program

CORE STRENGTH ROUTINE

Scorpion

Eagle

Russian Twist

Side Plank with Lateral Leg Lift

For each core exercise, complete 20 repetitions. No rest between exercises, but rest 1 minute between Core Routine and the beginning of either Strength Routine 1 or 2.

STRENGTH ROUTINE 1	STRENGTH ROUTINE 2
Single-Leg Squat	Lateral Shuffle
Balancing Single-Arm Row	Medicine Ball Pull-over
Medicine Ball Push-up	Medicine Ball Reach-Out
Medicine Ball Wood Chop	Medicine Ball Good Morning
Up/Down	Mountain Climber
Lateral Lunge	Step-up
For each exercise, complete 12 repetitions. Rest between exercises is 30 seconds. Repeat Core Strength + Strength Routine 1 three times; rest 2 minutes between cycles.	For each exercise, complete 12 repetitions. Rest between exercises is 30 seconds. Repeat Core Strength + Strength Routine 2 three times; rest 2 minutes between cycles.

Exercise Descriptions

CORE STRENGTH ROUTINE

SCORPION

Lying facedown with your arms straight out to your sides (you should look like a T), contract your glutes and lower back to lift your left foot up, then swing your left foot over to the right side of your body, bending your left knee and bringing your foot down until your left heel touches the floor. Try to extend as far as you can, without pain in your back, so your heel touches the ground as close to your right hand as possible. Rotate back to the starting position and repeat with your right foot. A touch to the floor on both sides completes one repetition (see Figures 8.1a, 8.1b, and 8.1c). Be careful not to perform this movement too fast. You're not trying to use momentum to "throw" your foot toward your opposite hand. You want the movement to be steady but controlled.

This movement engages many of the same muscles activated while running. It engages the hip extensors and lower back, not only in the sagittal (front to back) plane, but also in the transverse (rotational) plane.

FIGURE 8.1a

FIGURE 8.1b

FIGURE 8.1c

EAGLE (REVERSE SCORPION)

Lying faceup with your arms straight out to your sides, lift your right leg and, keeping your leg straight, use your abdominal muscles to rotate your right foot over your body and down to the floor on the left side. Your left leg should remain on the ground. Aim to get your right foot as close as you can to your left hand (see Figures 8.2a, 8.2b, and 8.2c). Rotate back to the starting position and repeat with your left leg. A touch to the floor on both sides completes one repetition.

This movement engages many of the same muscles activated while running, primarily the abdominal and hip flexor muscles in the sagittal and transverse planes.

FIGURE 8.2a

FIGURE 8.2b

FIGURE 8.2c

RUSSIAN TWIST

Start by sitting on the floor holding a medicine ball close to your chest, with your legs out in front of you and your knees slightly bent. Keep your back straight and lean back until your upper body is at about a 45-degree angle to the floor. From this position, slowly rotate your torso to the right, extending your arms to tap the medicine ball on the floor, and then rotate to the left side and tap the ball on the floor to complete one repetition (see Figures 8.3a, 8.3b, and 8.3c). Continue without pausing for the full set. Be careful to keep your back straight throughout this exercise; you don't want to hunch your shoulders forward. For a more advanced version of this exercise, lift your feet a few inches off the floor (see Figures 8.3d, 8.3e, and 8.3f).

Russian twist incorporates both the abdominal and lower back muscles in postural and transverse actions. Being strong in these areas will help to improve your form in both swimming and running.

FIGURE 8.3a

FIGURE 8.3d

FIGURE 8.3b

FIGURE 8.3e

FIGURE 8.3c

FIGURE 8.3f

SIDE PLANK WITH LATERAL LEG LIFT

To perform the side plank, start by lying on your side in a straight position from head to toe. Prop yourself up with your elbow and lower arm, so that your upper arm is perpendicular to the ground and your forearm is extending away from your body. Lift your hip off the floor so that your elbow and feet support your body, creating a straight line from head to toe. Place your top arm along your side. In a controlled motion, lift your top leg straight up. Bring your leg back down and repeat without pause until you complete the set (see Figures 8.4a and 8.4b). Support yourself on the other side and repeat the set (see Figures 8.4c and 8.4d). For a more advanced movement you can support your body by placing your hand on the ground instead of using the elbow. Be careful not to accelerate your leg upward too rapidly, as this will lead you to rely on momentum near the top of the movement instead of muscle.

This movement branches out core strengthening from the traditional abdominal and lower back muscle to include the hip joint and its abductors. It also requires some balance. The side plank will work your abdominals, lower back, and balance. The lateral leg lift will work your piriformis and IT band, frequent problem areas for triathletes.

FIGURE 8.4a

FIGURE 8.4b

FIGURE 8.4c

FIGURE 8.4d

STRENGTH ROUTINE 1

SINGLE-LEG SQUAT

Standing on your left leg, with your right leg bent at 90 degrees at the knee and your right foot off the floor, bend first at the hips, then at the knee, as you sit back into a squat. With single-leg squats it is often difficult for athletes to lower their hips as far as they can when performing a two-leg squat, so don't be surprised if you can't get down far enough for your thigh to be parallel to the ground. To keep your balance, move your arms as if running during the movement; as the left knee bends, the right arm comes forward and the left arm stays by your side or slightly to the rear. As the left leg straightens, the right arm moves backward. When you reach the bottom of the movement, drive with your hips and left leg to return to the starting position (see Figures 8.5a and 8.5b). Repeat for the full set, then perform the exercise with the right leg.

As this movement becomes easier, add a slight calf raise at the top of the movement to simulate the push-off in running. For an even bigger challenge, you can complete this exercise on a Bosu ball or a similarly unstable surface.

Single-leg squats simulate the drive phase of the running stride as well as challenging your balance.

FIGURE 8.5a   FIGURE 8.5b

BALANCING SINGLE-ARM ROW

Standing on your left leg with your knee slightly bent and holding a dumbbell (Figures 8.6a and 8.6b) or kettlebell (Figures 8.6c and 8.6d) in your right hand, bend forward at the waist while keeping your back straight, and simultaneously raise your right leg behind to act as a counterbalance. At this point your right arm should hang straight down toward the floor. Pull the weight up to the side of your chest in a slow, controlled motion and then lower it back to the starting position. Repeat for the full set, and then complete the exercise again with your left arm while balanced on your right leg. You may hold on to a stationary object with the left hand to assist your balance, but over time you should aim to complete this exercise balanced entirely on one foot. A more advanced version of this exercise can be completed while standing on an unstable surface like a Bosu ball.

This exercise is a simple one-armed row for your upper body, particularly the posterior portion of the shoulder, making it a good exercise for swimming strength and injury prevention. The body position adds a balance challenge and forces muscles in your hips and core to engage, not only to keep you from falling over, but to constantly correct as you move the dumbbell up and down.

FIGURE 8.6a

FIGURE 8.6b

FIGURE 8.6c

FIGURE 8.6d

MEDICINE BALL PUSH-UP

Move into the standard starting position for a push-up: body straight from shoulders to heels, weight supported on your hands and toes, with your hands a bit wider than shoulder-width apart. Then place a medium-size medicine ball under your right hand so your hand is on the top of the ball. Now your right hand should be even with your left hand (in terms of being in line with your shoulders), though a couple of inches higher off the floor. Keeping your shoulders level, lower your chest toward the floor, stopping when your chest reaches approximately the height of your right hand. Pushing with both sides equally, return to the starting position and continue until you complete the set (see Figures 8.7a and 8.7b). Move the ball to the left hand for the second set. When this becomes easy, switch your hand on the ball between repetitions.

Adding the medicine ball to the regular push-up adds a stabilizing requirement for the shoulder, strengthening the rotator cuff. This exercise is also an asymmetric challenge because you're asking your arms to push equally from two different positions. Both the neural and muscular components of this exercise are important for injury prevention.

FIGURE 8.7a

FIGURE 8.7b

MEDICINE BALL WOOD CHOP

Standing with your feet approximately shoulder-width apart and your knees slightly bent, keep your chest high and hold a medicine ball directly above your head with both hands. In a smooth, controlled motion, bending at the hips, knees, and back, bring the medicine ball across your body and down to the outside of your right foot. Reverse the movement to return the ball to the overhead position and then repeat on the left side to complete one repetition (see Figures 8.8a, 8.8b, and 8.8c). Continue without pause until you have completed the set. In the beginning this movement should be steady and controlled; be careful not to add speed until you have mastered the movement itself.

This is a very dynamic exercise that incorporates nearly every muscle from head to toe and involves movement in the sagittal and transverse planes.

FIGURE 8.8b

FIGURE 8.8a

FIGURE 8.8c

UP/DOWN

Standing with your feet hip-distance apart and arms at your sides, keep your chest high and sit back to lower into a squat, placing your hands to the outsides of your feet. Next jump your feet straight back while supporting your weight on your hands, so you end up in a classic push-up position with your head, hips, and legs in a straight line. Now jump your feet forward using your abdominal muscles to bring your feet to the insides of your hands, and then drive yourself upward to return to the starting position (see Figures 8.9a, 8.9b, and 8.9c). As you begin the drive upward, be careful to lead with your head and chest and drive with your hips and legs. You don't want to drive upward with the hips and legs with your back hunched forward.

Up/downs are another head-to-toe exercise at close to running speed and provide both a muscular and a cardiovascular stimulus.

FIGURE 8.9a

FIGURE 8.9b

FIGURE 8.9c

LATERAL LUNGE

This is one of my favorite exercises for endurance athletes, most of whom are in dire need of lateral stability and strength. Start with your feet together and your hands on your hips. Step to your right with your right foot, keeping your left leg straight and your left foot flat at its starting position. Keeping your right knee behind your right foot, and

FIGURE 8.10a   **FIGURE 8.10b**

FIGURE 8.10c   **FIGURE 8.10d**

your chest high and back straight, drop your hips as you sit into a squat. Aim to go low enough that your right thigh is parallel to the ground. Pause for 1 to 2 seconds, and then drive with your right leg to return to the starting position (see Figures 8.10a and 8.10b). As soon as you return to the starting position, step left with your left leg and repeat the same movement. One repetition of this exercise consists of lunging to both sides.

Beginners may want to step forward and to the side at about a 45-degree angle, as it can be easier to maintain your balance using this method. As you get stronger, gradually shift to stepping directly to the side (Figures 8.10c and 8.10d).

To make this exercise more challenging, you can hold a weight in front of your chest (Figures 8.10e and 8.10f). If you hold it close to your chest, you're mainly adding resistance for your legs. If you hold the weight out in front of your body, you will add an additional challenge to your back and shoulders. When you add a weight, like a medicine ball, make sure you don't roll your shoulders forward and curve your back.

FIGURE 8.10e   **FIGURE 8.10f**

STRENGTH ROUTINE 2

LATERAL SHUFFLE

Starting with your feet about shoulder-width apart and your hands on your hips, sit back into a half-squat position. Leading with your right leg first, quickly shuffle right for 20 yards (or count 15 to 20 footfalls with your leading foot), and then stop and shuffle back to the left without moving from the half squat (see Figures 8.11a–8.11d). Going to your right and then back to the starting position is one repetition. For a more advanced version of this exercise, you can do it slower but with an exercise band or elastic loop around your knees.

This exercise targets the piriformis and gluteus minimus for injury prevention but also challenges your abductors and adductors. Since moving laterally isn't an everyday occurrence for most triathletes, the lateral shuffle will help to improve your overall stability and athleticism.

FIGURE 8.11a   **FIGURE 8.11b**

FIGURE 8.11c   **FIGURE 8.11d**

MEDICINE BALL PULL-OVER

Lie on your back on a bench, holding a medicine ball close to your chest with both hands. The weight of the ball should be moderate; be careful not to use a heavier weight than you can control. Press the ball straight up off your chest, and then lower your hands toward the floor as if you were going to drop the ball behind your head (in other words, "over" your head as opposed to toward your feet). Lower the ball below the level of your head as far as possible without feeling pain in your shoulder or arching your back. Keeping a slight bend in your elbows and moving only at the shoulders, bring the medicine ball to the position directly above your chest to complete one repetition (see Figures 8.12a and 8.12b). Continue without pause to the end of the set.

The medicine ball pull-over works the latissimus dorsi and the small shoulder muscles (the teres complex), all of which are important for swimming and proper shoulder posture.

FIGURE 8.12a

FIGURE 8.12b

MEDICINE BALL REACH-OUT

Lying facedown on a bench, hold a medicine ball directly "above" your head (if you were standing it would be above your head) with both hands. Squeeze your shoulder blades together and extend your arms as far as possible without letting the medicine ball fall toward the ground. Bring the ball back until it lightly touches your head to complete one repetition (see Figures 8.13a and 8.13b). Continue without pause to the end of the set.

The medicine ball reach-out is another exercise that helps to strengthen the shoulder girdle against injury and will also work some of the accessory muscles used in swimming.

FIGURE 8.13a

FIGURE 8.13b

MEDICINE BALL GOOD MORNING

Stand with your feet approximately shoulder-width apart, knees slightly bent, holding a medicine ball behind your head with both hands at the base of your neck (not resting on your neck). Keeping your chest high, your head up, and your back flat, push your hips back and bend forward at the hips. Lower your shoulders until your upper body is parallel to the ground, or stop before that if you can't go any lower without arching your back. Come to a complete stop before returning to a standing position, leading with your head and shoulders (see Figures 8.14a and 8.14b). Continue without pause to the end of the set. Be careful not to let your shoulders slump forward, and keep the movement steady and controlled. Speed is not the objective. You can also perform this exercise with the medicine ball held close to your chest in front of you.

This exercise is another movement that promotes strength in the posterior chain, specifically the lower back and hip extensors, as well as the extensor muscles along the spine, all of which are important in all aspects of triathlon.

FIGURE 8.14a

FIGURE 8.14b

MOUNTAIN CLIMBER

Starting from the classic push-up position, quickly bring your right foot up toward your hands, making sure to angle your knee out so that your foot lands to the outside of your right hand. The foot should just tap the ground before you move it back to the starting position. Immediately bring your left foot up to tap the floor by your left hand. A tap to each side completes one repetition (see Figures 8.15a, 8.15b, and 8.15c). Continue without pause to the end of the set.

This exercise focuses predominantly on the flexion and extension of the hips. By taking the feet to the outside of the hands, however, more of the small stabilizing hip muscles are incorporated to help make hip extension stronger and more stable.

FIGURE 8.15a

FIGURE 8.15b

FIGURE 8.15c

STEP-UP

I particularly like the single-leg nature of this exercise because it develops strength and power that's not only useful in life but also applicable to your triathlon performance. Start by standing facing a bench that's at least knee height. Place your right foot on the bench and, keeping your back straight and chest high, use your hip extensors and leg to step up onto the bench. Bring your left foot even with your right foot, then step down in a controlled manner, leading with your left foot. Bring your right foot down to the floor and then step up with your left foot (see Figures 8.16a–8.16d).

FIGURE 8.16a

FIGURE 8.16b

FIGURE 8.16c

FIGURE 8.16d

CONTINUED

You can make this exercise more challenging by holding weights in your hands at your sides (Figures 8.16e–h). You can add an even greater challenge by holding a weight in front of you; this will bring a greater balance component to the exercise, but it's essential that the weight not be so heavy that it causes your shoulders to roll forward or pitch your upper body forward (Figures 8.16i–l).

FIGURE 8.16e

FIGURE 8.16f

FIGURE 8.16g

FIGURE 8.16h

If you don't have a bench, this exercise can be done on a staircase (step up onto the second step). The only issue with using a staircase is that you have to step a bit forward as you step up as well. This is a minor issue, but just make sure you're able to keep your chest high and back straight throughout the exercise. If you have to lean your upper body forward significantly in order to step up onto the second stair, your staircase may not be well suited to this exercise.

FIGURE 8.16i

FIGURE 8.16j

FIGURE 8.16k

FIGURE 8.16l

Acknowledgments

Chris Carmichael: To my wife, Paige: Our life together is a wonderful and exciting journey, and I am happy we are going "hand in hand" on it together.

To my children, Anna, Connor, and little Vivian: You all are wonderful, sparkling balls of life for Paige and me.

I would like to thank all the people who make up Carmichael Training Systems for your dedication to making my vision a reality. You all are the best. And to the athletes who continue to prove the effectiveness of the program presented in this book, thank you for providing the feedback and results that convinced me this program could help an even wider population of athletes to achieve their goals.

Of course, my thanks to all the athletes whom I have had the pleasure of coaching over many years. I cannot imagine a career more fulfilling than this one.

My mother and father, who were my first and always my best coaches, have my eternal gratitude. The same is true for my brother and sister, who have always been there for me.

Thank you to Ted Costantino and Renee Jardine at VeloPress for supporting this project from beginning to end.

And finally, a very special thank-you to Jim Rutberg, my close friend and colleague. It's hard to believe we've been at this for a decade.

Jim Rutberg: I am fortunate to work with a strong group of coaches and sports scientists at Carmichael Training Systems, and this book would not have come together without their help. Special thanks must be given to Abby Ruby, Lindsay Hyman, Patrick Valentine, Nick White, and Natalie Bojko for enduring my constant phone calls and requests to review materials. I also owe a debt of gratitude to the entire staff of Carmichael Training Systems for your support during the process of writing and editing this book. Thank you to Eric Peterson and Laurie Geisz for graciously participating in the photo shoots for the book. And of course I need to thank all the triathletes who were instrumental in proving that training programs such as the one presented in this book are an effective means to achieving high-performance, sport-specific fitness in limited training time. This book is written for athletes, and its development would not have been possible without the athletes who work with CTS coaches.

Thank you to Chris Carmichael for your guidance, ideas, and constant support during the process of writing this book. It's tremendously rewarding to look back over everything we've produced in the past 10 years, and I appreciate the confidence, friendship, and trust you've shown me for so many years.

Thank you to Ted Costantino and Dave Trendler at VeloPress for your tireless commitment to bringing this work to life and making it available to the athletic community.

And most of all, thank you to my wife, Leslie, for supporting me through the ups and downs of the book-writing process. Oliver and Elliot, I hope you know that coming home and going for walks and bike rides with you guys makes all the long days and nights worth the effort.

PACE RANGES FOR CTS

RUNNING WORKOUTS

TABLE A.1: Pace Ranges for CTS Running Workouts

FT. PACE (MIN./MILE)	ENDURANCERUN			STEADYSTATERUN			TEMPORUN			FARTLEK		
	Lower	Upper	Mid-Range	Lower	Upper	Mid-Range	Lower	Upper	Mid-Range	Lower	Upper	Mid-Range
5:33	8:19	5:42	7:01	5:59	5:39	5:49	5:39	5:26	5:33	5:39	5:06	5:23
5:34	8:21	5:44	7:02	6:00	5:40	5:50	5:40	5:27	5:34	5:40	5:07	5:23
5:35	8:22	5:45	7:03	6:01	5:41	5:51	5:41	5:28	5:35	5:41	5:08	5:24
5:36	8:24	5:46	7:05	6:02	5:42	5:52	5:42	5:29	5:36	5:42	5:09	5:25
5:37	8:25	5:47	7:06	6:03	5:43	5:53	5:43	5:30	5:37	5:43	5:10	5:26
5:38	8:27	5:48	7:07	6:05	5:44	5:54	5:44	5:31	5:38	5:44	5:10	5:27
5:39	8:28	5:49	7:08	6:06	5:45	5:55	5:45	5:32	5:39	5:45	5:11	5:28
5:40	8:30	5:50	7:10	6:07	5:46	5:57	5:46	5:33	5:40	5:46	5:12	5:29
5:41	8:31	5:51	7:11	6:08	5:47	5:58	5:47	5:34	5:41	5:47	5:13	5:30
5:42	8:33	5:52	7:12	6:09	5:48	5:59	5:48	5:35	5:42	5:48	5:14	5:31
5:43	8:34	5:53	7:13	6:10	5:49	6:00	5:49	5:36	5:43	5:49	5:15	5:32
5:44	8:36	5:54	7:15	6:11	5:50	6:01	5:50	5:37	5:44	5:50	5:16	5:33
5:45	8:37	5:55	7:16	6:12	5:51	6:02	5:51	5:38	5:45	5:51	5:17	5:34
5:46	8:39	5:56	7:17	6:13	5:52	6:03	5:52	5:39	5:46	5:52	5:18	5:35
5:47	8:40	5:57	7:18	6:14	5:53	6:04	5:53	5:40	5:47	5:53	5:19	5:36
5:48	8:42	5:58	7:20	6:15	5:54	6:05	5:54	5:41	5:48	5:54	5:20	5:37
5:49	8:43	5:59	7:21	6:16	5:55	6:06	5:55	5:42	5:49	5:55	5:21	5:38
5:50	8:45	6:00	7:22	6:18	5:57	6:07	5:57	5:43	5:50	5:57	5:22	5:39

5:55	8:52	6:05	7:29	6:23	6:02	6:12	6:02	5:47	5:55	6:02	5:26	5:44
6:00	9:00	6:10	7:35	6:28	6:07	6:18	6:07	5:52	6:00	6:07	5:31	5:49
6:05	9:07	6:15	7:41	5:34	6:12	6:23	6:12	5:57	6:05	6:12	5:35	5:54
6:10	9:15	6:21	7:48	5:39	6:17	6:28	6:17	6:02	6:10	6:17	5:40	5:58
6:15	9:22	6:26	7:54	6:45	6:22	6:33	6:22	6:07	6:15	6:22	5:45	6:03
6:20	9:30	6:31	8:00	6:50	6:27	6:39	6:27	6:12	6:20	6:27	5:49	6:08
6:25	9:37	6:36	8:07	6:55	6:32	6:44	6:32	6:17	6:25	6:32	5:54	6:13
6:30	9:45	6:41	8:13	7:01	6:37	6:49	6:37	6:22	6:30	6:37	5:58	6:18
6:35	9:52	6:46	8:19	7:06	6:42	6:54	6:42	6:27	6:35	6:42	6:03	6:23
6:40	10:00	6:52	8:26	7:12	6:48	7:00	6:48	6:32	6:40	6:48	6:08	6:28
6:45	10:07	6:57	8:32	7:17	6:53	7:05	6:53	6:36	6:45	6:53	6:12	6:32
6:50	10:15	7:02	8:38	7:22	6:58	7:10	6:58	6:41	6:50	6:58	6:17	6:37
6:55	10:22	7:07	8:44	7:28	7:03	7:15	7:03	6:46	6:55	7:03	6:21	6:42
7:00	10:30	7:12	8:51	7:33	7:08	7:21	7:08	6:51	7:00	7:08	6:26	6:47
7:05	10:37	7:17	8:57	7:39	7:13	7:26	7:13	6:56	7:05	7:13	6:31	6:52
7:10	10:45	7:22	9:03	7:44	7:18	7:31	7:18	7:01	7:10	7:18	6:35	6:57
7:15	10:52	7:28	9:10	7:49	7:23	7:36	7:23	7:06	7:15	7:23	6:40	7:01
7:20	11:00	7:33	9:16	7:55	7:28	7:42	7:28	7:11	7:20	7:28	6:44	7:06
7:25	11:07	7:38	9:22	8:00	7:33	7:47	7:33	7:16	7:25	7:33	6:49	7:11
7:30	11:15	7:43	9:29	8:06	7:39	7:52	7:39	7:21	7:30	7:39	6:54	7:16
7:35	11:22	7:48	9:35	8:11	7:44	7:57	7:44	7:25	7:35	7:44	6:58	7:21

CONTINUES

CONTINUED

TABLE A.1: Pace Ranges for CTS Running Workouts

FT. PACE (MIN./MILE)	ENDURANCE RUN			STEADY STATE RUN			TEMPO RUN			FARTLEK		
	Lower	Upper	Mid-Range	Lower	Upper	Mid-Range	Lower	Upper	Mid-Range	Lower	Upper	Mid-Range
7:40	11:30	7:53	9:41	8:16	7:49	8:03	7:49	7:30	7:40	7:49	7:03	7:26
7:45	11:37	7:58	9:48	8:22	7:54	8:08	7:54	7:35	7:45	7:54	7:07	7:31
7:50	11:45	8:04	9:54	8:27	7:59	8:13	7:59	7:40	7:50	7:59	7:12	7:35
7:55	11:52	8:09	10:00	8:33	8:04	8:18	8:04	7:45	7:55	8:04	7:17	7:40
8:00	12:00	8:14	10:07	8:38	8:09	8:24	8:09	7:50	8:00	8:09	7:21	7:45
8:05	12:07	8:19	10:13	8:43	8:14	8:29	8:14	7:55	8:05	8:14	7:26	7:50
8:10	12:15	8:24	10:19	8:49	8:19	8:34	8:19	8:00	8:10	8:19	7:30	7:55
8:15	12:22	8:29	10:26	8:54	8:24	8:39	8:24	8:05	8:15	8:24	7:35	8:00
8:20	12:30	8:35	10:32	9:00	8:30	8:45	8:30	8:10	8:20	8:30	7:40	8:05
8:25	12:37	8:40	10:38	9:05	8:35	8:50	8:35	8:14	8:25	8:35	7:44	8:09
8:30	12:45	8:45	10:45	9:10	8:40	8:55	8:40	8:19	8:30	8:40	7:49	8:14
8:35	12:52	8:50	10:51	9:16	8:45	9:00	8:45	8:24	8:35	8:45	7:53	8:19
8:40	13:00	8:55	10:57	9:21	8:50	9:06	8:50	8:29	8:40	8:50	7:58	8:24
8:45	13:07	9:00	11:04	9:27	8:55	9:11	8:55	8:34	8:45	8:55	8:03	8:29
8:50	13:15	9:05	11:10	9:32	9:00	9:16	9:00	8:39	8:50	9:00	8:07	8:34
8:55	13:22	9:11	11:16	9:37	9:05	9:21	9:05	8:44	8:55	9:05	8:12	8:38
9:00	13:30	9:16	11:23	9:43	9:10	9:27	9:10	8:49	9:00	9:10	8:16	8:43

APPENDIX B

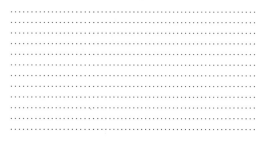

PACE RANGES FOR CTS
SWIMMING
WORKOUTS

TABLE B1: Pace Ranges for CTS Swimming Workouts

400 M TIME	100 M AVG.	BIS PER 100		PSS PER 100		LTS PER 100		VOS PER 100	
		Lower limit	Upper limit	Lower limit	Upper limit	Lower limit	Upper limit	Lower limit	Upper limit
4:30	1:07	1:10	1:21	1:07	1:13	1:03	1:09	0:50	1:02
4:35	1:08	1:11	1:22	1:08	1:14	1:04	1:10	0:51	1:03
4:40	1:10	1:12	1:24	1:10	1:16	1:05	1:12	0:52	1:05
4:45	1:11	1:14	1:25	1:11	1:17	1:06	1:13	0:53	1:06
4:50	1:12	1:15	1:27	1:12	1:19	1:08	1:14	0:54	1:07
4:55	1:13	1:16	1:28	1:13	1:20	1:09	1:15	0:55	1:08
5:00	1:15	1:18	1:30	1:15	1:21	1:10	1:17	0:56	1:09
5:05	1:16	1:19	1:31	1:16	1:23	1:11	1:18	0:57	1:10
5:10	1:17	1:20	1:33	1:17	1:24	1:12	1:19	0:58	1:12
5:15	1:18	1:21	1:34	1:18	1:25	1:14	1:21	0:59	1:13
5:20	1:20	1:23	1:36	1:20	1:27	1:15	1:22	1:00	1:14
5:25	1:21	1:24	1:37	1:21	1:28	1:16	1:23	1:00	1:15
5:30	1:22	1:25	1:39	1:22	1:29	1:17	1:24	1:01	1:16
5:35	1:23	1:27	1:40	1:23	1:31	1:18	1:26	1:02	1:17
5:40	1:25	1:28	1:42	1:25	1:32	1:19	1:27	1:03	1:19
5:45	1:26	1:29	1:43	1:26	1:34	1:21	1:28	1:04	1:20
5:50	1:27	1:31	1:45	1:27	1:35	1:22	1:30	1:05	1:21
5:55	1:28	1:32	1:46	1:28	1:36	1:23	1:31	1:06	1:22

6:00	1:30	1:33	1:48	1:30	:38	1:24	1:32	1:07	1:23
6:05	1:31	1:34	1:49	1:31	:39	1:25	1:33	1:08	1:24
6:10	1:32	1:36	1:51	1:32	1:40	1:26	1:35	1:09	1:26
6:15	1:33	1:37	1:52	1:33	1:42	1:28	1:36	1:10	1:27
6:20	1:35	1:38	1:54	1:35	1:43	1:29	1:37	1:11	1:28
6:25	1:36	1:40	1:55	1:36	1:44	1:30	1:39	1:12	1:29
6:30	1:37	1:41	1:57	1:37	1:46	1:31	1:40	1:13	1:30
6:35	1:38	1:42	1:58	1:38	:47	1:32	1:41	1:14	1:31
6:40	1:40	1:44	2:00	1:40	1:49	1:34	1:43	1:15	1:33
6:45	1:41	1:45	2:01	1:41	1:50	1:35	1:44	1:15	1:34
6:50	1:42	1:46	2:03	1:42	:51	1:36	1:45	1:16	1:35
6:55	1:43	1:47	2:04	1:43	1:53	1:37	1:46	1:17	1:36
7:00	1:45	1:49	2:06	1:45	1:54	1:38	1:48	1:18	1:37
7:05	1:46	1:50	2:07	1:46	1:55	1:39	1:49	1:19	1:38
7:10	1:47	1:51	2:09	1:47	1:57	1:41	1:50	1:20	1:39
7:15	1:48	1:53	2:10	1:48	1:58	1:42	1:52	1:21	1:41
7:20	1:50	1:54	2:12	1:50	1:59	1:43	1:53	1:22	1:42
7:25	1:51	1:55	2:13	1:51	2:01	1:44	1:54	1:23	1:43
7:30	1:52	1:57	2:15	1:52	2:02	1:45	1:55	1:24	1:44
7:35	1:53	1:58	2:16	1:53	2:03	1:46	1:57	1:25	1:45
7:40	1:55	1:59	2:18	1:55	2:05	1:48	1:58	1:26	1:46

CONTINUES

CONTINUED

TABLE B1: Pace Ranges for CTS Swimming Workouts

400 M TIME	100 M AVG.	BIS PER 100		PSS PER 100		LTS PER 100		VOS PER 100	
		Lower limit	Upper limit	Lower limit	Upper limit	Lower limit	Upper limit	Lower limit	Upper limit
7:45	1:56	2:00	2:19	1:56	2:06	1:49	1:59	1:27	1:48
7:50	1:57	2:02	2:21	1:57	2:08	1:50	2:01	1:28	1:49
7:55	1:58	2:03	2:22	1:58	2:09	1:51	2:02	1:29	1:50
8:00	2:00	2:04	2:24	2:00	2:10	1:52	2:03	1:30	1:51
8:05	2:01	2:06	2:25	2:01	2:12	1:53	2:04	1:30	1:52
8:10	2:02	2:07	2:27	2:02	2:13	1:55	2:06	1:31	1:53
8:15	2:03	2:08	2:28	2:03	2:14	1:56	2:07	1:32	1:55
8:20	2:05	2:10	2:30	2:05	2:16	1:57	2:08	1:33	1:56
8:25	2:06	2:11	2:31	2:06	2:17	1:58	2:10	1:34	1:57
8:30	2:07	2:12	2:33	2:07	2:18	1:59	2:11	1:35	1:58
8:35	2:08	2:13	2:34	2:08	2:20	2:01	2:12	1:36	1:59
8:40	2:10	2:15	2:36	2:10	2:21	2:02	2:13	1:37	2:00
8:45	2:11	2:16	2:37	2:11	2:23	2:03	2:15	1:38	2:02
8:50	2:12	2:17	2:39	2:12	2:24	2:04	2:16	1:39	2:03
8:55	2:13	2:19	2:40	2:13	2:25	2:05	2:17	1:40	2:04
9:00	2:15	2:20	2:42	2:15	2:27	2:06	2:19	1:41	2:05
9:05	2:16	2:21	2:43	2:16	2:28	2:08	2:20	1:42	2:06
9:10	2:17	2:23	2:45	2:17	2:29	2:09	2:21	1:43	2:07

9:15	2:18	2:24	2:46	2:18	2:31	2:10	2:22	1:44	2:09
9:20	2:20	2:25	2:48	2:20	2:32	2:11	2:24	1:45	2:10
9:25	2:21	2:26	2:49	2:21	2:33	2:12	2:25	1:45	2:11
9:30	2:22	2:28	2:51	2:22	2:35	2:13	2:26	1:46	2:12
9:35	2:23	2:29	2:52	2:23	2:36	2:15	2:28	1:47	2:13
9:40	2:25	2:30	2:54	2:25	2:38	2:16	2:29	1:48	2:14
9:45	2:26	2:32	2:55	2:26	2:39	2:17	2:30	1:49	2:16
9:50	2:27	2:33	2:57	2:27	2:40	2:18	2:31	1:50	2:17
9:55	2:28	2:34	2:58	2:28	2:42	2:19	2:33	1:51	2:18
10:00	2:30	2:36	3:00	2:30	2:43	2:21	2:34	1:52	2:19
10:05	2:31	2:37	3:01	2:31	2:44	2:22	2:35	1:53	2:20
10:10	2:32	2:38	3:03	2:32	2:46	2:23	2:37	1:54	2:21
10:15	2:33	2:39	3:04	2:33	2:47	2:24	2:38	1:55	2:22
10:20	2:35	2:41	3:06	2:35	2:48	2:25	2:39	1:56	2:24
10:25	2:36	2:42	3:07	2:36	2:50	2:26	2:40	1:57	2:25
10:30	2:37	2:43	3:09	2:37	2:51	2:28	2:42	1:58	2:26
10:35	2:38	2:45	3:10	2:38	2:53	2:29	2:43	1:59	2:27
10:40	2:40	2:46	3:12	2:40	2:54	2:30	2:44	2:00	2:28
10:45	2:41	2:47	3:13	2:41	2:55	2:31	2:46	2:00	2:29
10:50	2:42	2:49	3:15	2:42	2:57	2:32	2:47	2:01	2:31
10:55	2:43	2:50	3:16	2:43	2:58	2:33	2:48	2:02	2:32
11:00	2:45	2:51	3:18	2:45	2:59	2:35	2:49	2:03	2:33

References

Allen, Hunter, and Andrew Coggan. 2010. *Training and Racing with a Power Meter*, 2nd ed. Boulder, Colo.: VeloPress.

American College of Sports Medicine. "Exercise and Fluid Replacement." *Medicine and Science in Sports and Exercise* 39(2): 377–390.

Barnett, C., M. Carey, J. Proietto, E. Cerin, M. Febbraio, and D. Jenkins. 2004. Muscle metabolism during sprint exercise in man: Influence of sprint training. *Journal of Science and Medicine in Sport* 7(3) (September): 314–322.

Bickham, D. C., C. Gibbons, and P. F. Le Rossignol. 2004. VO$_2$ is attenuated above the lactate threshold in endurance-trained runners. *Medicine and Science in Sports and Exercise* 36(2) (February): 297–301.

Billat, V. 2001. Interval training for performance: A scientific and empirical practice. *Sports Medicine* 31(2): 75–90.

Brooks, G. A., and J. Mercier. 1994. Balance of carbohydrate and lipid utilization during exercise: The "crossover" concept. *Journal of Applied Physiology* 76: 2253–2261.

Burgomaster, K., S. Hughes, G. Heigenhauser, S. Bradwell, and M. Gibala. 2005. Six sessions of sprint interval training increases muscle oxidative potential and cycle endurance capacity in humans. *Journal of Applied Physiology* 98(6) (June): 1985–1990.

Cavanaugh, P. R., and K. R. Williams. 1982. The effect of stride length variation on oxygen uptake during distance running. *Medicine and Science in Sports and Exercise* 14(1): 30–35.

Coyle, E. F. 2004. Fluid and fuel intake during exercise. *Journal of Sports Sciences* 22: 39–55.

———. 2005. Very intense exercise training is extremely potent and time efficient: A reminder. *Journal of Applied Physiology* 98: 1983–1984.

Daniels, J., and N. Scardina. 1984. Interval training and performance. *Sports Medicine* 1(4) (July): 327–334.

Delextrat, A., J. Brisswalter, C. Hausswirth, T. Bernard, and J. M. Vallier. 2005. Does prior 1500-m swimming affect cycling energy expenditure in well-trained triathletes? *Applied Physiology Nutrition and Metabolism* 30(4): 392–403.

Dempsey, J. A. 1986. Is the lung built for exercise? *Medicine and Science in Sports and Exercise* 18: 143–155.

Dudley, G., W. Abraham, and R. Terjung. 1982. Influence of exercise intensity and duration on biochemical adaptations in skeletal muscle. *Journal of Applied Physiology* 53(4) (October): 844–850.

Esfarjani, F., and P. B. Laursen. 2007. Manipulating high-intensity interval training: Effects on VO_2max, the lactate threshold, and 3000 m running performance in moderately trained males. *Journal of Science and Medicine in Sport* 10(1) (February): 27–35. (E-publication July 28, 2006.)

Faria, E. W., D. K. Parker, and I. E. Faria. 2005. The science of cycling: Factors affecting performance—part 2. *Sports Medicine* 35: 313–337.

Faude, O., T. Meyer, J. Scharhag, F. Weins, A. Urhausen, and W. Kindermann. 2008. Volume versus intensity in the training of competitive swimmers. *International Journal of Sports Medicine* 29(11) (November): 906–912.

Fox, E. L., R. L. Bartels, and C. E. Billing. 1975. Frequency and duration of interval training programs and changes in aerobic power. *Journal of Applied Physiology* 38: 481–484.

Franch, J., K. Madsen, M. S. Djurhuus et al. 1998. Improved running economy following intensified training correlates with reduced ventilatory demands. *Medicine and Science in Sports and Exercise* 30: 1250–1256.

Gastin, P. 2001. Energy system interaction and relative contribution during maximal exercise. *Sports Medicine* 31(10): 725–741.

Gibala, M., J. Little, M. van Essen, G. Wilkin, K. Burgomaster, A. Safdar, S. Raha, and M. Tarnopolsky. 2006. Short-term sprint interval versus traditional endurance training: Similar initial adaptations in human skeletal muscle and exercise performance. *Journal of Physiology* 575(3): 901–911.

Gorostiaga, E. M., C. B. Walter, C. Foster et al. 1991. Uniqueness of interval and continuous training at the same maintained exercise intensity. *European Journal of Applied Physiology* 63: 101–107.

Gottschall, J. S., and B. M. Palmer. 2002. The acute effects of prior cycling cadence on running performance and kinematics. *Medicine and Science in Sports and Exercise* 34(9) (September): 1518–1522.

Hardman, A., C. Williams, and S. Wootton. 1986. The influence of short-term endurance training on maximum oxygen uptake, submaximum endurance, and the ability to perform brief, maximal exercise. *Journal of Sports Sciences* [online] 4(2) (Autumn): 109–116.

Harmer, A. R., M. J. McKenna, J. R. Sutto, R. J. Snow, P. A. Ruell, J. Booth, M. W. Thompson, N. A. Mackay, C. G. Stathis, R. M. Crameri, M. F. Carey, and D. M. Enger. 2000. Skeletal muscle metabolic and ionic adaptation during intense exercise following sprint training in humans. *Journal of Applied Physiology* 89: 1793–1803.

Hausswirth, C., A. X. Bigard, and C. Y. Guezennec. 1997. Relationships between running mechanics and energy cost of running at the end of a triathlon and a marathon. *International Journal of Sports Medicine* 18(5) (July): 330–339.

Hawley, J. A., K. H. Myburgh, T. D. Noakes et al. 1997. Training techniques to improve fatigue resistance and enhance endurance performance. *Journal of Sports Science* 15: 325–333.

Heiden, T., and A. Burnett. 2003. Triathlon. *Sports Biomechanics* 2(1): 35–49.

Helgerud, J., K. Høydal, E. Wang, T. Karlsen, P. Berg, M. Bjerkaas, T. Simonsen, C. Helgesen, N. Hjorth, R. Bach, and J. Hoff. 2007. Aerobic high-intensity intervals improve VO$_2$max more than moderate training. *Medicine and Science in Sports and Exercise* 39(4): 665–671.

Jacobs, I., M. Esbjoernsson, C. Sylven, I. Holm, and E. Jansson. 1987. Sprint training effects on muscle myoglobin, enzymes, fiber types, and blood lactate. *Medicine and Science in Sports and Exercise* 19(4) (August): 368–374.

Jones, A., and H. Carter. 2000. The effect of endurance training on parameters of aerobic fitness. *Sports Medicine* 6: 373–386.

Karp, Jason R. 2008. Chasing Pheidippides: The science of endurance. *IDEA Fitness Journal* 5(9) (October): 28.

Klika, R. J., M. Alderdice, J. Kvale, and J. Kearney. 2007. Efficacy of cycling training based on a power field test. *Journal of Strength and Conditioning Research* 21(1): 265–269.

Kreider, R., T. Boone, W. Thompson, S. Burkes, and C. Cortes. 1988. Cardiovascular and thermal responses of triathlon performance. *Medicine and Science in Sport and Exercise* 20: 385–390.

Krustrup, P., Y. Hellsten, and J. Bangsbo. 2004. Intense interval training enhances human skeletal muscle oxygen uptake in the initial phase of dynamic exercise at high but not at low intensities. *Journal of Physiology* 559(1): 335–345.

Kubukeli, Z. N., T. D. Noakes, and S. C. Dennis. 2002. Training techniques to improve endurance exercise performances. *Sports Medicine* 32(8): 489–509.

Laursen, P., M. Blanchard, and D. Jenkins. 2002. Acute high-intensity interval training improves T_{vent} and peak power output in highly trained males. *Canadian Journal of Applied Physiology* 27(4) (August): 336–348.

Laursen, P. B., and D. G. Jenkins. 2002. The scientific basis for high-intensity interval training: Optimising training programmes and maximising performance in highly trained endurance athletes. Sports Medicine 32(1): 53–73.

Laursen, P. B., C. M. Shing, J. M. Peake, J. S. Coombes, and D. G. Jenkins. 2002. Interval training program optimization in highly trained endurance cyclists. *Medicine and Science in Sports and Exercise* 34(11): 1801–1807.

———. 2005. Influence of high-intensity interval training on adaptations in well-trained cyclists. *Journal of Strength and Conditioning Research* 19(3) (August): 527–533.

Lindsay, F. H., J. A. Hawley, K. H. Myburgh et al. 1996. Improved athletic performance in highly trained cyclists after interval training. *Medicine and Science in Sports and Exercise* 28: 1427–1434.

Linossier, M. T., C. Dennis, D. Dormois et al. 1993. Ergometric and metabolic adaptation to a 5-s sprint training programmer. *European Journal of Applied Physiology* 67: 408–414.

Londeree, B. 1997. Effect of training on lactate/ventilatory thresholds: A meta-analysis. *Medicine and Science in Sports and Exercise* 29(6) (June): 837–843.

MacDougall, D., A. Hicks, J. MacDonald, R. McKelvie, H. Green, and K. Smith. 1998. Muscle performance and enzymatic adaptations to sprint interval training. *Journal of Applied Physiology* 84: 2138–2142.

Marles, A., R. Legrand, N. Blondel, P. Mucci, D. Bebeder, and F. Prieur. 2007. Effect of high-intensity interval training and detraining on extra VO_2 and on the VO_2 slow component. *European Journal of Applied Physiology* 99: 633–640.

McArdle, W. D., F. I. Katch, and V. L. Katch. 2000. *Essentials of Exercise Physiology*, 2nd ed. Baltimore: Lippincott Williams & Wilkins.

Midgley, A. W., L. R. McNaughton, and A. M. Jones. 2007. Training to enhance the physiological determinants of long-distance running performance. *Sports Medicine* 37(10): 857–880.

Millet, G. P., and V. E. Vleck. 2000. Physiological and biomechanical adaptations to the cycle to run transition in Olympic triathlon: Review and practical recommendations for training. *British Journal of Sports Medicine* 34: 384–390.

Millet, G. P., V. E. Vleck, and D. J. Bentley. 2009. Physiological differences between cycling and running: Lessons from triathletes. *Sports Medicine* 39(3): 179–206.

Mujika, I., and S. Padilla. 2003. Scientific bases for precompetition tapering strategies. *Medicine and Science in Sports and Exercise* 35(7) (July): 1182–1187.

Neufer, P. D. 1989. The effect of detraining and reduced training on the physiological adaptations to aerobic exercise training. *Sports Medicine* 8(5) (November): 302–320.

Parra, J., J. A. Cadefau, G. Rodas, N. Amigó, and R. Cussó. 2000. The distribution of rest periods affects performance and adaptations of energy metabolism induced by high-intensity training in human muscle. *Acta Physiologica Scandinavia* 169(2) (June): 157–165.

Peeling, P. D., D. J. Bishop, and G. J. Landers. 2005. Effect of swimming intensity on subsequent cycling and overall triathlon performance. *British Journal of Sports Medicine* 39(5): 960–964.

Rakobowchuk, M., S. Tanguay, K. Burgomaster, K. Howarth, M. Gibala, and M. MacDonald. 2008. Sprint interval and traditional endurance training induce similar improvements in peripheral arterial stiffness and flow-mediated dilation in healthy humans. *American Journal of Physiology—Regulatory, Integrative and Comparative Physiology* 295(1) (July): R236–R242.

Rodas, G., J. Ventura, J. Cadefau, R. Cusso, and J. Parra. 2000. A short training programme for the rapid improvement of both aerobic and anaerobic metabolism. *European Journal of Applied Physiology* 82: 480–486.

Seiler, S., and E. Tønnessen. 2009. Intervals, thresholds, and long slow distance: The role of intensity and duration in endurance training. *Sportscience* 13: 32–53.

Shaw, T., P. Howat, M. Trainer, and B. Maycock. 2004. Training patterns and sports injuries in triathletes. *Journal of Science and Medicine in Sport* 7(4) (December): 446–450.

Simoneau, J. A., G. Lortie, M. R. Boulay et al. 1986. Inheritance of human skeletal muscle and anaerobic capacity adaptation to high-intensity intermittent training: Human skeletal muscle fiber type alteration with high-intensity intermittent training. *International Journal of Sports Medicine* 7: 167–171.

Talanian, J., S. Galloway, G. Heigenhauser, A. Bonen, and L. Spriet. 2007. Two weeks of high-intensity aerobic interval training increases the capacity for fat oxidation during exercise in women. *Journal of Applied Physiology* 102: 1439–1447.

Tanaka, H., and D. R. Seals. 2008. Endurance exercise performance in masters athletes: Age-associated changes and underlying physiological mechanisms. *Journal of Physiology* 586(1) (January): 55–63.

Vercruyssen, F., R. Suriano, D. Bishop, C. Hausswirth, and J. Brisswalter. 2005. Cadence selection affects metabolic responses during cycling and subsequent running time to fatigue. *British Journal of Sports Medicine* 39(5): 267–272.

Westgarth-Taylor, C., J. Hawley, S. Rickard, K. Myburgh, T. Noakes, and S. Dennis. 1997. Metabolic and performance adaptations to interval training in endurance-trained cyclists. *European Journal of Applied Physiology* 75(4) (April): 298–304.

Weston, A. R., K. H. Myburgh, F. H. Lindsay, S. C. Dennis, T. D. Noakes, and J. A. Hawley. 1997. Skeletal muscle buffering capacity and endurance performance after high-intensity training by well-trained cyclists. *European Journal of Applied Physiology and Occupational Physiology* 75(1) (December): 7–13.

Willett, K. 2006. Mitochondria: The aerobic engines. www.biketechreview.com/performance/mitochondira.htm.

Index

About the Authors

Chris Carmichael started out as an Olympian and a professional cyclist before developing into a renowned coach, best-selling author, and entrepreneur. He was recognized as the U.S. Olympic Committee Coach of the Year in 1999 and was inducted into the United States Bicycling Hall of Fame in 2003. Chris founded Carmichael Training Systems, Inc. (CTS) in 2000 to make world-class coaching expertise available to the public.

Through Chris's leadership and an unsurpassed education program that develops the best-trained coaches in the industry, CTS immediately established itself as the premier destination for performance coaching, training camps, sports nutrition, and performance testing. As CTS celebrates its tenth anniversary in 2010, Chris's continued commitment to innovation has kept the company in a leadership position in the coaching industry. CTS is the Official Coaching Partner of Ironman, and CTS's proven track record for producing champions continues to attract top amateur and professional athletes.

Athletes who currently or in the past have relied on CTS include Ironman world champions Craig Alexander, Tim DeBoom, Normann Stadler, and Peter Reid; 2010 Ironman St. George champion Heather Wurtele; Olympic triathlon gold and silver medalist Simon Whitfield; seven-time Tour de France champion Lance Armstrong; NASCAR drivers Carl Edwards, Bobby Labonte, and Max Papis; six-time U.S. national cyclocross champion Katie Compton; two-time cyclocross national champion Ryan Trebon; and 2010 Women's Giro d'Italia champion Mara Abbott. In addition, Chris has created nearly two dozen training DVDs and authored six books, including *The Time-Crunched Cyclist* (2009), *The Ultimate Ride*

(2003), the *New York Times* best seller *Chris Carmichael's Food for Fitness* (2004), and *5 Essentials for a Winning Life* (2006).

Chris and his wife, Paige, live in Colorado Springs with their three children: Anna, Connor, and Vivian.

Jim Rutberg is the editorial director and a coach for Carmichael Training Systems and coauthor, with Chris Carmichael, of *The Time-Crunched Cyclist*, *The Ultimate Ride*, *Chris Carmichael's Food for Fitness*, *Chris Carmichael's Fitness Cookbook*, *The Carmichael Training Systems Cyclist's Training Diary*, *5 Essentials for a Winning Life*, and many articles. His work has appeared in *Bicycling*, *Outside*, *Men's Health*, *Men's Journal*, *VeloNews*, *Inside Triathlon*, and other magazines and journals. A graduate of Wake Forest University and former elite-level cyclist, Rutberg lives in Colorado Springs with his wife, Leslie, and their two sons, Oliver and Elliot.